W.H. Auden

SELECT POEMS

W.H. Auden

SELECT POEMS

[Edited with Complete Introduction, Biography, Author's Background, Complete Text, Study Questions, Select Criticism and Bibliography]

Aditya Nandwani

B.A. English (Hons), Delhi University;
M.A. (English), IGNOU; Print Journalism (English) YMCA

ANMOL PUBLICATIONS PVT. LTD.

NEW DELHI - 110 002 (INDIA)

ANMOL PUBLICATIONS PVT. LTD.

H.O.: 4374/4B, Ansari Road, Darya Ganj,
New Delhi-110 002 (India)
Ph.: 23278000, 23261597

B.O.: No. 1015, Ist Main Road, BSK IIIrd Stage
IIIrd Phase, IIIrd Block
Bangalore - 560 085 (India)
Visit us at: www.anmolpublications.com

First Published, 2009

PRINTED IN INDIA

Printed at Balaji Offset Press, Delhi.

Contents

Preface

W.H. Auden was a young, sensational English poet of the 1930s who became an elder statesman of Anglo-American literature by the time he died in 1973. He made his reputation while still at Oxford in the 1920s, and by the time he left England for New York to avoid World War II he was considered by many to be the spokes-poet of a generation -- an erudite, socially conscious and technically brilliant rising star. Once in America (1939), he wrote poems of all kinds (long and short), essays, films and speeches, as well as libretti and plays with more-than-just-pals Chester Kallman and Christopher Isherwood (respectively). He taught and lectured (he also kept up his relationship with Oxford) and became even more famous when won the 1948 Pulitzer for the long poem The Age of Anxiety. Critics and scholars still consider Auden one of the 20th century's great poets, but few of his poems are familiar to mainstream audiences. He spent his last years in New York, at Oxford and in Vienna, Austria (where he died). His poetry gained new notice in recent years, thanks to the film Four Weddings and a Funeral, which features Auden's poem "Funeral Blues".

Chapter 1

Introduction

W.H. Auden is ordinarily depicted as the most influential and, in many cases, best-loved member of his generation of English poets, the generation falling between the airy heights of T.S. Eliot and the grim postmodernism of Philip Larkin. Just as John Ashberry managed to decamp from the high-spirited group known to us now as the New York School, Auden gained notoriety and reverence that left him at a remove from his contemporaries in The Movement.

His intimate alliance with such dapper figures as Stephen Spender, Louis MacNeice, Christopher Isherwood, and Benjamin Britten lent dramatic proportions to his career and personal life, as his intellectual light reflected well on them (although such collaborations as arose were not without their faults: Auden composed the libretto to Britten's dreadful opera *Paul Bunyon*, co-authored three forgivable plays and *Journey to War* with Isherwood, and published the limp *Letters from Iceland* with MacNeice; he redeemed himself later with the stunning libretto to Igor Stravinsky's opera *The Rake's Progress*). Though hardly the most handsome of his generation at Oxford, he was nevertheless bathed in warm admiration and outright loyalty from a wide circle of companions, as much for his intellectual powers as his bold charm and humour. His wit is renowned, and a survey of any anthology of quotations will surface more than a few by Wystan, including such favorites as "thank God for books as an alternative to conversation" and "one cannot review a bad book without showing off."

Fame came quickly and at a young age for Auden. Upon arriving at Oxford, he insisted, when asked what future profession he intended to assume, that he would be a poet. By his second year at Christ Church college, he was at the heart of a burgeoning group of young poets and intellectuals, who sought his opinion on a variety of subjects. Though he graduated with astonishingly low marks, he had already distinguished himself as a poet, self-publishing his first chapbook while at university and placing his first book, Poems, with Faber and Faber when only 21.

A few years later, King George VI presented him with the Gold Medal for Poetry. After some time spent exploring the homosexual café world of Berlin with Isherwood, he found himself, by his mid-twenties, considered the most important poet of his generation. Later in life, he would return to Oxford to take up the post of Professor of Poetry and hold his daily informal salon at a café in the Covered Market, at the centre of Oxford. Much later in life, having grown somewhat disenchanted with his annual routine of a half year in lower Manhattan interpolated by seasons in either Italy or Austria, he returned to Christ Church to take up residence in meager accommodations on the college grounds. Sadly, he found himself isolated by fame and left alone most of the time by the students he hoped to tutor. Today, undergraduates slurp cucumber soup and exchange jokes in the Christ Church dining hall beneath his admonishing portrait.

As with such giants as Henri Mattisse and Ludwig von Beethoven, it is customary to divide W.H. Auden's career into two distinct phases, bisected, in his case, by the Second World War. The earlier poetry, particularly that of the thirties, is defined by a preoccupation with political and historical matters, while that of the forties, fifties, and particularly the sixties, is concerned with more modest affairs such as friendship and the household. Needless to say, this split, however accurate it may seem from a distance, is a preconceived notion which his readers would do well to dispense with entirely. There is, however, a clear shift in mid-career from peripatetic European to convivial New Yorker, when he took up residence in various apartments in Brooklyn (with Paul Bowles, Thomas Mann's son, and uber-stripper

Gypsy Rose Lee and friends) and the West Village (where he shared an apartment with the younger American poet Chester Kallman). Around this time he also became an American citizen and embraced conservative Christianity, despite his homosexuality, which was open in his circles but hardly advertised publicly as was Allen Ginsberg's (a young composer once remarked at a dinner that Auden "doesn't love God. He's just attracted to him").

A devoted formalist, it can be said that the rigorous technical consistency of his poetry mirrors its moral depth, a type of well-wrought urn, though hardly the reflexive sort envisioned by the famous critic Cleanth Brooks (who had John Donne and his fellow Metaphysicals in mind). One is surprised by the dramatist's flair and composure of Auden's early recordings. From "The Wanderer" in 193 on to "In Time of War" in 1938, his voice is congenial and already avuncular in spite of his young age. Unfortunately, his lifestyle caught up with him, and his once agreeable voice went gravelly. Heavy smoking and daily drinking took their toll, and from the scarcely intelligible (which is to say poorly preserved) recording of "In Memory of W.B. Yeats" onward, his voice becomes harder to take. By the midpoint of "Friday's Child", recorded in 1958, he sounds as though he's just climbed a fifth-floor walkup. These recordings also have substantial scholarly value. Auden not only substitutes individual words during performance (for instance, "invade" for "invest" in the first line of the eighteenth stanza of "Thanksgiving for a Habitat") but whole titles. "Fish in the Unruffled Lakes" is announced simply as "Song", and "Death's Echo" as the more forceful "The Dead Echo". The recordings also make apparent his use of slant rhyme and what could uncharitably be referred to as "eye" rhyme. In the otherwise chiming final section of "In Memory of W.B. Yeats", one witnesses, or rather hears, the following lunge:

Earth, receive an honoured guest:
William Yeats is laid to rest.
Let the Irish vessel lie
Emptied of its poetry.

Of course one thinks of Blake's rhyming of "eye" with "symmetry" in "The Tiger" and is reminded that such deviations from pure form are acceptable. Image is far from central in his poetry; philosophical and ethical assertion mingle with political opinion or fact to form what could be called tracts or aphorisms:

The sons of Hermes love to play,
And only do their best when they
Are told they oughtn't;
Apollo's children never shrink
From boring jobs but have to think
Their work important.

Both Georgian traditionalists and many Imagist moderns were repelled by Auden's poems, saturated as they are with leftist utopian ideology and studded with Greek gods, indignant jabs, and nimble pranks. J.D. McClatchy writes that Auden's early poems seem as if written "by an anarchic Boy Scout on speed. There was a cocky, conspiratorial, shocking edge to them, and he would use schoolboy slang, Norse sagas, liturgy and metallurgy, camp or conscience-whatever suppressed energies might be available."

Auden coined the term Age of Anxiety (securing the Pulitzer Prize for the book of that title in 1947), and has been described as the first English poet to feel at home in the twentieth century. The most prominent quality of his work is compassion, his belief in a world where "one could weep because another wept," his vision of "Agape," or uncorrupted love. Attempts to peg a programme or project to his career are ill-fated; like any great thinker, he evolved. Unlike a Geoffrey Hill (widely considered the finest living English poet), who never retracts a sentiment or line of poetry, Auden turned his back on much of his own writing. The most enduring and popular line from "September 1st, 1939" (the day Hitler's panzers jumped the border into Poland, effectively sparking the Second World War)—"We must love one another or die"—was thought unsuitable by Auden because, strictly speaking, it isn't true. It was perfectly timed, in an historical sense, on the eve of the most destructive war in history, but, as Auden later lamented, not a word of poetry could have prevented the horrors of the Second World War. Of course, great poetry is often at once true and a bit of a reassuring fib. He changed the line to "we must love one another and die" because love cannot avert—even if it may forestall—death (though Dante Alighieri and possibly even Dylan Thomas might dispute that, and John Donne and Christina Rossetti suggest it a bit harsh). He then realized how unlovely the line had become once relieved of its original rhetorical punch, so he eliminated it altogether. It was only much later, when assembling a selected poems, that he was persuaded by friends to reinstate the line. Auden's utopian meditations were formed in the shadow of the looming figures of Karl Marx and Sigmund Freud, but he famously dismissed the political potency of poetry. It is interesting that this is, in a sense, a reversal of Theodor Adorno's insistence that after Auschwitz there can be no lyric poetry, by which he meant that no poem could exist in an entirely personal casing but must partake of the sweep and pull of history.

Whatever can be said of Auden today—his naïve ideological entanglements, his tendency to repeat himself to interviewers in his later days, his slovenly lifestyle—he must be remembered for two things: first, his compelling commitment to friendship and its attendant compassion, which was extended to universal dimensions in his poetry; and second, his dedication to the life of a poet, as man of letters, editor, teacher, critic, as manifested in his tireless involvement in forming the cultural landscape of England and America. For these things, we are indebted, and the recordings in this series are indispensable to understanding the man and his works.

Chapter 2

Biography

W. H. Auden - Wystan Hugh Auden

English-born poet, whose world view developed from youthful rebellion to rediscovered Anglo-Catholicism. In his work Auden reconciled tradition and modernism. Auden is widely considered among the greatest literary figures of the 2th century.

"But time is always guilty. Someone must pay for
Our loss of happiness, our happiness itself."
(from 'Detective Story' in Collected Poems, 1991)

Wystan Hugh Auden was born in York, North Yorkshire, as the son of George Augustus Auden, a distinguished physician, and Rosalie Auden. Solihull in the West Midlands, where Auden was brought up, remained important to him as a poet. Auden was educated at St. Edmund's Hindhood and then at Gresham's School, Holt, Norfolk. In 1925 he entered Christ Church, Oxford. Auden's studies and writing progressed without much success: he took a disappointing third-class degree in English. And his first collection of poems was rejected by T. S. Eliot at Faber & Faber. At one time in his undergraduate years he planned to become a biologist. From 1928 to 1929 he lived in Berlin, where he took advantage of the sexually liberal atmosphere, and was introduced to the psychological theories of Homer Lane.

After returning to England Auden taught at a prep school, in 193 privately in London, at Larchfield Academy, a boys' school in Helensburgh , and at Downs School, Colwall, Herefordshire in 1932-35. He was staff member of GPO film

Unit , making documentaries such as 'Night Mail' . Music for this film was provided by Benjamin Brittein, with whom Auden collaborated on the song-cycle 'Our Hunting Fathers 'and on the unsuccessful folk-opera 'Paul Bunyan'. In 1936 Auden traveled in Iceland with Louis MacNeice - Auden believed himself to be of Icelandic descent.

Auden first gained attention in 193 when his short verse play called "Paid on Both Sides" was published in T. S. Eliot's periodical The Criterion. In the same year appeared Auden's POEMS, his first commercially published book, in which he carefully avoided Yeatsian romantic self-expression - the poems were short, untitled, and slightly cryptic. Auden soon gained fame as a leftist intellectual. He showed interest in Marx and Freud and he wrote passionately on social problems, among others in LOOK, STRANGER! .

However, by 1962 he argued that art and politics were best kept apart, stating in his essay 'The Poet and the City' that "All political theories which, like Plato, are based on analogies drawn from artistic fabrication are bound, if put into practice, to turn into tyrannies." Compressed figures of speech, direct statement, and musical effect characterized ON THIS ISLAND and ANOTHER TIME . In the late 193s Auden's poems were perhaps less radical politically, suffering and injustice are not rejected as a part of ordinary life. The last works from this decade astonished readers with their light comic tone and domesticity.

Auden married in 1935 Thomas Mann's daughter Erika Mann, a lesbian actress and journalist, so that she could get a British passport. They met for the first time on their "wedding day". Of women he once said: "When people are talking they should retire to the kitchen." In 1937 Auden went to Spain as a civilian and gave radio broadcasts to help the Republican forces. These experiences he recorded in SPAIN . However, he did not actively continue his campaign. Like George Orwell and Arthur Koestler, he became disillusioned with the politics of the struggle. In stead of being welcomed as a supporter of the Republican cause he was ignored because he wasn't a member of the Communist Party.

In the 193s Auden collaborated with Christopher Isherwood in several plays, and travelled with him in China in 1938. Sex, according to Isherwood, gave their friendship an extra dimension. In January 1939 they emigrated to America and in 1946 Auden became a US citizen. In the 194s he turned into a religious thinker under the influence of Kierkegaard and Reinhold Niebuhr , the foremost American Protestant theologian. Auden depicted his conversion to Anglicanism, his mother's faith, in the THE SEA AND THE MIRROR and FOR THE TIME BEING , in which 'The Sea and the Mirror', subtitled 'A Commentary on Shakespeare's The Tempest', presented a Christian-allegorical reading of Shakespeare's work. The poem can be understood as an allegorical drama, with Prospero representing the conscious ego, Ariel the imagination, and Caliban material needs of fallen creatures. But Auden's original mind leaves much to interpretations - his poems challenge the reader to abandon preconceived expectations.

When Statesmen gravely say 'We must be realistic',
The chances are they're weak and, therefore, pacifistic,
But when they speak of Principles, look out: perhaps
Their generals are already poring over maps.
(from Shorts in Collected Shorter Poems 1927-1957)

From 1939 to 1953 Auden taught at various schools and universities. T.S. Eliot believed that Auden's long career as a teacher left too much traces on his work - "One tires," Eliot stated, "of having things explained and being preached at." Auden's pupils remember his heavy smoking, tireless energy, large black Flemish hat, and umbrella he waved. "We called him Uncle Wiz," one student told later. (W.H. Auden: A Biography by Humphrey Carpenter, 1981) Auden believed that criticism is live conversation. When he was lecturing in New York in 1946-47 on Shakespeare he discarded his manuscripts after each session. However, Alan Ansen and other members of the audience managed to collect his texts which were published in 21. Later Ansen became Auden's secretary and friend.

During World War II Auden was granted temporary status as Major when he went with the U.S. Army to Germany to report on the psychological effects of bombing on civilians. From 1956 to 1961 he was a professor of poetry at Oxford and from 1954 a member of the American Academy. Auden lived primarly in New York, though he also spent summers in Kirchstetten, Austria. He was a member of the editorial board of Decision magazine , Delos magazine , and editor of the Yale Series of Young Poets .

ABOUT THE HOUSE represents Auden's mature period, technically playful and intellectually sharp and witty. The poems corresponded to the rooms of Auden's Austrian house, the boundaries of his everyday life. Auden also wrote opera librettos with the American poet Chester Kallman, who was only 18 when Auden fell in love with him, and who lived with him over 2 years. In 1972 Auden left New York and returned to Oxford, living in a cottage provided by Christ Church. He died of a heart-attack after giving a poetry reading in Vienna on September 29, 1973. Auden was buried in nearby Kirchstetten. Kallman died in 1975, penniless, in Athens.

'Every man carries with him through life a mirror, as unique and impossible to get rid of as his shadow.'

Auden often returned to his early poems and revised them from his later viewpoint as a Christian. He talked of himself as a colonizer of modern verse, when such poets as Marianne Moore or Ezra Pound were explorers. In 'Psychology and Art To-Day,' Auden claimed that art consists in telling parables "from which each according to his immediate and peculiar needs may draw his own conclusions." Sometimes Auden used the parable as a means of speaking about Christianity at a distance, as in the 1954 essay 'Balaam and his Ass.'

In 'The Guilty Vicarage' Auden found in the detective story a Christian parable of existential guilt. Among Auden's single most popular poems is 'Funeral Blues' which was used in the film Four Weddings and a Funeral : "Stop all the clocks, cut off the telephone. / Prevent the dog from barking with a juicy bone. / Silence the pianos and with muffled drum / Bring out the coffin, let the mourners come. /"

Later Auden

In the late 194's, W.H. Auden became enamored of the idea that every writer's mind is a household containing three personalities. T.S. Eliot's, he wrote, included an archdeacon, an old peasant grandmother and a young boy who liked to play practical jokes. His own, as described in his poem "A Household," was a paterfamilias tormented by his "miserable runt" of a son and his "slatternly hag" of a mother.

In fact, Auden's poetry has dozens of inhabitants, as various as the members of his actual household at 7 Middagh Street in Brooklyn (which included, among others, Benjamin Britten, Carson McCullers and Gypsy Rose Lee). Auden is the author of love lyrics ("Lay your sleeping head, my love") and ominous prophecies ("It is time for the destruction of error"); socialist lectures ("Today the struggle") and Christian hymns ("Let us praise our Maker, with true passion extol Him"); crystalline songs ("Deftly, admiral, cast your fly") and fantastically complex allegories (such as The Age of Anxiety, in which the four Jungian personality types converse in the meter of Beowulf).

But the most important of the many fractures in Auden's life and work is that between Early and Later. The poet broke his life in two, quite intentionally, in 1939, when he abandoned England for New York City on the eve of war. Before the year was out, two more events would complete the break: his return to Christianity, after a decade's obsession with Freud and Marx; and his "Vision of Eros" in the form of Chester Kallman, an 18-year-old Jewish boy from Brooklyn.

Auden lived in New York for the next 3 years, and the details of his life here are almost folkloric. He was as successful, and nearly as famous, in America as he ever was in England; but a large part of the legend focuses on the unhappier aspects of his later years. Auden had always been slovenly in his personal habits, but by the 5's, when he was living at 77 St. Mark's Place, his situation was really appalling; Hannah Arendt remembered times "when his slum apartment was so cold that the water no longer functioned and he had to use the toilet in the liquor store at the corner, when his suit was ...

worn so thin that his trousers would suddenly split from top to bottom." Alcohol and tobacco and Benzedrine began to take their toll on his appearance, until his deeply wrinkled face–in his own words–looked "like a wedding cake left out in the rain." When he tried to give Dorothy Day a check for $25 to avert the closing of her Catholic Worker shelter, she thought he was a bum handing over $2.5.

Auden's long relationship with Chester Kallman–it lasted from the day they met until the day Auden died in 1973–has also proved a rich source of gossip. The younger man was considered Auden's inferior in every way by most of his friends, and his biographers continue to be puzzled by the attachment. (Richard Davenport-Hines, whose 1995 biography, Auden, is psychologically very acute, can find nothing nicer to say about Kallman than that "it was impossible to be indifferent about" him.) And the pain that Kallman frequently caused Auden, with his infidelities and public scenes, leaks into Auden's writing–his essay on Shakespeare's sonnets is practically a roman à clef about their affair. Yet Kallman always represented for Auden the possibility of real love, from which he had felt excluded by his homosexuality and his precocity. Auden only wore a wedding ring for the first few months after meeting Kallman; but it remained a marriage, if a troubled one, to the end.

The stories of Auden's life in New York have been well told by several biographers, and will surely be told again. But they have almost no place in Edward Mendelson's new study, Later Auden, which completes the work he began in 1981 with Early Auden. Probably no one alive knows Auden's poetry and prose better than Mr. Mendelson, and it shows: His close readings are always meticulous and insightful, and he draws detailed connections between what Auden read and what he wrote. Later Auden is invaluable for a complete understanding of Auden, and it should be kept on the shelf right next to the Collected Poems.

Mr. Mendelson's two-volume division is entirely appropriate, for ever since 1939, the Early and Later Audens have almost seemed like two different poets, and have done battle in the minds of critics and readers. For some–including Philip Larkin, who wrote an essay in 196 called "What's Become of Wystan?"–Auden's emigration was a disaster. In the 3's, on this view, Auden thrived on the atmosphere of impending crisis, writing taut, nervous poems that expressed the mood of a generation; by moving to America, he lost touch with his natural audience and became merely "literary." For the other camp–which includes Mr. Mendelson–Early Auden is still a genius, but Later Auden is an even bigger genius. His emigration allowed him to pare away inauthenticity and rhetoric from his verse, and in America he wrote his best poems, meditations on simple but timeless themes like the nature of happiness and the relation between art and justice.

It's appropriate that Mr. Mendelson should defend the Later Auden, since it was the Later Auden who in 1972 plucked him from the ranks of academia to be his literary executor. Mr. Mendelson, now a professor at Columbia University, is still best known for his work with Auden's literary remains. It was a difficult assignment, made even harder by the poet's tendency to revise or renounce poems he had written decades earlier, including some of his most famous. Mr. Mendelson has performed his role expertly, mediating between the poet's wishes and his readers'. The Collected Poems follows Auden's instructions, omitting, for example, "September 1, 1939" ("the most dishonest poem I have ever written"); but the Selected Poems and the invaluable volume The English Auden fill in the gaps.

In Later Auden, Mr. Mendelson's focus is on the intellectual content of Auden's poems; and while this approach is generally illuminating, it does have the defects of its virtues. Mr. Mendelson pays relatively little attention to prosody, of which Auden was the greatest 2th-century master, and ventures only a few esthetic judgments of his own. He tends to treat Auden as a thinker, or at least as a philosophical poet, and he regards the changes in Auden's thought as deliberate advances: "In almost every poem Auden wrote at this time, he remembered and corrected the content and tone of poems he had written earlier." The problem with this approach is that

Auden's ideas were usually confused, and not seldom flimsy. Though educated at Oxford University, he had an autodidact's mind, full of eccentric theories and explanations; the books that influenced him most were by "polymath generalizers"–or, less charitably, cranks, most of them now forgotten–who "rushed breathlessly across vast tracts of history, tracing patterns unimagined by others."

As a child, Auden preferred machinery to people, and later on he reached irritably for mechanistic explanations–whether Freudian, Marxist or Christian-existentialist–to supply the basic human understanding that he often seemed to lack. (Until meeting Kallman, Mr. Mendelson writes, "the word 'person' was not ... part of [Auden's] moral vocabulary"–rather a large gap for a 32-year-old.) His lifelong habit of analyzing human nature in terms of spurious categories–the Prolific and the Devourer, A and B, Self and I, Alice and Mabel, Eden and New Jerusalem–is another symptom of the same deficiency.

But again: Auden's household contains multitudes. If one doesn't like the philosopher and synthesizer that Mr. Mendelson depicts, there is always the songwriter, the prosodist, the narrator with an eye for novelistic detail. Auden, as he himself wrote of W.B. Yeats, has also become his admirers, and he can be admired in as many different ways as he has readers. As Later Auden proves, no one reads him better than Edward Mendelson.

Chapter 3

Major Work

Auden is best known as a poet of great erudition, wisdom, and remarkable lyrical gifts. His early verse in *Poems* is characterized by terse exposition, alluring abstraction, and inventive use of language, bearing the influence of Eliot and Thomas Hardy, Auden's initial master, as well as Laura Riding, Wilfred Owen, and Gerard Manley Hopkins. Auden's early poems also adumbrate his penchant for Anglo-Saxon phrasing, syncopated rhythms, traditional forms, the allegorical imagery of science and geology, and his deep-felt humanitarian concerns. Drawing on eclectic sources for the verse drama *Paid on Both Sides*, inspired by the lively dramatic action of the parlor charade and the plays of Bertolt Brecht and William Butler Yeats, Auden merges the archaic style and blood-feud theme of Anglo-Saxon poetry with structural elements of Greek tragedy and the fragmentary modernist presentation of Eliot's *The Waste Land*.

Auden built upon these early experiments in the prose and verse of *The Orators*, drawing on Freudian psychoanalysis, Marxist doctrine, and the avant-garde techniques of Eliot, James Joyce, and Gertrude Stein to present a surreal vision of the revolutionary hero and a warning against the danger of fascism. Peppered with private jokes and allusions to his friends, *The Orators* laments and satirizes the stagnation of English society and the dubious promise of untamed modernism. Similar political and psychological concerns are echoed in Auden's collaborative verse dramas with Isherwood from this period, including *The Dog Beneath the Skin, The Ascent of F6* and *On the Frontier. Look, Stranger!* , reprinted as *On This*

Island, marks Auden's entrance into leftist politics and his shift toward an increasingly formal aesthetic. Turning away from the obtuseness of modernism and the subjective idealism of the Romantics, Auden invokes the directness and clarity of light verse to give serious expression to his strong ethical stance and to impose order upon the chaos preceding the Second World War. His poem "Spain," composed immediately after witnessing the brutal internecine combat in that country, reflects Auden's disillusionment with political causes and the indiscriminate violence of war.

"In Time of War." a sequence of sonnets which appeared in *Journey to a War*, reveals the maturation of Auden's civic voice and liberal humanist creed. Published shortly thereafter, *Another Time* displays the full emergence of Auden's unique synthesis of technical mastery, moral probity, and spirited lyricism. This volume, his first American publication, contains many of his greatest poems, including "As I Walked Out One Evening," "Musée des Beaux Arts," "Lay Your Sleeping Head, My Love," "September 1, 1939," "The Unknown Citizen," "Letter to Lord Byron," and elegies to poets Matthew Arnold, A. E. Housman, and Yeats. The full impact of Auden's self-imposed exile and acute spiritual crisis, which led to his reversion to Christianity, is evident in *The Double Man.*

This volume contains "New Year Letter," an extended epistolary poem on the evils of modern civilization rendered in Augustan form, and the sonnet sequence "The Quest." Influenced by the existentialist thought of Soren Kierkegaard and American theologian Rheinhold Neibuhr, Auden moved still further toward a cerebral style that sought universal harmony in a system of religious ideals.

For the Time Being contains "For the Time Being: A Christmas Oratorio," an overt Christian allegory based on the Nativity in which he employs the terminology of science and psychology to rationalize religious faith, and "The Sea and the Mirror: A Commentary on Shakespeare's *The Tempest*," an ambitious allegorical work that examines the complex relationship between life and art and the creative potential of literary interpretation. His next major work, *The Age of Anxiety*, subtitled "a baroque eclogue," relates the inner consciousness of four disparate characters as they converse among themselves in a New York City bar during the Second World War. Returning to the alliterative Anglo-Saxon versification of his early poetry, Auden explores the spiritual dimensions of their ordinary lives and individual failings within a religious context. The height of Auden's mature, intellectual style is evident in *Nones*, which contains "In Praise of Limestone," *The Shield of Achilles* , featuring "Horae Canonicae" and "Bucolics," and *Homage to Clio* , which includes "The Cave of Making" and "Tonight at Seven-Thirty."

Devoid of the frivolity of his earlier poetry, the serene meditations of these late volumes, frequently in neo-classical or pastoral modes, displays Auden's unsurpassed technical control and deep insights into the nature of human existence and experience, particularly as informed by the philosophy of Martin Heidegger, medieval Christianity, history, and nature. Auden's highly perceptive critical essays, reviews, and lectures in *The Enchafèd Flood* . *The Dyer's Hand* , and *Forewords and Afterwords* document his intellectual concerns and artistic principles during his American period.

Poetry

Poems (privately printed, 1928)
Poems
The Orators prose and verse
Look, Stranger! in America: On This Island
Spain
Another Time
The Double Man
The Quest
For the Time Being
The Sea and the Mirror
Collected Poetry
The Age of Anxiety: A Baroque Eclogue
Collected Shorter Poems 193-1944
Nones
The Shield of Achilles

Selected Poetry
The Old Man's Road
Homage to Clio
About the House About the House
Collected Shorter Poems 1927-1957
Collected Longer Poems
City without Walls
Academic Graffiti
Epistle to a Godson
Thank You, Fog: Last Poems
Selected Poems
Collected Poems

Prose

Letters from Iceland
Journey to a War
Enchaféd Flood
The Dyer's Hand
Selected Essays
Forewords and Afterwords

Anthology

Selected Poems by Gunnar Ekelöf

Drama

Paid On Both Sides
The Dance of Death
The Dog Beneath the Skin: or, Where is Francis?
The Ascent of F.6
On the Frontier

Chapter 4

Chronology of W.H. Auden

1970 Wystan Hugh Auden born on February 21 in York, third son of George Augustus and Constance Rosalie Auden.

1980 The family moved to Birmingham, where Dr. Auden be- came Medical Officer and Professor of Public Health in Birmingham University.

1915-20 St. Edmund's School (preparatory). Met Christopher Isherwood, who was three years older and left in

1918-25 Gresham's School Holt . Specialized in biology. In an essay in The Old School (ed. Graham Greene, London & N.Y., 1934), Auden describes the school with gener- osity and himself with candor: "The son of book-loving, Anglo-Catholic parents of the professional class, the youngest of three brothers, I was... mentally precocious, physically backward, short-sighted, a rabbit at all games, very untidy and grubby, a nail-biter, a physical coward, dishonest, sentimental, with no community sense what- ever, in fact a typical little highbrow and difficult child".

1922 Discovery of vocation. "One afternoon in March at half- past three / When walking in a ploughed field with a friend; /... he turned to me / And said, 'Tell me, do you write poetry?' / I never had, and said so, but I knew / That very moment what I wished to do" (Letters from Iceland, p. 28). The friend was Robert Medley, accord- ing to Julian Symons (The Thirties, London, 196, p. 78); Medley became a painter and theatrical designer and was associated with Auden in the Group Theatre. First poem published in Public Schools Verse, 1924 ("It is a lovely sight and good").

1930-35 Schoolmaster at Larchfield Academy, Helensburgh, Scot-land, and at The Downs School, Colwall, near Malvern

1933 The Dance of Death (dedicated to Robert Medley and Rupert Doone) published by Faber & Faber in November. Written for the Group Theatre, with which Auden had worked since 1932, and of which Medley was art director and Doone director. Reviews in The Criterion of The Evolution of Sex, by Dr. Maranon and The Biological Tragedy of Women, by A. Nemilov; Dark Places in Education, by Dr. Schohaus ; The Poems of William Dunbar ; The Book of Talbot, by V. Clifton . Reviews in Scrutiny of Thoughts and Adventures, by W. Churchill ; Alfred Mond, by H. Bolitho.

1934 Poems published by Random House, New York, containing. The Orators and The Dance of Deatb as well as the 1933 Poems. "The Group Movement and the Middle Classes," in Oxford and the Groups, ed. Richard Crossman. "Honour (Gresham's School, Holt)," in The Old School, ed. Graham Greene. "T. E. Lawrence," in Now and Then, Spring 1934. Reviews in The Criterion of Gerard Manley Hopkins, by E. E. Phare; English Poetry for Children, ed. R. L. Mégroz. Reviews in Scrutiny of Lessons from the Varsity of Life, by Lord Baden-Powell ; G. L. Dick-inson, by E. M. Forster. 1941-42 Taught at the University of Michigan.

1941 Paul Bunyan, a choral operetta, written with Benjamin Britten, produced in May. Both collaborators were dis- satisfied with it and it has never been published. The Double Man published by Random House in March; the Faber & Faber edition was called New Year Letter. Dedicated to Elizabeth Mayer. " Criticism in a Mass Society," in The Intent of the Critic, ed. D. A. Stauffer. "The Role of Intellectuals in Political Affairs," in De- cision, Jan. 1941. "A Note on Order," in The Nation, Feb. 1, 1941. "Opera on an American Legend," in the New York

Times, May 4, 1941. (About Paul Bunyan.) Reviews in Decision of Where Do We Go From Here?, by Harold Laski ; Towards a Philosophy of History, by Ortega y Gasset ("The Masses Defined," May 1941). Reviews in The Nation of Christianity and Power Poli- tics, by Reinhold Niebuhr ("Tract for the Times," Jan. 4, 1941); Love in the Western World, by Denis de Rougemont ("Eros and Agape," June 28, 1941). Reviews in The New Republic of translations of Kafka ("The Wandering Jew," Feb. 1, 1941); Darwin, Marx and Freud, by J. Barzun ("Ambiguous Answers," June 23, 1941); The Nature and Destiny of Man, by Reinhold Niebuhr ("The Means of Grace," June 2, 1941); The Philos- ophy of Literary Form, by Kenneth Burke ("A Grammar of Assent," July 14, 1941).

1948 Awarded Pulitzer Prize in May. Began spending the spring and summer of each year on the Italian island of Ischia. Edited The Portable Greek Reader (New York: Vik- ing). Edited A Beginning, by Robert Horan (Vol. 46 of Yale Series of Younger Poets). "Squares and Oblongs," in Poets at Work, ed. Charles D. Abbot (New York: Harcourt, Brace; partially in- cluded in The Dyer's Hand, 1962). "Yeats as an Example," in Kenyon Review, Spring 1948. "The Guilty Vicarage: Notes on the Detective Story by an Addict," in Harper's, May 1948 (included in The Dyer's Hand, 1962). "Henry James and the Artist in America," in Harper's, July 1948. "Opera Addict," Vogue, July 1948.

1949 Edited The Grasshopper's Man, by Rosalie Moore (Vol. 47 of Yale Series of Younger Poets). "The Heresy of our Time," Renascence, Spring 1949. "The Question of Ezra Pound," Partisan Review, May 1949. "A Note on Graham Greene," The Wind and the Rain, Summer 1949. "The Ironic Hero: Some Reflections on Don Quixote," Horizon, Aug. 1949. Review of Notes Towards a Definition of Culture, by T. S. Eliot, in The New Yorker, April 23, 1949 ("Port and Nuts with the Eliots"). Review of A Writer's Notebook, by Somerset Maugham, in The New York Times Book Review, October 23, 1949.

Chapter 5

Auden and the Limits of Poetry

His verse was brilliant, ironic, often funny, wide-ranging in its reference — equally at home in the worlds of Anglo-Saxon heroic poetry and the technology of mining — and sometimes impenetrably obscure. His poetic voice was from the beginning so distinctive that in 1933, when Auden was just twenty-six years old, Graham Greene could employ the word "Audenesque" in a movie review, confident that readers would know what he meant. The phrase "the Auden age" was in use before the poet turned thirty. But this widely recognized leader of the British intellectual avant-garde was an unhappy and confused young man.

Auden had been unable to believe in God since his adolescence. His loss of faith and his discovery of poetry had come, interestingly enough, at almost the same time. But in the late thirties, as Auden's uncertainty about his role as a poet grew (along with political and social tensions in Europe) some odd things began to happen to him. When in Spain during that country's Civil War, for instance, he was shocked and disturbed to see that supporters of the Republican cause had closed or burned many of Barcelona's churches — but he could not account for his own reaction. Soon afterward, he met the English writer and editor Charles Williams, and felt himself to be "in the presence of personal sanctity" — though what sanctity meant in a world without God he could not say.

In December 1939 Auden had his most decisive experience of this kind. He went to a theater in what was then a German-speaking section of Manhattan to see a newsreel about the German invasion of Poland, which had occurred three months before. But it was not the film so much as the audience that Auden later remembered. Whenever the Poles appeared on the screen—as prisoners, of course, in the hands of the Wehrmacht—members of the audience would shout in German, "Kill them! Kill them!" Auden was stunned. "There was no hypocrisy," he recalled many years later: these people were unashamed of their feelings and attempted to put no "civilized" face upon them. "I wondered, then, why I reacted as I did against this denial of every humanistic value." On what grounds did he have a right to demand, or even a reason to expect, a more "humanistic" response?

His inability to answer this question, he explained much later, "brought me back to the Church." By the fall of 194 he was going to church again, for the first time since childhood, and would affirm the Christian faith for the rest of his days. However, the many readers who have rejoiced in the work of Auden's fellow British Christians, the Inklings — Lewis, Tolkien, Charles Williams, and (peripheral to their circle) Dorothy Sayers—have paid little attention to this remarkable man or the extraordinary work that emerged from his embrace of the Christian faith. This is, as we shall see, an understandable but deeply lamentable state of affairs.

Edward Mendelson's marvelous recent book about Auden ends with the words, "and his work was done." This conclusion provides the key to understanding Mendelson's project not only in this book but also in its predecessor, 1981's *Early Auden*. In these two rich and resourceful volumes, Mendelson has written the definitive account of one of the greatest poetic careers of the last century.

The story he tells is not the story of Auden's life in the usual sense of the word, though all elements of that life naturally enter into the story; rather, he narrates for us the complex and fascinating history of a body of work, the fruit of a calling. Mendelson gives us the biography of Auden's vocation.

Not long after he began writing poetry at age fifteen, Auden came to understand that words were the medium in which he should work. But who or what imposed this "should" upon him? And how should he use the words he was called upon to use? In *Early Auden*—which began with Auden's first adult poems, written in 1927 when he was twenty years old, and ended with his leaving England in January 1939 — Mendelson traced Auden's oscillations among several divergent and probably irreconcilable descriptions of the poet: conjurer, teacher, servant, prophet, redeemer. *Later Auden* begins with the poet in a new land, a place famous for encouraging new beginnings. When, with his friend Christopher Isherwood, Auden boarded a ship for America, he was the most celebrated young poet in England, but he knew that his career was at an impasse. All of the models for the writing life which he had tried out in the previous decade had come to seem empty, sterile, and in some cases repulsive. But he had no idea what could replace them. The germ of a new understanding, Mendelson shows, can be found in a word that Auden began using just before he left England: he said that the poet had a gift.

The presence of a gift implies the activity of a giver. But who, or what, gives the gift of poetry? Auden's conversion, less than two years later, indicated that he had found an answer to that question. But Auden's conversion did not resolve his puzzlement about his life as a poet: What should he do with the gift that God had given him? During the war years, from his apartment in New York, his pursuit of an answer to that question led him upon a remarkable intellectual and spiritual journey. In reviews and essays commissioned by major American periodicals, he would explore thinkers and ideas that he hoped would help him figure out what he was supposed to do, as a poet and a man: he considered Kierkegaard, Reinhold Niebuhr, and Paul Tillich, along with a host of less well-known figures like the historian Charles Norris Cochrane and, a little later on, the polymathic but eccentric philosopher-historian Eugen Rosenstock-Huessy.

As Mendelson demonstrates, Auden's essays and reviews consistently depicted these figures as having some significant contribution to make to the interpretation of Western culture at that particular and terrible moment. But in the poems Auden was writing at the same time, Mendelson convincingly argues, he was preoccupied with the questions he could not answer, with the doubts that even the greatest of his intellectual helpers left unassuaged. Among these poems are some of Auden's finest achievements, including the three long poems he wrote between 1941 and 1947, "For the Time Being: A Christmas Oratorio," "The Sea and the Mirror: A Commentary on *The Tempest*," and "The Age of Anxiety: a Baroque Eclogue."

The first and last of these, Mendelson contends, have brilliant passages but are flawed in either their concept or execution; and even the masterful "The Sea and the Mirror" fails to offer a clear and satisfying account of the problem it sets out to address, namely, whether art can have spiritual significance. (Auden told his friend Ursula Niebuhr — the wife of Reinhold — that the poem was "really about the Christian conception of art.") Mendelson fully recognizes the greatness of this poem, and the extraordinarily intelligent ambitions of the other two. His point is not that the poems are less than they could have been, but rather that none of them satisfied its author. In the thirties, Auden had nurtured hopes that the poet might be a prophet to — or even a redeemer of — a sick and chaotic society. In the aftermath of his conversion, his thinking dominated by what he later called a "neo-Calvinist (i.e., Barthian) exaggeration of God's transcendence," he found poetry valuable only when it acknowledged its hopeless, incompetent distance from anything true or good that it tried to represent. One sees this notion vividly illustrated in one of the concluding speeches of "The Sea and the Mirror," a poem that adapts and transforms various elements of Shakespeare's *The Tempest*.

In this passage, Auden's Caliban explains what he thinks to be the only kind of situation in which the artist receives any genuine illumination. He asks us to imagine "the greatest grandest opera rendered by a very provincial touring company indeed." Paradoxically, it is the very poverty and ineptitude of the production that makes it valuable to its actors, for even though "there was not a single aspect of our whole performance, not even the huge stuffed bird of happiness, for which a kind word could, however patronizingly, be said," nevertheless it is "at this very moment [that] we do at last see ourselves as we are." And, more important, "for the first time in our lives we hear... the real Word which is our only raison d'être." At the moment when all pretense to aesthetic achievement helplessly falls away, and the actors are confronted with the authentic selves which they had used their performances to escape, they come to see God precisely in their distance from Him: ... we are blessed with that Wholly Other Life from which we are separated by an essential emphatic gulf of which our contrived fissures of mirror and proscenium arch—we understand them at last—are feebly figurative signs.... It is just here, among the ruins and the bones, that we may rejoice in the perfected Work that is not ours.

Similarly, Auden's Prospero, musing on the kind of life he will live after giving up his magical powers, says "I never dreamed the way of truth / Was a way of silence." But if Prospero is right, what can the poet do except stop writing? One suspects that at this point in his career Auden was contemplating just that — that is, making his adaptation of The Tempest his farewell to poetry, just as *The Tempest* itself has always been read as Shakespeare's (and not just Prospero's) farewell to the dramatic arts. And yet, Auden continued to believe that poetry was the vocation to which he had been called, not just by his temperament or aptitudes, but by God himself, "the author and giver of all good things" (as he wrote in a 194 poem). But how, given the incapacity of language to grasp the most important things in and beyond this world, could he fulfill that calling?

In thinking through this problem, Auden gained insight from Kierkegaard; he found especially useful the Danish thinker's notion of "indirect communication." (This is a theme that Mendelson makes too little of, but since almost every other critic of Auden has made too much of it, the fault is easily pardonable.) Many of Kierkegaard's works — in fact, all of his most famous ones — are not explicitly Christian. Such books are easily identifiable because Kierkegaard did not sign his name to them: they appeared under various pseudonyms.

These works approach the questions with which Christianity is most concerned, but they do not offer Christian answers to those questions; indeed, their failure to produce compelling responses is just what leads the reader toward the Christian faith that alone can provide what we need. "An illusion can never be destroyed directly," Kierkegaard wrote, "and only by indirect means can it be radically removed."

Auden adopted this approach, and adapted it to his poetic needs. In the great poems of his maturity, Christianity appears as the missing piece of the puzzle, the answer to a question no one thought to ask. In "The Shield of Achilles," for instance — one of the greatest poems of the twentieth century — the blacksmith god Hephaestos, watched by Achilles' mother Thetis, portrays our world as it appears to the carnal eye, the eye unillumined by faith. He inscribes on the shield "three pale figures" being bound to three posts; the poem indicates their condition:

The mass and majesty of this world, all
That carries weight and always weighs the same
Lay in the hands of others; they were small
And could not hope for help and no help came:
What their foes liked to do was done, their shame
Was all the worst could wish; they lost their pride
And died as men before their bodies died.

A little later we see another figure:

A ragged urchin, aimless and alone,
Loitered about that vacancy; a bird
Flew up to safety from his well-aimed stone:
That girls are raped, that two boys knife a third,
Were axioms to him, who'd never heard
Of any world where promises were kept,
Or one could weep because another wept.

In the Christian understanding, we indeed live in a world where such events occur. But the cold eye of Hephaestos, while it sees with terrifying clarity, is blind to some things: that one of those three bound figures may be different than the other two; that somewhere promises are kept; and that people weep with their brothers and sisters who weep. In Auden's poem the Christian interpretation of history is evoked all the more powerfully by its absence: the indirect communication of "The Shield of Achilles" has a force more overt testimonials often lack. The Christian faith helped Auden to keep writing in another way as well, by offering him—though not immediately, and not without years of profound study and reflection—a way of comprehending a problem that had obsessed him for many years: the relationship between freedom and necessity. In almost every major poem he wrote after coming to America, says Mendelson, Auden in some way "incorporated the significant events of his life. But he confronted each time a new variation on his inner debate: whether those events were better understood as the product of involuntary necessity or of free choice." Mendelson begins his book by reflecting on this obsession of Auden's, and one of the great achievements of *Later Auden* is the skillful patience and critical tact with which he explores Auden's changing views on this vital subject.

Auden came to formulate the problem in this way: alone among the creatures, human beings live in history as well as in nature. In the natural world all obey the laws that govern their being; only we make choices and live out the consequences of them. That's what history means. In a lovely poem called "Their Lonely Betters," Auden sits in a chair in his garden, listens, and thinks about what he hears:

A robin with no Christian name ran through
The Robin-Anthem which was all it knew,
And rustling flowers for some third party waited
To say which pairs, if any, should get mated.
Not one of them was capable of lying,
There was not one which knew that it was dying
Or could have with a rhythm or a rhyme
Assumed responsibility for time.
Let them leave language to their lonely betters
Who count some days and long for certain letters;
We, too, make noises when we laugh or weep:
Words are for those with promises to keep.

The robin cannot decide what song to sing; the flowers

cannot select their mates. These creatures, living wholly in nature, neither celebrate the wisdom nor lament the folly of their choices, for they have no choices to make. We, on the other hand, must and do choose, and thereby enter into the historical world of accountability ("responsibility for time"). We know what it means to have "promises to keep" — and what it means to break them.

But we are not just historical beings. We are also participants in nature, and in that sense we too are part of the Creation. And Mendelson shows, as no other critic has yet shown, how Auden came to wrestle with — and ultimately to accept, with gratitude — the limits and circumscriptions of our natural, our bodily, lives.

I have said that Auden was deeply influenced by Kierkegaard, but he gradually came to understand that there were some valuable and necessary things that Kierkegaard didn't understand. Late in his life, Auden would write of Kierkegaard that, "like all heretics, conscious or unconscious, he is a monodist, who can hear with particular acuteness one theme in the New Testament—in his case, the theme of suffering and self-sacrifice—but is deaf to its rich polyphony.... The Passion of Christ was to Kierkegaard's taste, the Nativity and Epiphany were not." Auden contends that, while Kierkegaard's consciously held beliefs were scrupulously orthodox, he was "in his sensibility" a Manichee, who felt strongly the evil and degradation of matter, of our bodies. Indeed, Auden wrote in another essay, with pardonable exaggeration, "A planetary visitor might read through the whole of his voluminous works without discovering that human beings are not ghosts but have bodies of flesh and blood." And to have bodies of flesh and blood is to live in the world of nature's necessity as well as in the world of history, of existential choice.

Auden thus increasingly came to believe that we are emphatically compound beings, subject always to natural laws and yet called upon to "assume responsibility for time" by making decisions — decisions whose inevitable consequences are yet another form of necessity. For Auden, this peculiar situation is, above all, comic. There is something intrinsically funny about our mixed identity, as we try to exercise Divine powers of decision and yet always find our bodies getting in the way. "A sense of humour develops in a society to the degree that its members are simultaneously conscious of being each a unique person and of being all in common subjection to unalterable laws." And this sense of humour about one's condition is for Auden absolutely necessary to spiritual health. He may have dreamed in his youth of redeeming the world through his poetic power or being destroyed in the effort, but as an older man he found himself, as he often remarked, just a "martyr to corns," which afflicted his feet and made him comfortable only in carpet slippers.

By the 1950s most of the people who had admired the young Auden had rejected his mature poetry as trivial. But the heart of Mendelson's book, in many respects, is his demonstration that in this later poetry Auden is working "at the height of his powers," though in a poetic idiom that was incomprehensible to those who loved the gnomic and hieratic pronouncements of Auden's earlier verse. In 1948, Mendelson notes, Auden began to write poems about the inarticulate human body...: the body that never asks to be regimented or idealized, feels no abstract hatred or intellectual envy, believes no theories, and is moved by impulses that, fortunately for us, are not exactly the same as our own. He dedicated to the body some of his most profound poems, works whose depth and breadth have been underestimated because their treatment of their subject matter was novel and unexpected in an age whose writers hesitated to see the body as "simply, publicly, there." And because he learned to value the body as sacred in itself, Auden learned to believe in it as the means and promise of salvation.

"Means" is perhaps not quite right. It is not through the body that we are saved, but we are saved as embodied creatures, and saved for a future of embodiment. Auden came to believe the doctrine of the resurrection of the body a vital one and a necessary corrective to the implicit Gnosticism and Manicheanism of his existentialist influences. But Mendelson's argument is compelling, and if there is any justice in the world it will put an end to the ill-informed dismissals of Auden's later verse. Auden's poems about the body are often poems of gratitude and thanksgiving. In a poem dedicated to his senses, "Precious Five," he concludes by invoking

That singular command
I do not understand,
Bless what there is for being,
Which has to be obeyed, for
What else am I made for,
Agreeing or disagreeing?

In one sense this recurrent emphasis on blessing and thankfulness is a correction of the theology that dominated Auden's early years as a Christian. I have already noted how important for Auden was Kierkegaard's statement that "before God we are always in the wrong." In that movie theater in Manhattan, Auden confronted his own infinite capacity for sinfulness as well as that of the Germans. One of Auden's friends relates that he taught Sunday School in 1942, and once asked the class, "Do you know what the Devil looks like?" He then answered his own question: "The Devil looks like me." Not too long afterward, he wrote of his conviction that Jesus is Lord: "I believe because he fulfills none of my dreams, because he is in every respect the opposite of what he would be if I could have made him in my own image." But why not one of the other great teachers, like Buddha or Muhammad? Because, Auden wrote, chillingly, "none of the others arouse all sides of my being to cry 'Crucify Him.'" Auden never rejected this deep conviction of his depravity, but he came to realise that if he tried to build his whole theology around it he would become, like Kierkegaard, a "monodist" and an inadvertent heretic. Thus the necessary poems of praise and thanksgiving.

It is in light of this sought theological balance that we may best understand Auden's sequence of poems "Horae Canonicae," based on the "canonical hours" that govern time in monastic communities and many churches. These poems have rarely been given serious attention, but Mendelson points out that they "occupied [Auden's] attention longer than any other" work of his career — seven years, off and on — and believes that they constitute "arguably his greatest work." In these poems, some of which are deceptively casual in tone, Auden attempts to do no less than to encompass self-censure and gratitude, necessity and freedom.

The first poem, "Prime," begins with an awakening. In this first preconscious moment of opening eyes Auden is (as we all are) an "Adam still previous to any act"; but he is also (as we all are) "Afraid of our living task, the dying / Which the coming day will ask." In the next poem he speaks of "our victim," the one who will do the dying, the one who "knows that by sundown / We shall have had a good Friday." Writes Mendelson, "The day in which the events [of this sequence] occur is Good Friday, and also any day; and the place where they occur is Jerusalem with its law court and temple, and also the Italian fishing village where the poems were written, or anywhere." This juxtaposition of times and situations is made possible by the understanding of time embodied in the canonical hours. In them, as in the larger calendar of the church year, unrepeatable events (the pronouncement of judgment, the Crucifixion, the deposition from the Cross) are remembered and in a sense reenacted. But of course this remembrance is done day after day, year after year, according to the necessary rhythms of the seasons and our bodies. Thus the sequence ends, not with the evening prayer of "Compline," but with "Lauds," the song of another morning.

This second morning song not only emphasizes the repetitive nature of bodily actions, including worship, but also indicates, in Mendelson's eloquent words, the blessed movement "from fatal memory to unconditional hope."

This is no transcendent escape from the physical world but an undignified, saving scramble back into it. In imagining it, [Auden] found himself at home not only in both his work and his body — their reconciliation is one of the private achievements of the poem — but also in the double world of nature and history, neither an imaginary past nor a visionary future, but the place he lived now.

Only if we live in the world where God has placed us can we fulfill the vocations to which He has called us.

Why are Christians so indifferent to Auden? It is a question made compelling by Mendelson's brilliant and sympathetic analysis. It is certainly true that Auden is not nearly as accessible a writer as Lewis, Tolkien, Sayers, or Charles Williams. Neither, however, is T. S. Eliot, and yet Eliot continues to hold a totemic status for Christians interested in modern literature, while Auden is almost completely neglected. This state of affairs bears reflection.

The first problem is an obvious one: throughout Auden's life he was a practicing homosexual. After his conversion to Christianity, such sexual activity became problematic for him. His good friend Christopher Isherwood wrote of Auden's attitude toward his homosexuality that "his religion condemned it and he agreed that it was sinful, though he fully intended to go on sinning."

This is only partly right. In a letter to Isherwood — a letter that may have been the source of Isherwood's comment — Auden wrote, "Though I believe it sinful to be queer, it has at least saved me from becoming a pillar of the Establishment." The comment is illuminating. Auden tried to resist his sexual temptations, but felt them to be stronger than he was. In one poem he ruefully echoes a famous prayer of Augustine's, writing "I am sorry I'm not sorry... / Make me chaste, Lord, but not yet." But his determination to "bless what there is for being" led him to seek ways to be grateful to God even for his sins and afflictions, through which he believed God to work for His own purposes. Hence his thankfulness not to have become an Establishment figure. He also believed that the homosexual was less likely to engage in the idolatry of eros that is so common among heterosexuals. In his view his sexuality was, therefore, an affliction that bore the seeds of potential blessings.

But however complex Auden's attitude toward these matters, the mere fact that he was homosexual has written him off the books of many Christians — even Christians who are quick to forgive C. S. Lewis' peculiar liaison with Mrs. Moore, or Charles Williams' penchant for spanking and being spanked by young women. The Christian world has its hierarchy of sins, and may be right in its judgments. But it is singularly unfortunate that, even if we have judged Auden's sins rightly, we should allow that judgment to stand in the way of learning from the wisdom contained in his writings.

In any case, homosexuality alone is not enough to explain the Christian neglect of Auden. More important, perhaps, is his Kierkegaardian emphasis on indirect communication. This emphasis stemmed from Auden's determination to repent of his, and his fellow poets', prideful assertions of their own importance. But Christian readers, for the most part, don't want their poets to be humble: being somewhat Romantic in taste, they tend to prefer their poets to be seers, prophets, "unacknowledged legislators of the world" (as Shelley put it) — just as long as they are Christian seers, prophets, legislators. As they often say, they like poems that are "redemptive." But Auden understood that nothing and no one is redemptive except Jesus Christ — and thus he called Shelley's famous line "the silliest remark ever made about poets." As he wrote to Clio, the mythological Muse of History,

Approachable as you seem,
I dare not ask you if you bless the poets,
For you do not look as if you ever read them,
Nor can I see a reason why you should.

He sent this poem to J. R. R. Tolkien, and in an accompanying letter referred to it as "a hymn to Our Lady." Mary, as the mother of Christ, presides over the world's moments of ultimate significance: What can poetry add to the Incarnation or the Passion of our Lord?

Auden consistently repudiated the notion that poetry has any privileged access to truth, any especially sanctified role to play. Poetry was certainly his vocation, and he loved it. As Mendelson writes, "Vocation, for Auden, is the most innocent form of love, a voluntary loss of self in an object." He knew he would be wrong not to love his work, not to achieve what he called "that eye-on-the-object look" characteristic of people who are "forgetting themselves in a function." But he would never claim that his calling was superior to any other. In this sense he was purely Lutheran, emphasizing the dignity of every calling before God. It is not surprising that he wrote a poem based on the medieval legend of *le jong-leur de Dieu*, the poor "clown of God" who can offer nothing to the Christ Child but his juggling — and whose offering is received, not because it has special value, but because he gave what he had to give.

As a result of this penitential humility, Auden came to insist over and over again that one cannot in poetry speak the Truth directly and unequivocally. In one of his most powerful poems, "Friday's Child," he remembers, in a characteristically oblique way, the martyr's death of Dietrich Bonhoeffer. (The title is typical of Auden's approach: he trusts us to remember that "Friday's child is loving and giving," and trusts us also to understand that the old Mother Goose rhyme draws on the memory of Good Friday, when God loved and gave most fully.) The poem concludes with an invocation, and a recommendation, of silence in the face of an evil that cannot be comprehended and a faith that, as Kierkegaard said, can be neither explained nor justified:

Now, did He really break the seal
And rise again? We dare not say;
But conscious unbelievers feel
Quite sure of Judgment Day.
Meanwhile, a silence on the cross
As dead as we shall ever be,
Speaks of some total gain or loss,
And you and I are free
To guess from the insulted face
Just what Appearances He saves
By suffering in a public place
A death reserved for slaves.

The key phrase here, I believe, is "We dare not say." It is not the same as "We dare not believe" — though Auden often confessed in his later years to dark times of doubt — nor does it mean "We dare not proclaim," since undoubtedly Auden often did proclaim, in church at least, "On the third day he rose again in accordance with the Scriptures." Auden's "we" does not refer to Christians, but to poets, whose tendency (as he writes in another poem) to "utter some resonant lie" makes them unfit bearers of the gospel proclamation. As Auden said repeatedly, almost obsessively, "Orthodoxy is reticence"; orthodoxy is knowing when to shut up. This is not a teaching that many Christian readers want to hear from their poets. But Auden knew what poetry can't do, and always felt the need to put himself and other poets in their proper place. Thus the wittily self-deflating question in "Compline": "Can poets (can men in television) / Be saved?"

Late in his life, he said in a lecture that he and his "fellow-citizens of the Republic of Letters" — a phrase coined by Voltaire — had but one "political duty": "To love the Word and defend it against its enemies." And who or what are those enemies? The "principal enemies of the True Word are two: the Idle Word and the Black Magician." On the one hand, he came to see much of his early poetry as intolerably careless not only in its technique but in its disregard for whether it meant what it said. It was full of idle words. But the other enemy was more dangerous still. The Black Magician encourages poets to believe that they can be prophets and redeemers. Or, as Auden put it once in a review, he tries to make a person attempt "to do for himself or others by the writing of poetry what can only be done in some other way, by action, or study, or prayer." Auden uses poetry to remind us of what poetry can never give us. But, in the end, this assigns poetry a genuine and important role, as it points always beyond itself in a strangely mute witness to that of which it is unable definitively to speak. As Auden wrote in one of his later poems,

> *We can only*
> *do what it seems to us we were made for, look at*
> *this world with a happy eye*
> *but from a sobre perspective.*

Chapter 6

Complete Text of Poems by W.H. Auden

A New Age

So an age ended, and its last deliverer died
In bed, grown idle and unhappy; they were safe:
The sudden shadow of a giant's enormous calf
Would fall no more at dusk across their lawns outside.
They slept in peace: in marshes here and there no doubt
A sterile dragon lingered to a natural death,
But in a year the spoor had vanished from the heath:
A kobold's knocking in the mountain petered out.
Only the scupltors and the poets were half sad,
And the pert retinue from the magician's house
Grumbled and went elsewhere. The vanished powers were glad
To be invisible and free; without remorse
Struck down the sons who strayed in their course,
And ravished the daughters, and drove the fathers mad.

After Reading a Child's Guide to Modern Physics

If all a top physicist knows
About the Truth be true,
Then, for all the so-and-so's,
Futility and grime,
Our common world contains,
We have a better time
Than the Greater Nebulae do,

Or the atoms in our brains.
Marriage is rarely bliss
But, surely it would be worse
As particles to pelt
At thousands of miles per sec
About a universe
Wherein a lover's kiss
Would either not be felt
Or break the loved one's neck.
Though the face at which I stare
While shaving it be cruel
For, year after year, it repels
An ageing suitor, it has,
Thank God, sufficient mass
To be altogether there,
Not an indeterminate gruel
Which is partly somewhere else.
Our eyes prefer to suppose
That a habitable place
Has a geocentric view,
That architects enclose
A quiet Euclidian space:
Exploded myths - but who
Could feel at home astraddle
An ever expanding saddle?
This passion of our kind
For the process of finding out
Is a fact one can hardly doubt,
But I would rejoice in it more
If I knew more clearly what
We wanted the knowledge for,
Felt certain still that the mind
Is free to know or not.
It has chosen once, it seems,
And whether our concern
For magnitude's extremes
Really become a creature
Who comes in a median size,

Or politicizing Nature
Be altogether wise,
Is something we shall learn.

Another Time

For us like any other fugitive,
Like the numberless flowers that cannot number
And all the beasts that need not remember,
It is today in which we live.
So many try to say Not Now,
So many have forgotten how
To say I Am, and would be
Lost, if they could, in history.
Bowing, for instance, with such old-world grace
To a proper flag in a proper place,
Muttering like ancients as they stump upstairs
Of Mine and His or Ours and Theirs.
Just as if time were what they used to will
When it was gifted with possession still,
Just as if they were wrong
In no more wishing to belong.
No wonder then so many die of grief,
So many are so lonely as they die;
No one has yet believed or liked a lie,
Another time has other lives to live.

Are You There?

Each lover has some theory of his own
About the difference between the ache
Of being with his love, and being alone:
Why what, when dreaming, is dear flesh and bone
That really stirs the senses, when awake,
Appears a simulacrum of his own.
Narcissus disbelieves in the unknown;
He cannot join his image in the lake
So long as he assumes he is alone.
The child, the waterfall, the fire, the stone,
Are always up to mischief, though, and take

The universe for granted as their own.
The elderly, like Proust, are always prone
To think of love as a subjective fake;
The more they love, the more they feel alone.
Whatever view we hold, it must be shown
Why every lover has a wish to make
Some kind of otherness his own:
Perhaps, in fact, we never are alone.

At Last the Secret is Out

At last the secret is out,
as it always must come in the end,
the delicious story is ripe to tell
to tell to the intimate friend;
over the tea-cups and into the square
the tongues has its desire;
still waters run deep, my dear,
there's never smoke without fire.
Behind the corpse in the reservoir,
behind the ghost on the links,
behind the lady who dances
and the man who madly drinks,
under the look of fatigue
the attack of migraine and the sigh
there is always another story,
there is more than meets the eye.
For the clear voice suddenly singing,
high up in the convent wall,
the scent of the elder bushes,
the sporting prints in the hall,
the croquet matches in summer,
the handshake, the cough, the kiss,
there is always a wicked secret,
a private reason for this.

A Walk After Dark by W.H. Auden

A cloudless night like this
Can set the spirit soaring:

After a tiring day
The clockwork spectacle is
Impressive in a slightly boring
Eighteenth-century way.
It soothed adolescence a lot
To meet so shameless a stare;
The things I did could not
Be so shocking as they said
If that would still be there
After the shocked were dead
Now, unready to die
Bur already at the stage
When one starts to resent the young,
I am glad those points in the sky
May also be counted among
The creatures of middle-age.
It's cosier thinking of night
As more an Old People's Home
Than a shed for a faultless machine,
That the red pre-Cambrian light
Is gone like Imperial Rome
Or myself at seventeen.
Yet however much we may like
The stoic manner in which
The classical authors wrote,
Only the young and rich
Have the nerve or the figure to strike
The lacrimae rerum note.
For the present stalks abroad
Like the past and its wronged again
Whimper and are ignored,
And the truth cannot be hid;
Somebody chose their pain,
What needn't have happened did.
Occurring this very night
By no established rule,
Some event may already have hurled
Its first little No at the right

Of the laws we accept to school
Our post-diluvian world:
But the stars burn on overhead,
Unconscious of final ends,
As I walk home to bed,
Asking what judgment waits
My person, all my friends,
And these United States.

As I Walked Out One Evening

As I walked out one evening,
Walking down Bristol Street,
The crowds upon the pavement
Were fields of harvest wheat.
And down by the brimming river
I heard a lover sing
Under an arch of the railway:
"Love has no ending.
"I'll love you, dear, I'll love you
Till China and Africa meet,
And the river jumps over the mountain
And the salmon sing in the street,
"I'll love you till the ocean
Is folded and hung up to dry
And the seven stars go squawking
Like geese about the sky.
"The years shall run like rabbits,
For in my arms I hold
The Flower of the Ages,
And the first love of the world."
But all the clocks in the city
Began to whirr and chime:
"O let not Time deceive you,
You cannot conquer Time.
"In the burrows of the Nightmare
Where Justice naked is,
Time watches from the shadow
And coughs when you would kiss.

"In headaches and in worry
Vaguely life leaks away,
And Time will have his fancy
To-morrow or to-day.
"Into many a green valley
Drifts the appalling snow;
Time breaks the threaded dances
And the diver's brilliant bow.
"O plunge your hands in water,
Plunge them in up to the wrist;
Stare, stare in the basin
And wonder what you've missed.
"The glacier knocks in the cupboard,
The desert sighs in the bed,
And the crack in the tea-cup opens
A lane to the land of the dead.
"Where the beggars raffle the banknotes
And the Giant is enchanting to Jack,
And the Lily-white Boy is a Roarer,
And Jill goes down on her back.
"O look, look in the mirror?
O look in your distress:
Life remains a blessing
Although you cannot bless.
"O stand, stand at the window
As the tears scald and start;
You shall love your crooked neighbour
With your crooked heart."
It was late, late in the evening,
The lovers they were gone;
The clocks had ceased their chiming,
And the deep river ran on.

August 1968

The Ogre does what ogres can,
Deeds quite impossible for Man,
But one prize is beyond his reach,
The Ogre cannot master Speech:

About a subjugated plain,
Among its desperate and slain,
The Ogre stalks with hands on hips,
While drivel gushes from his lips.

Epitaph on A Tyrant

Perfection, of a kind, was what he was after,
And the poetry he invented was easy to understand;
He knew human folly like the back of his hand,
And was greatly interested in armies and fleets;
When he laughed, respectable senators burst
with laughter,
And when he cried the little children died in the streets.

The Fall of Rome

The piers are pummelled by the waves;
In a lonely field the rain
Lashes an abandoned train;
Outlaws fill the mountain caves.
Fantastic grow the evening gowns;
Agents of the Fisc pursue
Absconding tax-defaulters through
The sewers of provincial towns.
Private rites of magic send
The temple prostitutes to sleep;
All the literati keep
An imaginary friend.
Cerebrotonic Cato may
Extol the Ancient Disciplines,
But the muscle-bound Marines
Mutiny for food and pay.
Caesar's double-bed is warm
As an unimportatnt clerk
Writes I DO NOT LIKE MY WORK
On a pink official form.
Unendowed with wealth or pity
Little birds with scalet legs,
Sitting on their speckled eggs,

Eye each flu-infected city.
Altogether elsewhere, vast
Herds of reindeer move across
Miles and miles of golden moss,
Silently and very fast.

Funeral Blues

Stop all the clocks, cut off the telephone,
Prevent the dog from barking with a juicy bone,
Silence the pianos and with muffled drum
Bring out the coffin, let the mourners come.
Let aeroplanes circle moaning overhead
Scribbling on the sky the message He is Dead.
Put crepe bows round the white necks of the public doves,
Let the traffic policemen wear black cotton gloves.
He was my North, my South, my East and West,
My working week and my Sunday rest,
My noon, my midnight, my talk, my song;
I thought that love would last forever: I was wrong.
The stars are not wanted now; put out every one,
Pack up the moon and dismantle the sun,
Pour away the ocean and sweep up the wood;
For nothing now can ever come to any good.

If I Could Tell You

Time will say nothing but I told you so,
Time only knows the price we have to pay;
If I could tell you I would let you know.
If we should weep when clowns put on their show,
If we should stumble when musicians play,
Time will say nothing but I told you so.
There are no fortunes to be told, although,
Because I love you more than I can say,
If I could tell you I would let you know.
The winds must come from somewhere when they blow,
There must be reasons why the leaves decay;
Time will say nothing but I told you so.
Perhaps the roses really want to grow,

The vision seriously intends to stay;
If I could tell you I would let you know.
Suppose all the lions get up and go,
And all the brooks and soldiers run away;
Will Time say nothing but I told you so?
If I could tell you I would let you know.
{Sh] In Memory Of W.B. Yeats

I

He disappeared in the dead of winter:
The brooks were frozen, the airports almost deserted,
The snow disfigured the public statues;
The mercury sank in the mouth of the dying day.
What instruments we have agree
The day of his death was a dark cold day.
Far from his illness
The wolves ran on through the evergreen forests,
The peasant river was untempted by the
fashionable quays;
By mourning tongues
The death of the poet was kept from his poems.
But for him it was his last afternoon as himself,
An afternoon of nurses and rumours;
The provinces of his body revolted,
The squares of his mind were empty,
Silence invaded the suburbs,
The current of his feeling failed; he became his admirers.
Now he is scattered among a hundred cities
And wholly given over to unfamiliar affections,
To find his happiness in another kind of wood
And be punished under a foreign code of conscience.
The words of a dead man
Are modified in the guts of the living.
But in the importance and noise of to-morrow
When the brokers are roaring like beasts
on the floor of the Bourse,
And the poor have the sufferings to which they
are fairly accustomed,

And each in the cell of himself is almost convinced of his freedom,
A few thousand will think of this day
As one thinks of a day when one did something slightly unusual.
What instruments we have agree
The day of his death was a dark cold day.

II

You were silly like us; your gift survived it all:
The parish of rich women, physical decay,
Yourself. Mad Ireland hurt you into poetry.
Now Ireland has her madness and her weather still,
For poetry makes nothing happen: it survives
In the valley of its making where executives
Would never want to tamper, flows on south
From ranches of isolation and the busy griefs,
Raw towns that we believe and die in; it survives,
A way of happening, a mouth.

III

Earth, receive an honoured guest:
William Yeats is laid to rest.
Let the Irish vessel lie
Emptied of its poetry.
In the nightmare of the dark
All the dogs of Europe bark,
And the living nations wait,
Each sequestered in its hate;
Intellectual disgrace
Stares from every human face,
And the seas of pity lie
Locked and frozen in each eye.
Follow, poet, follow right
To the bottom of the night,
With your unconstraining voice
Still persuade us to rejoice.
With the farming of a verse

Make a vineyard of the curse,
Sing of human unsuccess
In a rapture of distress.
In the deserts of the heart
Let the healing fountains start,
In the prison of his days
Teach the free man how to praise.

In Praise Of Limestone

If it form the one landscape that we, the inconstant ones,
Are consistently homesick for, this is chiefly
Because it dissolves in water. Mark these rounded slopes
With their surface fragrance of thyme and, beneath,
A secret system of caves and conduits; hear the springs
That spurt out everywhere with a chuckle,
Each filling a private pool for its fish and carving
Its own little ravine whose cliffs entertain
The butterfly and the lizard; examine this region
Of short distances and definite places:
What could be more like Mother or a fitter background
For her son, the flirtatious male who lounges
Against a rock in the sunlight, never doubting
That for all his faults he is loved; whose works are but
Extensions of his power to charm? From
weathered outcrop
To hill-top temple, from appearing waters to
Conspicuous fountains, from a wild to a formal vineyard,
Are ingenious but short steps that a child's wish
To receive more attention than his brothers, whether
By pleasing or teasing, can easily take.
Watch, then, the band of rivals as they climb up and down
Their steep stone gennels in twos and threes, at times
Arm in arm, but never, thank God, in step; or engaged
On the shady side of a square at midday in
Voluble discourse, knowing each other too well to think
There are any important secrets, unable
To conceive a god whose temper-tantrums are moral
And not to be pacified by a clever line

Or a good lay: for accustomed to a stone that responds,
They have never had to veil their faces in awe
Of a crater whose blazing fury could not be fixed;
Adjusted to the local needs of valleys
Where everything can be touched or reached by walking,
Their eyes have never looked into infinite space
Through the lattice-work of a nomad's comb; born lucky,
Their legs have never encountered the fungi
And insects of the jungle, the monstrous forms and lives
With which we have nothing, we like to hope, in common.
So, when one of them goes to the bad, the
way his mind works
Remains incomprehensible: to become a pimp
Or deal in fake jewellery or ruin a fine tenor voice
For effects that bring down the house,
could happen to all
But the best and the worst of us...
That is why, I suppose,
The best and worst never stayed here long but sought
Immoderate soils where the beauty was not so external,
The light less public and the meaning of life
Something more than a mad camp. 'Come!' cried the
granite wastes,
"How evasive is your humour, how accidental
Your kindest kiss, how permanent is
death." (Saints-to- be
Slipped away sighing.) "Come!" purred the
clays and gravels,
"On our plains there is room for armies to drill; rivers
Wait to be tamed and slaves to construct you a tomb
In the grand manner: soft as the earth is mankind and both
Need to be altered." (Intendant Caesars rose and
Left, slamming the door.) But the really reckless
were fetched
By an older colder voice, the oceanic whisper:
"I am the solitude that asks and promises nothing;
That is how I shall set you free. There is no love;
There are only the various envies, all of them sad."

They were right, my dear, all those voices were right
And still are; this land is not the sweet home that it looks,
Nor its peace the historical calm of a site
Where something was settled once and for all:
A back ward
And dilapidated province, connected
To the big busy world by a tunnel, with a certain
Seedy appeal, is that all it is now? Not quite:
It has a worldy duty which in spite of itself
It does not neglect, but calls into question
All the Great Powers assume; it disturbs our rights.
The poet,
Admired for his earnest habit of calling
The sun the sun, his mind Puzzle, is made uneasy
By these marble statues which so obviously doubt
His antimythological myth; and these gamins,
Pursuing the scientist down the tiled colonnade
With such lively offers, rebuke his concern for Nature's
Remotest aspects: I, too, am reproached, for what
And how much you know. Not to lose time,
not to get caught,
Not to be left behind, not, please! to resemble
The beasts who repeat themselves, or a thing like water
Or stone whose conduct can be predicted, these
Are our common prayer, whose greatest comfort is music
Which can be made anywhere, is invisible,
And does not smell. In so far as we have to look forward
To death as a fact, no doubt we are right: But if
Sins can be forgiven, if bodies rise from the dead,
These modifications of matter into
Innocent athletes and gesticulating fountains,
Made solely for pleasure, make a further point:
The blessed will not care what angle they are
regarded from,
Having nothing to hide. Dear, I know nothing of
Either, but when I try to imagine a faultless love
Or the life to come, what I hear is the murmur
Of underground streams, what I see is a
limestone landscape.

Law Like Love

Law, say the gardeners, is the sun,
Law is the one
All gardeners obey
To-morrow, yesterday, to-day.
Law is the wisdom of the old,
The impotent grandfathers feebly scold;
The grandchildren put out a treble tongue,
Law is the senses of the young.
Law, says the priest with a priestly look,
Expounding to an unpriestly people,
Law is the words in my priestly book,
Law is my pulpit and my steeple.
Law, says the judge as he looks down his nose,
Speaking clearly and most severely,
Law is as I've told you before,
Law is as you know I suppose,
Law is but let me explain it once more,
Law is The Law.
Yet law-abiding scholars write:
Law is neither wrong nor right,
Law is only crimes
Punished by places and by times,
Law is the clothes men wear
Anytime, anywhere,
Law is Good morning and Good night.
Others say, Law is our Fate;
Others say, Law is our State;
Others say, others say
Law is no more,
Law has gone away.
And always the loud angry crowd,
Very angry and very loud,
Law is We,
And always the soft idiot softly Me.
If we, dear, know we know no more
Than they about the Law,
If I no more than you

Know what we should and should not do
Except that all agree
Gladly or miserably
That the Law is
And that all know this
If therefore thinking it absurd
To identify Law with some other word,
Unlike so many men
I cannot say Law is again,
No more than they can we suppress
The universal wish to guess
Or slip out of our own position
Into an unconcerned condition.
Although I can at least confine
Your vanity and mine
To stating timidly
A timid similarity,
We shall boast anyway:
Like love I say.
Like love we don't know where or why,
Like love we can't compel or fly,
Like love we often weep,
Like love we seldom keep.

Lay Your Sleeping Head, My Love

Lay your sleeping head, my love,
Human on my faithless arm;
Time and fevers burn away
Individual beauty from
Thoughtful children, and the grave
Proves the child ephermeral:
But in my arms till break of day
Let the living creature lie,
Mortal, guilty, but to me
The entirely beautiful.
Soul and body have no bounds:
To lovers as they lie upon
Her tolerant enchanted slope

In their ordinary swoon,
Grave the vision Venus sends
Of supernatural sympathy,
Universal love and hope;
While an abstract insight wakes
Among the glaciers and the rocks
The hermit's sensual ecstasy.
Certainty, fidelity
On the stroke of midnight pass
Like vibrations of a bell,
And fashionable madmen raise
Their pedantic boring cry:
Every farthing of the cost,
All the dreadful cards foretell,
Shall be paid, but not from this night
Not a whisper, not a thought,
Not a kiss nor look be lost.
Beauty, midnight, vision dies:
Let the winds of dawn that blow
Softly round your dreaming head
Such a day of sweetness show
Eye and knocking heart may bless.
Find the mortal world enough;
Noons of dryness see you fed
By the involuntary powers,
Nights of insult let you pass
Watched by every human love.

Let History Be My Judge

We made all possible preparations,
Drew up a list of firms,
Constantly revised our calculations
And allotted the farms,
Issued all the orders expedient
In this kind of case:
Most, as was expectd, were obedient,
Though there were murmurs, of course;
Chiefly against our exercising

Our old right to abuse:
Even some sort of attempt at rising,
But these were mere boys.
For never serious misgiving
Occurred to anyone,
Since there could be no question of living
If we did not win.
The generally accepted view teaches
That there was no excuse,
Though in the light of recent researches
Many would find the cause
In a not uncommon form of terror;
Others, still more astute,
Point to possibilities of error
At the very start.
As for ourselves there is left remaining
Our honour at least,
And a reasonable chance of retaining
Our faculties to the last.

Like A Vocation

Not as that dream Napoleon, rumour's dread and centre,
Before who's riding all the crowds divide,
Who dedicates a column and withdraws,
Nor as that general favourite and breezy visitor
To whom the weather and the ruins mean so much,
Nor as any of those who always will be welcome,
As luck or history or fun,
Do not enter like that: all these depart.
Claim, certainly, the stranger's right to pleasure:
Ambassadors will surely entertain you
With knowledge of operas and men,
Bankers will ask for your opinion
And the heiress' cheek lean ever so slightly towards you,
The mountains and the shopkeepers accept you
And all your walks be free.
But politeness and freedom are never enough,
Not for a life. They lead

Up to a bed that only looks like marriage;
Even the disciplined and distant admiration
For thousands who obviously want nothing
Becomes just a dowdy illness. These have their moderate success;
They exist in the vanishing hour.
But somewhere always, nowhere particularly unusual,
Almost anywhere in the landscape of water and houses,
His crying competing unsuccessfully with the cry
Of the traffic or the birds, is always standing
The one who needs you, that terrified
Imaginative child who only knows you
As what the uncles call a lie,
But knows he has to be the future and that only
The meek inherit the earth, and is neither
Charming, successful, nor a crowd;
Alone among the noise and policies of summer,
His weeping climbs towards your life like a vocation.

Lullaby

Lay your sleeping head, my love,
Human on my faithless arm;
Time and fevers burn away
Individual beauty from
Thoughtful children, and the grave
Proves the child ephemeral:
But in my arms till break of day
Let the living creature lie,
Mortal, guility, but to me
The entirely beautiful.
Soul and body have no bounds:
To lovers as they lie upon
Her tolerant enchanted slope
In their ordinary swoon,
Grave the vision Venus sends
Of supernatural sympathy,
Universal love and hope;
While abstract insight wakes

Among the glaciers and the rocks
The hermit's sensual ecstasy.
Certainty, fidelity
On the stroke of midnight pass
Like vibrations of a bell,
And fashionable madmen raise
Their pedantic boring cry:
Every farthing of the cost,
All the dreaded cards foretell,
Shall be paid, but from this night
Not a whisper, not a thought,
Not a kiss nor look be lost.
Beauty, midnight, vision dies:
Let the winds of dawn that blow
Softly round your dreaming head
Such a day of sweetness show
Eye and knocking heart may bless,
Find your mortal world enough;
Noons of dryness see you fed
By the involuntary powers,
Nights of insult let you pass
Watched by every human love..

The More Loving One

Looking up at the stars, I know quite well
That, for all they care, I can go to hell,
But on earth indifference is the least
We have to dread from man or beast.
How should we like it were stars to burn
With a passion for us we could not return?
If equal affection cannot be,
Let the more loving one be me.
Admirer as I think I am
Of stars that do not give a damn,
I cannot, now I see them, say
I missed one terribly all day.
Were all stars to disappear or die,

I should learn to look at an empty sky
And feel its total dark sublime,
Though this might take me a little time.

Musée des Beaux Arts

About suffering they were never wrong,
The Old Masters; how well, they understood
Its human position; how it takes place
While someone else is eating or opening a
window or just walking dully along;
How, when the aged are reverently, passionately waiting
For the miraculous birth, there always must be
Children who did not specially want it to happen, skating
On a pond at the edge of the wood:
They never forgot
That even the dreadful martyrdom must run its course
Anyhow in a corner, some untidy spot
Where the dogs go on with their doggy
life and the torturer's horse
Scratches its innocent behind on a tree.
In Breughel's Icarus, for instance: how
everything turns away
Quite leisurely from the disaster; the ploughman may
Have heard the splash, the forsaken cry,
But for him it was not an important failure; the sun shone
As it had to on the white legs disappearing into the green
Water; and the expensive delicate ship that must have seen
Something amazing, a boy falling out of the sky,
had somewhere to get to and sailed calmly on.

The Novelist

Encased in talent like a uniform,
The rank of every poet is well known;
They can amaze us like a thunderstorm,
Or die so young, or live for years alone.
They can dash forward like hussars: but he
Must struggle out of his boyish gift and learn
How to be plain and awkward, how to be

One after whom none think it worth to turn.
For, to achieve his lightest wish, he must
Become the whole of boredom, subject to
Vulgar complaints like love, among the Just
Be just, among the Filthy filthy too,
And in his own weak person, if he can,
Must suffer dully all the wrongs of Man.

Old People's Home

All are limitory, but each has her own
nuance of damage. The elite can dress
and decent themselves,
are ambulant with a single stick, adroit
to read a book all through, or play
the slow movements of
easy sonatas. (Yet, perhaps their very
carnal freedom is their spirit's bane: intelligent
of what has happened and why, they are obnoxious
to a glum beyond tears.) Then come those on
wheels, the average
majority, who endure T.V. and, led by
lenient therapists, do community-singing, then
the loners, muttering in Limbo, and last
the terminally incompetent, as improvident,
unspeakable, impeccable as the plants
they parody. (Plants may sweat profusely but never
sully themselves.) One tie, though, unites them: all
appeared when the world, though much was
awry there, was more
spacious, more comely to look at, it's Old Ones
with an audience and secular station. Then a child,
in dismay with Mamma, could refuge with Gran
to be revalued and told a story. As of now,
we all know what to expect, but their generation
is the first to fade like this, not at home but assigned
to a numbered frequent ward, stowed out of conscience
as unpopular luggage.
As I ride the subway

to spend half-an-hour with one, I revisage
who she was in the pomp and sumpture of her hey-day,
when week-end visits were a presumptive joy,
not a good work. Am I cold to wish for a speedy
painless dormition, pray, as I know she prays,
that God or Nature will abrupt her earthly function?

Petition

Sir, no man's enemy, forgiving all
But will his negative inversion, be prodigal:
Send to us power and light, a sovereign touch
Curing the intolerable neural itch,
The exhaustion of weaning, the liar's quinsy,
And the distortions of ingrown virginity.
Prohibit sharply the rehearsed response
And gradually correct the coward's stance;
Cover in time with beams those in retreat
That, spotted, they turn though the reverse were great;
Publish each healer that in city lives
Or country houses at the end of drives;
Harrow the house of the dead; look shining at
New styles of architecture, a change of heart.

September 1, 1939

I sit in one of the dives
On Fifty-second Street
Uncertain and afraid
As the clever hopes expire
Of a low dishonest decade:
Waves of anger and fear
Circulate over the bright
And darkened lands of the earth,
Obsessing our private lives;
The unmentionable odour of death
Offends the September night.
Accurate scholarship can
Unearth the whole offence
From Luther until now

That has driven a culture mad,
Find what occurred at Linz
What huge imago made
A psychopathic god:
I and the public know
What all schoolchildren learn,
Those to whom evil is done
Do evil in return.
Exiled Thucydides knew
All that a speech can say
About Democracy,
And what dictators do,
The elderly rubbish they talk
To an apathetic grave;
Analysed all in his book,
The enlightenment driven away,
The habit-forming pain,
Mismanagement and grief:
We must suffer them all again.
Into this neutral air
Where blind skyskrapers use
Their full height to proclaim
The strength of Collective Man,
Each language pours its vain
Competitive excuse:
But who can live for long
In an euphoric dream;
Out of the mirror they stare,
Imperialism's face
And the international wrong.
Faces along the bar
Cling to their average day:
The lights must never go out,
The music must always play,
All the conventions conspire
To make this fort assume
The furniture of home;
Lest we should see where we are,

Lost in a haunted wood,
Children afraid of the night
Who have never been happy or good.
The windiest militant trash
Important Persons shout
Is not so crude as our wish:
What mad Nijinsky wrote
About Diaghilev
Is true of the normal heart;
For the error bred in the bone
Of each woman and each man
Craves what it cannot have,
Not universal love
But to be loved alone.
From the conservative dark
Into the ethical life
The dense commuters come,
Repeating their morning vow;
'I will be true to the wife,
I'll concentrate more on my work,'
And helpless governors wake
To resume their compulsory game:
Who can release them now,
Who can reach the deaf,
Who can speak for the dumb?
All I have is a voice
To undo the folded lie,
The romantic lie in the brain
Of the sensual man-in-the-street
And the lie of Authority
Whose buildings grope the sky:
There is no such thing as the State
And no one exists alone;
Hunger allows no choice
To the citizen or the police;
We must love one another or die.
Defenceless under the night
Our world in stupor lies;

Yet, dotted everywhere,
Ironic points of light
Flash out wherever the Just
Exchange their messages:
May I, composed like them
Of Eros and of dust,
Beleaguered by the same
Negation and despair,
Show an affirming flame.

The Shield Of Achilles

She looked over his shoulder
For vines and olive trees,
Marble well-governed cities
And ships upon untamed seas,
But there on the shining metal
His hands had put instead
An artificial wilderness
And a sky like lead.
A plain without a feature, bare and brown,
No blade of grass, no sign of neighborhood,
Nothing to eat and nowhere to sit down,
Yet, congregated on its blankness, stood
An unintelligible multitude,
A million eyes, a million boots in line,
Without expression, waiting for a sign.
Out of the air a voice without a face
Proved by statistics that some cause was just
In tones as dry and level as the place:
No one was cheered and nothing was discussed;
Column by column in a cloud of dust
They marched away enduring a belief
Whose logic brought them, somewhere else, to grief.
She looked over his shoulder
For ritual pieties,
White flower-garlanded heifers,
Libation and sacrifice,
But there on the shining metal

Where the altar should have been,
She saw by his flickering forge-light
Quite another scene.
Barbed wire enclosed an arbitrary spot
Where bored officials lounged (one cracked a joke)
And sentries sweated for the day was hot:
A crowd of ordinary decent folk
Watched from without and neither moved nor spoke
As three pale figures were led forth and bound
To three posts driven upright in the ground.
The mass and majesty of this world, all
That carries weight and always weighs the same
Lay in the hands of others; they were small
And could not hope for help and no help came:
What their foes like to do was done, their shame
Was all the worst could wish; they lost their pride
And died as men before their bodies died.
She looked over his shoulder
For athletes at their games,
Men and women in a dance
Moving their sweet limbs
Quick, quick, to music,
But there on the shining shield
His hands had set no dancing-floor
But a weed-choked field.
A ragged urchin, aimless and alone,
Loitered about that vacancy; a bird
Flew up to safety from his well-aimed stone:
That girls are raped, that two boys knife a third,
Were axioms to him, who'd never heard
Of any world where promises were kept,
Or one could weep because another wept.
The thin-lipped armorer,
Hephaestos, hobbled away,
Thetis of the shining breasts
Cried out in dismay
At what the god had wrought
To please her son, the strong

Iron-hearted man-slaying Achilles
Who would not live long.

Three Short Poems

"The underground roads
Are, as the dead prefer them,
Always tortuous."
"When he looked the cave in the eye,
Hercules
Had a moment of doubt."
Leaning out over
The dreadful precipice,
One contemptuous tree."

The Two

You are the town and we are the clock.
We are the guardians of the gate in the rock.
The Two.
On your left and on your right
In the day and in the night,
We are watching you.
Wiser not to ask just what has occurred
To them who disobeyed our word;
To those
We were the whirlpool, we were the reef,
We were the formal nightmare, grief
And the unlucky rose.
Climb up the crane, learn the sailor's words
When the ships from the islands laden with birds
Come in.
Tell your stories of fishing and other men's wives:
The expansive moments of constricted lives
In the lighted inn.
But do not imagine we do not know
Nor that what you hide with such care won't show
At a glance.
Nothing is done, nothing is said,
But don't make the mistake of believing us dead:
I shouldn't dance.

We're afraid in that case you'll have a fall.
We've been watching you over the garden wall
For hours.
The sky is darkening like a stain,
Something is going to fall like rain
And it won't be flowers.
When the green field comes off like a lid
Revealing what was much better hid:
Unpleasant.
And look, behind you without a sound
The woods have come up and are standing round
In deadly crescent.
The bolt is sliding in its groove,
Outside the window is the black removers' van.
And now with sudden swift emergence
Come the woman in dark glasses and
humpbacked surgeons
And the scissors man.
This might happen any day
So be careful what you say
Or do.
Be clean, be tidy, oil the lock,
Trim the garden, wind the clock,
Remember the Two.

Under Which Lyre

A REACTIONARY TRACT FOR THE TIMES

(Phi Beta Kappa Poem, Harvard, 1946)

Ares at last has quit the field,
The bloodstains on the bushes yield
To seeping showers,
And in their convalescent state
The fractured towns associate
With summer flowers.
Encamped upon the college plain
Raw veterans already train
As freshman forces;
Instructors with sarcastic tongue
Shepherd the battle-weary young

Through basic courses.
Among bewildering appliances
For mastering the arts and sciences
They stroll or run,
And nerves that steeled themselves to slaughter
Are shot to pieces by the shorter
Poems of Donne.
Professors back from secret missions
Resume their proper eruditions,
Though some regret it;
They liked their dictaphones a lot,
T hey met some big wheels, and do not
Let you forget it.
But Zeus' inscrutable decree
Permits the will-to-disagree
To be pandemic,
Ordains that vaudeville shall preach
And every commencement speech
Be a polemic.
Let Ares doze, that other war
Is instantly declared once more
'Twixt those who follow
Precocious Hermes all the way
And those who without qualms obey
Pompous Apollo.
Brutal like all Olympic games,
Though fought with smiles and Christian names
And less dramatic,
This dialectic strife between
The civil gods is just as mean,
And more fanatic.
What high immortals do in mirth
Is life and death on Middle Earth;
Their a-historic
Antipathy forever gripes
All ages and somatic types,
The sophomoric
Who face the future's darkest hints

With giggles or with prairie squints
As stout as Cortez,
And those who like myself turn pale
As we approach with ragged sail
The fattening forties.
The sons of Hermes love to play
And only do their best when they
Are told they oughtn't;
Apollo's children never shrink
From boring jobs but have to think
Their work important.
Related by antithesis,
A compromise between us is
Impossible;
Respect perhaps but friendship never:
Falstaff the fool confronts forever
The prig Prince Hal.
If he would leave the self alone,
Apollo's welcome to the throne,
Fasces and falcons;
He loves to rule, has always done it;
The earth would soon, did Hermes run it,
Be like the Balkans.
But jealous of our god of dreams,
His common-sense in secret schemes
To rule the heart;
Unable to invent the lyre,
Creates with simulated fire
Official art.
And when he occupies a college,
Truth is replaced by Useful Knowledge;
He pays particular
Attention to Commercial Thought,
Public Relations, Hygiene, Sport,
In his curricula.
Athletic, extrovert and crude,
For him, to work in solitude
Is the offence,

The goal a populous Nirvana:
His shield bears this device: Mens sana
Qui mal y pense.
Today his arms, we must confess,
From Right to Left have met success,
His banners wave
From Yale to Princeton, and the news
From Broadway to the Book Reviews
Is very grave.
His radio Homers all day long
In over-Whitmanated song
That does not scan,
With adjectives laid end to end,
Extol the doughnut and commend
The Common Man.
His, too, each homely lyric thing
On sport or spousal love or spring
Or dogs or dusters,
Invented by some court-house bard
For recitation by the yard
In filibusters.
To him ascend the prize orations
And sets of fugal variations
On some folk-ballad,
While dietitians sacrifice
A glass of prune-juice or a nice
Marsh-mallow salad.
Charged with his compound of sensational
Sex plus some undenominational
Religious matter,
Enormous novels by co-eds
Rain down on our defenceless heads
Till our teeth chatter.
In fake Hermetic uniforms
Behind our battle-line, in swarms
That keep alighting,
His existentialists declare
That they are in complete despair,

Yet go on writing.
No matter; He shall be defied;
White Aphrodite is on our side:
What though his threat
To organize us grow more critical?
Zeus willing, we, the unpolitical,
Shall beat him yet.
Lone scholars, sniping from the walls
Of learned periodicals,
Our facts defend,
Our intellectual marines,
Landing in little magazines
Capture a trend.
By night our student Underground
At cocktail parties whisper round
From ear to ear;
Fat figures in the public eye
Collapse next morning, ambushed by
Some witty sneer.
In our morale must lie our strength:
So, that we may behold at length
Routed Apollo's
Battalions melt away like fog,
Keep well the Hermetic Decalogue,
Which runs as follows:—
Thou shalt not do as the dean pleases,
Thou shalt not write thy doctor's thesis
On education,
Thou shalt not worship projects nor
Shalt thou or thine bow down before
Administration.
Thou shalt not answer questionnaires
Or quizzes upon World-Affairs,
Nor with compliance
Take any test. Thou shalt not sit
With statisticians nor commit
A social science.
Thou shalt not be on friendly terms

With guys in advertising firms,
Nor speak with such
As read the Bible for its prose,
Nor, above all, make love to those
Who wash too much.
Thou shalt not live within thy means
Nor on plain water and raw greens.
If thou must choose
Between the chances, choose the odd;
Read The New Yorker, trust in God;
And take short views.

The Unknown Citizen

(To JS/7/M/378/ This Marble Monument
Is Erected by the State)
He was found by the Bureau of Statistics to be
One against whom there was no official complaint,
And all the reports on his conduct agree
That, in the modern sense of an old-fashioned
word, he was a saint, For in everything he did
he served the Greater Community.
Except for the War till the day he retired
He worked in a factory and never got fired
But satisfied his employers, Fudge Motors Inc.
Yet he wasn't a scab or odd in his views,
For his Union reports that he paid his dues,
(Our report on his Union shows it was sound)
And our Social Psychology workers found
That he was popular with his mates and liked a drink.
The Press are convinced that he bought a paper every day
And that his reactions to advertisements were
normal in every way.
Policies taken out in his name prove that
he was fully insured,
And his Health-card shows he was once in
hospital but left it
cured.
Both Producers Research and High-Grade Living declare

He was fully sensible to the advantages of the
Installment Plan
And had everything necessary to the Modern Man,
A phonograph, a radio, a car and a frigidaire.
Our researchers into Public Opinion are content
That he held the proper opinions for the time of year;
When there was peace, he was for peace:
when there was war, he went.
He was married and added five children
to the population,
Which our Eugenist says was the right
number for a parent of his generation.
And our teachers report that he never interfered
with their education.
Was he free? Was he happy? The question is absurd:
Had anything been wrong, we should
certainly have heard.

Voltaire At Ferney

Almost happy now, he looked at his estate.
An exile making watches glanced up as he passed,
And went on working; where a hospital was rising fast
A joiner touched his cap; an agent came to tell
Some of the trees he'd planted were progressing well.
The white alps glittered. It was summer.
He was very great.
Far off in Paris, where his enemies
Whsipered that he was wicked, in an upright chair
A blind old woman longed for death and letters.
He would write
"Nothing is better than life." But was it? Yes, the fight
Against the false and the unfair
Was always worth it. So was gardening. Civilise.
Cajoling, scolding, screaming, cleverest of them all,
He'd had the other children in a holy war
Against the infamous grown-ups, and, like a
child, been sly
And humble, when there was occassion for

The two-faced answer or the plain protective lie,
But, patient like a peasant, waited for their fall.
And never doubted, like D'Alembert, he would win:
Only Pascal was a great enemy, the rest
Were rats already poisoned; there was much,
though, to be done,
And only himself to count upon.
Dear Diderot was dull but did his best;
Rousseau, he'd always known, would blubber
and give in.
So, like a sentinel, he could not sleep.
The night was full of wrong,
Earthquakes and executions. Soon he would be dead,
And still all over Europe stood the horrible nurses
Itching to boil their children. Only his verses
Perhaps could stop them: He must go on
working: Overhead
The uncomplaining stars composed their lucid song.

A Walk After Dark

A cloudless night like this
Can set the spirit soaring:
After a tiring day
The clockwork spectacle is
Impressive in a slightly boring
Eighteenth-century way.
It soothed adolescence a lot
To meet so shamelesss a stare;
The things I did could not
Be so shocking as they said
If that would still be there
After the shocked were dead
Now, unready to die
Bur already at the stage
When one starts to resent the young,
I am glad those points in the sky
May also be counted among
The creatures of middle-age.

It's cosier thinking of night
As more an Old People's Home
Than a shed for a faultless machine,
That the red pre-Cambrian light
Is gone like Imperial Rome
Or myself at seventeen.
Yet however much we may like
The stoic manner in which
The classical authors wrote,
Only the young and rich
Have the nerve or the figure to strike
The lacrimae rerum note.
For the present stalks abroad
Like the past and its wronged again
Whimper and are ignored,
And the truth cannot be hid;
Somebody chose their pain,
What needn't have happened did.
Occuring this very night
By no established rule,
Some event may already have hurled
Its first little No at the right
Of the laws we accept to school
Our post-diluvian world:
But the stars burn on overhead,
Unconscious of final ends,
As I walk home to bed,
Asking what judgment waits
My person, all my friends,
And these United States.

Who's Who

A shilling life will give you all the facts:
How Father beat him, how he ran away,
What were the struggles of his youth, what acts
Made him the greatest figure of his day;
Of how he fought, fished, hunted, worked all night,
Though giddy, climbed new mountains; named a sea;

Some of the last researchers even write
Love made him weep his pints like you and me.
With all his honours on, he sighed for one
Who, say astonished critics, lived at home;
Did little jobs about the house with skill
And nothing else; could whistle; would sit still
Or potter round the garden; answered some
Of his long marvellous letters but kept none.

Atlantis

Being set on the idea
Of getting to Atlantis,
You have discovered of course
Only the Ship of Fools is
Making the voyage this year,
As gales of abnormal force
Are predicted, and that you
Must therefore be ready to
Behave absurdly enough
To pass for one of The Boys,
At least appearing to love
Hard liquor, horseplay and noise.
Should storms, as may well happen,
Drive you to anchor a week
In some old harbour-city
Of Ionia, then speak
With her witty scholars, men
Who have proved there cannot be
Such a place as Atlantis:
Learn their logic, but notice
How its subtlety betrays
Their enormous simple grief;
Thus they shall teach you the ways
To doubt that you may believe.
If, later, you run aground
Among the headlands of Thrace,
Where with torches all night long
A naked barbaric race

Leaps frenziedly to the sound
Of conch and dissonant gong:
On that stony savage shore
Strip off your clothes and dance, for
Unless you are capable
Of forgetting completely
About Atlantis, you will
Never finish your journey.
Again, should you come to gay
Carthage or Corinth, take part
In their endless gaiety;
And if in some bar a tart,
As she strokes your hair, should say
"This is Atlantis, dearie,"
Listen with attentiveness
To her life-story: unless
You become acquainted now
With each refuge that tries to
Counterfeit Atlantis, how
Will you recognise the true?
Assuming you beach at last
Near Atlantis, and begin
That terrible trek inland
Through squalid woods and frozen
Thundras where all are soon lost;
If, forsaken then, you stand,
Dismissal everywhere,
Stone and now, silence and air,
O remember the great dead
And honour the fate you are,
Travelling and tormented,
Dialectic and bizarre.
Stagger onward rejoicing;
And even then if, perhaps
Having actually got
To the last col, you collapse
With all Atlantis shining
Below you yet you cannot

Descend, you should still be proud
Even to have been allowed
Just to peep at Atlantis
In a poetic vision:
Give thanks and lie down in peace,
Having seen your salvation.
All the little household gods
Have started crying, but say
Good-bye now, and put to sea.
Farewell, my dear, farewell: may
Hermes, master of the roads,
And the four dwarf Kabiri,
Protect and serve you always;
And may the Ancient of Days
Provide for all you must do
His invisible guidance,
Lifting up, dear, upon you
The light of His countenance.

Base Words Are Uttered

Base words are uttered only by the base
And can for such at once be understood,
But noble platitudes:—ah, there's a case
Where the most careful scrutiny is needed
To tell a voice that's genuinely good
From one that's base but merely has succeeded

Canzone

When shall we learn, what should be clear as day,
We cannot choose what we are free to love?
Although the mouse we banished yesterday
Is an enraged rhinoceros today,
Our value is more threatened than we know:
Shabby objections to our present day
Go snooping round its outskirts; night and day
Faces, orations, battles, bait our will
As questionable forms and noises will;
Whole phyla of resentments every day

Give status to the wild men of the world
Who rule the absent-minded and this world.
We are created from and with the world
To suffer with and from it day by day:
Whether we meet in a majestic world
Of solid measurements or a dream world
Of swans and gold, we are required to love
All homeless objects that require a world.
Our claim to own our bodies and our world
Is our catastrophe. What can we know
But panic and caprice until we know
Our dreadful appetite demands a world
Whose order, origin, and purpose will
Be fluent satisfaction of our will?
Drift, Autumn, drift; fall, colours, where you will:
Bald melancholia minces through the world.
Regret, cold oceans, the lymphatic will
Caught in reflection on the right to will:
While violent dogs excite their dying day
To bacchic fury; snarl, though, as they will,
Their teeth are not a triumph for the will
But utter hesitation. What we love
Ourselves for is our power not to love,
To shrink to nothing or explode at will,
To ruin and remember that we know
What ruins and hyaenas cannot know.
If in this dark now I less often know
That spiral staircase where the haunted will
Hunts for its stolen luggage, who should know
Better than you, beloved, how I know
What gives security to any world.
Or in whose mirror I begin to know
The chaos of the heart as merchants know
Their coins and cities, genius its own day?
For through our lively traffic all the day,
In my own person I am forced to know
How much must be forgotten out of love,
How much must be forgiven, even love.

Dear flesh, dear mind, dear spirit, O dear love,
In the depths of myself blind monsters know
Your presence and are angry, dreading Love
That asks its image for more than love;
The hot rampageous horses of my will,
Catching the scent of Heaven, whinny: Love
Gives no excuse to evil done for love,
Neither in you, nor me, nor armies, nor the world
Of words and wheels, nor any other world.
Dear fellow-creature, praise our God of Love
That we are so admonished, that no day
Of conscious trial be a wasted day.
Or else we make a scarecrow of the day,
Loose ends and jumble of our common world,
And stuff and nonsense of our own free will;
Or else our changing flesh may never know
There must be sorrow if there can be love.

Cocaine Lil and Morphine Sue

Did you ever hear about Cocaine Lil?
She lived in Cocaine town on Cocaine hill,
She had a cocaine dog and a cocaine cat,
They fought all night with a cocaine rat.
She had cocaine hair on her cocaine head.
She had a cocaine dress that was poppy red:
She wore a snowbird hat and sleigh-riding clothes,
On her coat she wore a crimson, cocaine rose.
Big gold chariots on the Milky Way,
Snakes and elephants silver and gray.
Oh the cocaine blues they make me sad,
Oh the cocaine blues make me feel bad.
Lil went to a snow party one cold night,
And the way she sniffed was sure a fright.
There was Hophead Mag with Dopey Slim,
Kankakee Liz and Yen Shee Jim.
There was Morphine Sue and the Poppy Face Kid,
Climbed up snow ladders and down they skid;
There was the Stepladder Kit, a good six feet,

And the Sleigh-riding Sister who were hard to beat.
Along in the morning about half past three
They were all lit up like a Christmas tree;
Lil got home and started for bed,
Took another sniff and it knocked her dead.
They laid her out in her cocaine clothes:
She wore a snowbird hat with a crimson rose;
On her headstone you'll find this refrain:
She died as she lived, sniffing cocaine

Dear, Though the Night Is Gone

Dear, though the night is gone,
Its dream still haunts today,
That brought us to a room
Cavernous, lofty as
A railway terminus,
And crowded in that gloom
Were beds, and we in one
In a far corner lay.
Our whisper woke no clocks,
We kissed and I was glad
At everything you did,
Indifferent to those
Who sat with hostile eyes
In pairs on every bed,
Arms round each other's neck,
Inert and vaguely sad.
O but what worm of guilt
Or what malignant doubt
Am I the victim of,
That you then, unabashed,
Did what I never wished,
Confessed another love;
And I, submissive, felt
Unwanted and went out?

For Friends Only

(for John and Teckla Clark)

Ours yet not ours, being set apart
As a shrine to friendship,
Empty and silent most of the year,
This room awaits from you
What you alone, as visitor, can bring,
A weekend of personal life.
In a house backed by orderly woods,
Facing a tractored sugar-beet country,
Your working hosts engaged to their stint,
You are unlike to encounter
Dragons or romance: were drama a craving,
You would not have come.
Books we do have for almost any
Literate mood, and notepaper, envelopes,
For a writing one (to "borrow" stamps
Is the mark of ill-breeding):
Between lunch and tea, perhaps a drive;
After dinner, music or gossip.
Should you have troubles (pets will die
Lovers are always behaving badly)
And confession helps, we will hear it,
Examine and give our counsel:
If to mention them hurts too much,
We shall not be nosey.
Easy at first, the language of friendship
Is, as we soon discover,
Very difficult to speak well, a tongue
With no cognates, no resemblance
To the galimatias of nursery and bedroom,
Court rhyme or shepherd's prose,
And, unless spoken often, soon goes rusty.
Distance and duties divide us,
But absence will not seem an evil
If it make our re-meeting
A real occasion. Come when you can:
Your room will be ready.
In Tum-Tum's reign a tin of biscuits
On the bedside table provided

For nocturnal munching. Now weapons have changed,
And the fashion of appetites:
There, for sunbathers who count their calories,
A bottle of mineral water.
Felicissima notte! May you fall at once
Into a cordial dream, assured
That whoever slept in this bed before
Was also someone we like,
That within the circle of our affection
Also you have no double

For What As Easy

For what as easy
For what thought small,
For what is well
Because between,
To you simply
From me I mean.
Who goes with who
The bedclothes say,
As I and you
Go kissed away,
The data given,
The senses even.
Fate is not late,
Nor the speech rewritten,
Nor one word forgotten,
Said at the start
About heart,
By heart, for heart.

Ganymede

He looked in all His wisdom from the throne
Down on that humble boy who kept the sheep,
And sent a dove; the dove returned alone:
Youth liked the music, but soon fell asleep.
But He had planned such future for the youth:
Surely, His duty now was to compel.

For later he would come to love the truth,
And own his gratitude. His eagle fell.
It did not work. His conversation bored
The boy who yawned and whistled and made faces,
And wriggled free from fatherly embraces;
But with the eagle he was always willing
To go where it suggested, and adored
And learnt from it so many ways of killing.

Give me a Doctor

Give me a doctor partridge-plump,
Short in the leg and broad in the rump,
An endomorph with gentle hands
Who'll never make absurd demands
That I abandon all my vices
Nor pull a long face in a crisis,
But with a twinkle in his eye
Will tell me that I have to die

In Memory of Sigmund Freud

When there are so many we shall have to mourn,
when grief has been made so public, and exposed
to the critique of a whole epoch
the frailty of our conscience and anguish,
of whom shall we speak? For every day they die
among us, those who were doing us some good,
who knew it was never enough but
hoped to improve a little by living.
Such was this doctor: still at eighty he wished
to think of our life from whose unruliness
so many plausible young futures
with threats or flattery ask obedience,
but his wish was denied him: he closed his eyes
upon that last picture, common to us all,
of problems like relatives gathered
puzzled and jealous about our dying.
For about him till the very end were still
those he had studied, the fauna of the night,

and shades that still waited to enter
the bright circle of his recognition
turned elsewhere with their disappointment as he
was taken away from his life interest
to go back to the earth in London,
an important Jew who died in exile.
Only Hate was happy, hoping to augment
his practice now, and his dingy clientele
who think they can be cured by killing
and covering the garden with ashes.
They are still alive, but in a world he changed
simply by looking back with no false regrets;
all he did was to remember
like the old and be honest like children.
He wasn't clever at all: he merely told
the unhappy Present to recite the Past
like a poetry lesson till sooner
or later it faltered at the line where
long ago the accusations had begun,
and suddenly knew by whom it had been judged,
how rich life had been and how silly,
and was life-forgiven and more humble,
able to approach the Future as a friend
without a wardrobe of excuses, without
a set mask of rectitude or an
embarrassing over-familiar gesture.
No wonder the ancient cultures of conceit
in his technique of unsettlement foresaw
the fall of princes, the collapse of
their lucrative patterns of frustration:
if he succeeded, why, the Generalised Life
would become impossible, the monolith
of State be broken and prevented
the co-operation of avengers.
Of course they called on God, but he went his way
down among the lost people like Dante, down
to the stinking fosse where the injured
lead the ugly life of the rejected,

and showed us what evil is, not, as we thought,
deeds that must be punished, but our lack of faith,
our dishonest mood of denial,
the concupiscence of the oppressor.
If some traces of the autocratic pose,
the paternal strictness he distrusted, still
clung to his utterance and features,
it was a protective coloration
for one who'd lived among enemies so long:
if often he was wrong and, at times, absurd,
to us he is no more a person
now but a whole climate of opinion
under whom we conduct our different lives:
Like weather he can only hinder or help,
the proud can still be proud but find it
a little harder, the tyrant tries to
make do with him but doesn't care for him much:
he quietly surrounds all our habits of growth
and extends, till the tired in even
the remotest miserable duchy
have felt the change in their bones and are cheered
till the child, unlucky in his little State,
some hearth where freedom is excluded,
a hive whose honey is fear and worry,
feels calmer now and somehow assured of escape,
while, as they lie in the grass of our neglect,
so many long-forgotten objects
revealed by his undiscouraged shining
are returned to us and made precious again;
games we had thought we must drop as we grew up,
little noises we dared not laugh at,
faces we made when no one was looking.
But he wishes us more than this. To be free
is often to be lonely. He would unite
the unequal moieties fractured
by our own well-meaning sense of justice,
would restore to the larger the wit and will
the smaller possesses but can only use

for arid disputes, would give back to
the son the mother's richness of feeling:
but he would have us remember most of all
to be enthusiastic over the night,
not only for the sense of wonder
it alone has to offer, but also
because it needs our love. With large sad eyes
its delectable creatures look up and beg
us dumbly to ask them to follow:
they are exiles who long for the future
that lives in our power, they too would rejoice
if allowed to serve enlightenment like him,
even to bear our cry of 'Judas',
as he did and all must bear who serve it.
One rational voice is dumb. Over his grave
the household of Impulse mourns one dearly loved:
sad is Eros, builder of cities,
and weeping anarchic Aphrodite.

In the Time of War, XII

And the age ended, and the last deliverer died.
In bed, grown idle and unhappy; they were safe:
The sudden shadow of the giant's enormous calf
Would fall no more at dusk across the lawn outside.
They slept in peace: in marshes here and there no doubt
A sterile dragon lingered to a natural death,
But in a year the spoor had vanished from the heath;
The kobold's knocking in the mountain petered out.
Only the sculptors and the poets were half sad,
And the pert retinue from the magician's house
Grumbled and went elsewhere.
The vanished powers were glad
To be invisible and free: without remorse
Struck down the sons who strayed their course,
And ravished the daughters, and drove the fathers mad.

Lady

Lady, weeping at the crossroads

Would you meet your love
In the twilight with his greyhounds,
And the hawk on his glove?
Bribe the birds then on the branches
Bribe them to be dumb,
Stare the hot sun out of heaven
That the night may come.
Starless are the night of travel,
Bleak the winter wind;
Run with terror all before you
And regret behind.
Run until you hear the ocean's
Everlasting cry;
Deep though it may be and bitter
You must drink it dry.
Wear out patience in the lowest
Dungeons of the sea,
Searching through the stranded shipwrecks
For the golden key.
Push on to the world's end, pay the
Dread guard with a kiss;
Cross the rotten bridge that totters
Over the abyss.
There stands the deserted castle
Ready to explore;
Enter, climb the marble staircase
Open the locked door.
Cross the silent ballroom,
Doubt and danger past;
Blow the cobwebs from the mirror
See yourself at last.
Put your hand behind the wainscot,
You have done your part;
Find the penknife there and plunge it
Into your false heart.]

Lay Your Sleeping Head, My Love

Lay your sleeping head, my love,

Human on my faithless arm;
Time and fevers burn away
Individual beauty from
Thoughtful children, and the grave
Proves the child ephemeral:
But in my arms till break of day
Let the living creature lie,
Mortal, guilty, but to me
The entirely beautiful.
Soul and body have no bounds:
To lovers as they lie upon
Her tolerant enchanted slope
In their ordinary swoon,
Grave the vision Venus sends
Of supernatural sympathy,
Universal love and hope;
While an abstract insight wakes
Among the glaciers and the rocks
The hermit's sensual ecstasy.
Certainty, fidelity
On the stroke of midnight pass
Like vibrations of a bell,
And fashionable madmen raise
Their pedantic boring cry:
Every farthing of the cost,
All the dreadful cards foretell,
Shall be paid, but not from this night
Not a whisper, not a thought,
Not a kiss nor look be lost.
Beauty, midnight, vision dies:
Let the winds of dawn that blow
Softly round your dreaming head
Such a day of sweetness show
Eye and knocking heart may bless.
Find the mortal world enough;
Noons of dryness see you fed
By the involuntary powers,
Nights of insult let you pass
Watched by every human love.

Miranda

My dear one is mine as mirrors are lonely,
As the poor and sad are real to the good king,
And the high green hill sits always by the sea.
Up jumped the Black Man behind the elder tree,
Turned a somersault and ran away waving;
My Dear One is mine as mirrors are lonely.
The Witch gave a squawk; her venomous body
Melted into light as water leaves a spring,
And the high green hill sits always by the sea.
At his crossroads, too, the Ancient prayed for me,
Down his wasted cheeks tears of joy were running:
My dear one is mine as mirrors are lonely.
He kissed me awake, and no one was sorry;
The sun shone on sails, eyes, pebbles, anything,
And the high green hill sits always by the sea.
So to remember our changing garden, we
Are linked as children in a circle dancing:
My dear one is mine as mirrors are lonely,
And the high, green hill sits always by the sea.

Night Mail

I

This is the night mail crossing the Border,
Bringing the cheque and the postal order,
Letters for the rich, letters for the poor,
The shop at the corner, the girl next door.
Pulling up Beattock, a steady climb:
The gradient's against her, but she's on time.
Past cotton-grass and moorland boulder
Shovelling white steam over her shoulder,
Snorting noisily as she passes
Silent miles of wind-bent grasses.
Birds turn their heads as she approaches,
Stare from bushes at her blank-faced coaches.
Sheep-dogs cannot turn her course;

They slumber on with paws across.
In the farm she passes no one wakes,
But a jug in a bedroom gently shakes.

II

Dawn freshens, Her climb is done.
Down towards Glasgow she descends,
Towards the steam tugs yelping down a glade of cranes
Towards the fields of apparatus, the furnaces
Set on the dark plain like gigantic chessmen.
All Scotland waits for her:
In dark glens, beside pale-green lochs
Men long for news.

III

Letters of thanks, letters from banks,
Letters of joy from girl and boy,
Receipted bills and invitations
To inspect new stock or to visit relations,
And applications for situations,
And timid lovers' declarations,
And gossip, gossip from all the nations,
News circumstantial, news financial,
Letters with holiday snaps to enlarge in,
Letters with faces scrawled on the margin,
Letters from uncles, cousins, and aunts,
Letters to Scotland from the South of France,
Letters of condolence to Highlands and Lowlands
Written on paper of every hue,
The pink, the violet, the white and the blue,
The chatty, the catty, the boring, the adoring,
The cold and official and the heart's outpouring,
Clever, stupid, short and long,
The typed and the printed and the spelt all wrong.

IV

Thousands are still asleep,
Dreaming of terrifying monsters

Or of friendly tea beside the band in
Cranston's or Crawford's:
Asleep in working Glasgow, asleep in well-set Edinburgh,
Asleep in granite Aberdeen,
They continue their dreams,
But shall wake soon and hope for letters,
And none will hear the postman's knock
Without a quickening of the heart,
For who can bear to feel himself forgotten?

Nocturne

Now through night's caressing grip
Earth and all her oceans slip,
Capes of China slide away
From her fingers into day
And th'Americas incline
Coasts towards her shadow line.
Now the ragged vagrants creep
Into crooked holes to sleep:
Just and unjust, worst and best,
Change their places as they rest:
Awkward lovers like in fields
Where disdainful beauty yields:
While the splendid and the proud
Naked stand before the crowd
And the losing gambler gains
And the beggar entertains:
May sleep's healing power extend
Through these hours to our friend.
Unpursued by hostile force,
Traction engine, bull or horse
Or revolting succubus;
Calmly till the morning break
Let him lie, then gently wake.

O Tell Me The Truth About Love

Some say love's a little boy,
And some say it's a bird,

Some say it makes the world go around,
Some say that's absurd,
And when I asked the man next-door,
Who looked as if he knew,
His wife got very cross indeed,
And said it wouldn't do.
Does it look like a pair of pyjamas,
Or the ham in a temperance hotel?
Does its odour remind one of llamas,
Or has it a comforting smell?
Is it prickly to touch as a hedge is,
Or soft as eiderdown fluff?
Is it sharp or quite smooth at the edges?
O tell me the truth about love.
Our history books refer to it
In cryptic little notes,
It's quite a common topic on
The Transatlantic boats;
I've found the subject mentioned in
Accounts of suicides,
And even seen it scribbled on
The backs of railway guides.
Does it howl like a hungry Alsatian,
Or boom like a military band?
Could one give a first-rate imitation
On a saw or a Steinway Grand?
Is its singing at parties a riot?
Does it only like Classical stuff?
Will it stop when one wants to be quiet?
O tell me the truth about love.
I looked inside the summer-house;
It wasn't over there;
I tried the Thames at Maidenhead,
And Brighton's bracing air.
I don't know what the blackbird sang,
Or what the tulip said;
But it wasn't in the chicken-run,
Or underneath the bed.

Can it pull extraordinary faces?
Is it usually sick on a swing?
Does it spend all its time at the races,
or fiddling with pieces of string?
Has it views of its own about money?
Does it think Patriotism enough?
Are its stories vulgar but funny?
O tell me the truth about love.
When it comes, will it come without warning
Just as I'm picking my nose?
Will it knock on my door in the morning,
Or tread in the bus on my toes?
Will it come like a change in the weather?
Will its greeting be courteous or rough?
Will it alter my life altogether?
O tell me the truth about love.

O What Is That Sound

O what is that sound which so thrills the ear
Down in the valley drumming, drumming?
Only the scarlet soldiers, dear,
The soldiers coming.
O what is that light I see flashing so clear
Over the distance brightly, brightly?
Only the sun on their weapons, dear,
As they step lightly.
O what are they doing with all that gear,
What are they doing this morning, morning?
Only their usual manoeuvres, dear,
Or perhaps a warning.
O why have they left the road down there,
Why are they suddenly wheeling, wheeling?
Perhaps a change in their orders, dear,
Why are you kneeling?
O haven't they stopped for the doctor's care,
Haven't they reined their horses, horses?
Why, they are none of them wounded, dear,
None of these forces.

O is it the parson they want, with white hair,
Is it the parson, is it, is it?
No, they are passing his gateway, dear,
Without a visit.
O it must be the farmer that lives so near.
It must be the farmer so cunning, so cunning?
They have passed the farmyard already, dear,
And now they are running.
O where are you going? Stay with me here!
Were the vows you swore deceiving, deceiving?
No, I promised to love you, dear,
But I must be leaving.
O it's broken the lock and splintered the door,
O it's the gate where they're turning, turning;
Their boots are heavy on the floor
And their eyes are burning.

O Where Are You Going?

"O where are you going?" said reader to rider,
"That valley is fatal when furnaces burn,
Yonder's the midden whose odors will madden,
That gap is the grave where the tall return."
"O do you imagine," said fearer to farer,
"That dusk will delay on your path to the pass,
Your diligent looking discover the lacking
Your footsteps feel from granite to grass?"
"O what was that bird," said horror to hearer,
"Did you see that shape in the twisted trees?
Behind you swiftly the figure comes softly,
The spot on your skin is a shocking disease?"
"Out of this house" , said rider to reader,
"Yours never will" , said farer to fearer,
"They're looking for you" , said hearer to horror,
As he left them there, as he left them there.

On the Circuit

Among pelagian travelers,
Lost on their lewd conceited way
To Massachusetts, Michigan,

Miami or L.A.,
An airborne instrument I sit,
Predestined nightly to fulfill
Columbia-Giesen-Management's
Unfathomable will,
By whose election justified,
I bring my gospel of the Muse
To fundamentalists, to nuns,
to Gentiles and to Jews,
And daily, seven days a week,
Before a local sense has jelled,
From talking-site to talking-site
Am jet-or-prop-propelled.
Though warm my welcome everywhere,
I shift so frequently, so fast,
I cannot now say where I was
The evening before last,
Unless some singular event
Should intervene to save the place,
A truly asinine remark,
A soul-bewitching face,
Or blessed encounter, full of joy,
Unscheduled on the Giesen Plan,
With, here, an addict of Tolkien,
There, a Charles Williams fan.
Since Merit but a dunghill is,
I mount the rostrum unafraid:
Indeed, 'twere damnable to ask
If I am overpaid.
Spirit is willing to repeat
Without a qualm the same old talk,
But Flesh is homesick for our snug
Apartment in New York.
A sulky fifty-six, he finds
A change of mealtime utter hell,
Grown far too crotchety to like
A luxury hotel.
The Bible is a goodly book
I always can peruse with zest,

But really cannot say the same
For Hilton's Be My Guest.
Nor bear with equanimity
The radio in students' cars,
Muzak at breakfast, or—dear God!—
Girl-organists in bars.
Then, worst of all, the anxious thought,
Each time my plane begins to sink
And the No Smoking sign comes on:
What will there be to drink?
Is this ma milieu where I must
How grahamgreeneish! How infra dig!
Snatch from the bottle in my bag An analeptic swig?
Another morning comes: I see,
Dwindling below me on the plane,
The roofs of one more audience
I shall not see again.
God bless the lot of them, although
I don't remember which was which:
God bless the U.S.A., so large,
So friendly, and so rich.

One Evening

As I walked out one evening,
Walking down Bristol Street,
The crowds upon the pavement
Were fields of harvest wheat.
And down by the brimming river
I heard a lover sing
Under an arch of the railway:
'Love has no ending.
I'll love you, dear, I'll love you
Till China and Africa meet,
And the river jumps over the mountain
And the salmon sing in the street.
I'll love you till the ocean
Is folded and hung up to dry,
And the seven stars go squawking
Like geese about the sky.

The years shall run like rabbits,
For in my arms I hold
The Flower of the Ages,
And the first love of the world.'
But all the clocks in the city
Began to whirr and chime:
'O let not Time deceive you,
You cannot conquer Time.
'In the burrows of the Nightmare
Where Justice naked is,
Time watches from the shadow
And coughs when you would kiss.
'In headaches and in worry
Vaguely life leaks away,
And Time will have his fancy
To-morrow or today.
'Into many a green valley
Drifts the appalling snow;
Time breaks the threaded dances
And the diver's brilliant bow.
'O plunge your hands in water,
Plunge them in up to the wrist;
Stare, stare at the basin
And wonder what you've missed.
'The glacier knocks in the cupboard,
The desert sighs in the bed,
And the crack in the tea-cup opens
A lane to the land of the dead.
'Where the beggars raffle the banknotes
And the Giant in enchanting to Jack,
And the Lily-white Boy is a Roarer,
And Jill goes down on her back.
'O look, look in the mirror,
O look in your distress;
Life remains a blessing
Although you cannot bless.
'O stand, stand in the window
As the tears scald and start;
You shall love your crooked neighbour

With your crooked heart.'
It was late, late in the evening
The lovers they were gone;
The clocks had ceased their chiming,
And the deep river ran on.

Refugee Blues

Say this city has ten million souls,
Some are living in mansions, some are living in holes:
Yet there's no place for us, my dear, yet
there's no place for us.
Once we had a country and we thought it fair,
Look in the atlas and you'll find it there:
We cannot go there now, my dear,
we cannot go there now.
In the village churchyard there grows an old yew,
Every spring it blossoms anew:
Old passports can't do that, my dear,
old passports can't do that.
The consul banged the table and said,
"If you've got no passport you're officially dead":
But we are still alive, my dear, but we are still alive.
Went to a committee; they offered me a chair;
Asked me politely to return next year:
But where shall we go to-day, my dear, but
where shall we go to-day?
Came to a public meeting; the speaker got up and said;
"If we let them in, they will steal our daily bread":
He was talking of you and me, my dear,
he was talking of you and me.
Thought I heard the thunder rumbling in the sky;
It was Hitler over Europe, saying, "They must die":
O we were in his mind, my dear, O we were in his mind.
Saw a poodle in a jacket fastened with a pin,
Saw a door opened and a cat let in:
But they weren't German Jews, my dear, but they weren't
German Jews.
Went down the harbour and stood upon the quay,
Saw the fish swimming as if they were free:

Only ten feet away, my dear, only ten feet away.
Walked through a wood, saw the birds in the trees;
They had no politicians and sang at their ease:
They weren't the human race, my dear,
they weren't the human race.
Dreamed I saw a building with a thousand floors,
A thousand windows and a thousand doors:
Not one of them was ours, my dear, not one of
them was ours.
Stood on a great plain in the falling snow;
Ten thousand soldiers marched to and fro:
Looking for you and me, my dear,
looking for you and me.

Roman Wall Blues

Over the heather the wet wind blows,
I've lice in my tunic and a cold in my nose.
The rain comes pattering out of the sky,
I'm a Wall soldier, I don't know why.
The mist creeps over the hard grey stone,
My girl's in Tungria; I sleep alone.
Aulus goes hanging around her place,
I don't like his manners, I don't like his face.
Piso's a Christian, he worships a fish;
There'd be no kissing if he had his wish.
She gave me a ring but I diced it away;
I want my girl and I want my pay.
When I'm a veteran with only one eye
I shall do nothing but look at the sky.

Seascape

Look, stranger, at this island now
The leaping light for your delight discovers,
Stand stable here
And silent be,
That through the channels of the ear
May wander like a river
The swaying sound of the sea.
Here at the small field's ending pause

Where the chalk wall falls to the foam, and its tall ledges
Oppose the pluck
And knock of the tide,
And the shingle scrambles
after the sucking surf,
and the gull lodges
A moment on its sheer side.
Far off like floating seeds the ships
Diverge on urgent voluntary errands;
And the full view
Indeed may enter
And move in memory as now these clouds do,
That pass the harbour mirror
And all the summer through the water saunter.

Song Of The Master And Boatswain

At Dirty Dick's and Sloppy Joe's
We drank our liquor straight,
Some went upstairs with Margery,
And some, alas, with Kate;
And two by two like cat and mouse
The homeless played at keeping house.
There Wealthy Meg, the Sailor's Friend,
And Marion, cow-eyed,
Opened their arms to me but I
Refused to step inside;
I was not looking for a cage
In which to mope my old age.
The nightingales are sobbing in
The orchards of our mothers,
And hearts that we broke long ago
Have long been breaking others;
Tears are round, the sea is deep:
Roll them overboard and sleep.

The Fall of Rome

(for Cyril Connolly)
The piers are pummelled by the waves;
In a lonely field the rain

Lashes an abandoned train;
Outlaws fill the mountain caves.
Fantastic grow the evening gowns;
Agents of the Fisc pursue
Absconding tax-defaulters through
The sewers of provincial towns.
Private rites of magic send
The temple prostitutes to sleep;
All the literati keep
An imaginary friend.
Cerebrotonic Cato may
Extol the Ancient Disciplines,
But the muscle-bound Marines
Mutiny for food and pay.
Caesar's double-bed is warm
As an unimportant clerk
Writes I DO NOT LIKE MY WORK
On a pink official form.
Unendowed with wealth or pity,
Little birds with scarlet legs,
Sitting on their speckled eggs,
Eye each flu-infected city.
Altogether elsewhere, vast
Herds of reindeer move across
Miles and miles of golden moss,
Silently and very fast.

The Geography of the House

(for Christopher Isherwood)
Seated after breakfast
In this white-tiled cabin
Arabs call the House where
Everybody goes,
Even melancholics
Raise a cheer to Mrs.
Nature for the primal
Pleasure She bestows.
Sex is but a dream to
Seventy-and-over,

But a joy proposed un-
-til we start to shave:
Mouth-delight depends on
Virtue in the cook, but
This She guarantees from
Cradle unto grave.
Lifted off the potty,
Infants from their mothers
Hear their first impartial
Words of worldly praise:
Hence, to start the morning
With a satisfactory
Dump is a good omen
All our adult days.
Revelation came to
Luther in a privy
(Crosswords have been solved there)
Rodin was no fool
When he cast his Thinker,
Cogitating deeply,
Crouched in the position
Of a man at stool.
All the arts derive from
This ur-act of making,
Private to the artist:
Makers' lives are spent
Striving in their chosen
Medium to produce a
De-narcissus-ized en-
During excrement.
Freud did not invent the
Constipated miser:
Banks have letter boxes
Built in their façade
Marked For Night Deposits,
Stocks are firm or liquid,
Currencies of nations
Either soft or hard.
Global Mother, keep our

Bowels of compassion
Open through our lifetime,
Purge our minds as well:
Grant us a king ending,
Not a second childhood,
Petulant, weak-sphinctered,
In a cheap hotel.
Keep us in our station:
When we get pound-notish,
When we seem about to
Take up Higher Thought,
Send us some deflating
Image like the pained ex-
-pression on a Major
Prophet taken short.
(Orthodoxy ought to
Bless our modern plumbing:
Swift and St. Augustine
Lived in centuries
When a stench of sewage
Made a strong debating
Point for Manichees.)
Mind and Body run on
Different timetables:
Not until our morning
Visit here can we
Leave the dead concerns of
Yesterday behind us,
Face with all our courage
What is now to be.

The Hidden Law

The Hidden Law does not deny
Our laws of probability,
But takes the atom and the star
And human beings as they are,
And answers nothing when we lie.
It is the only reason why
No government can codify,

And verbal definitions mar
The Hidden Law.
Its utter patience will not try
To stop us if we want to die;
If we escape it in a car,
If we forget It in a bar,
These are the ways we're punished by
The Hidden Law

The Labyrinth

Anthropos apteros for days
Walked whistling round and round the Maze,
Relying happily upon
His temperment for getting on.
The hundredth time he sighted, though,
A bush he left an hour ago,
He halted where four alleys crossed,
And recognized that he was lost.
"Where am I?" Metaphysics says
No question can be asked unless
It has an answer, so I can
Assume this maze has got a plan.
If theologians are correct,
A Plan implies an Architect:
A God-built maze would be, I'm sure,
The Universe in minature.
Are data from the world of Sense,
In that case, valid evidence?
What in the universe I know
Can give directions how to go?
All Mathematics would suggest
A steady straight line as the best,
But left and right alternately
Is consonant with History.
Aesthetics, though, believes all Art
Intends to gratify the heart:
Rejecting disciplines like these,
Must I, then, go which way I please?
Such reasoning is only true

If we accept the classic view,
Which we have no right to assert,
According to the Introvert.
His absolute pre-supposition
Is - Man creates his own condition:
This maze was not divinely built,
But is secreted by my guilt.
The centre that I cannot find
Is known to my unconscious Mind;
I have no reason to despair
Because I am already there.
My problem is how not to will;
They move most quickly who stand still;
I'm only lost until I see
I'm lost because I want to be.
If this should fail, perhaps I should,
As certain educators would,
Content myself with the conclusion;
In theory there is no solution.
All statements about what I feel,
Like I-am-lost, are quite unreal:
My knowledge ends where it began;
A hedge is taller than a man."
Anthropos apteros, perplexed
To know which turning to take next,
Looked up and wished he were a bird
To whom such doubts must seem absurd.

The More Loving One

Looking up at the stars, I know quite well
That, for all they care, I can go to hell,
But on earth indifference is the least
We have to dread from man or beast.
How should we like it were stars to burn
With a passion for us we could not return?
If equal affection cannot be,
Let the more loving one be me.
Admirer as I think I am
Of stars that do not give a damn,

I cannot, now I see them, say
I missed one terribly all day.
Were all stars to disappear or die,
I should learn to look at an empty sky
And feel its total dark sublime,
Though this might take me a little time.

The Quest

I The Door

Out of it steps our future, through this door
Enigmas, executioners and rules,
Her Majesty in a bad temper or
A red-nosed Fool who makes a fool of fools.
Great persons eye it in the twilight for
A past it might so carelessly let in,
A widow with a missionary grin,
The foaming inundation at a roar.
We pile our all against it when afraid,
And beat upon its panels when we die:
By happening to be open once, it made
Enormous Alice see a wonderland
That waited for her in the sunshine and,
Simply by being tiny, made her cry.

II The Preparations

All had been ordered weeks before the start
From the best firms at such work: instruments
To take the measure of all queer events,
And drugs to move the bowels or the heart.
A watch, of course, to watch impatience fly,
Lamps for the dark and shades against the sun;
Foreboding, too, insisted on a gun,
And coloured beads to soothe a savage eye.
In theory they were sound on Expectation,
Had there been situations to be in;
Unluckily they were their situation:
One should not give a poisoner medicine,
A conjurer fine apparatus, nor

A rifle to a melancholic bore.

III The Crossroads

Two friends who met here and embraced are gone,
Each to his own mistake; one flashes on
To fame and ruin in a rowdy lie,
A village torpor holds the other one,
Some local wrong where it takes time to die:
This empty junction glitters in the sun.
So at all quays and crossroads: who can tell
These places of decision and farewell
To what dishonour all adventure leads,
What parting gift could give that friend protection,
So orientated his vocation needs
The Bad Lands and the sinister direction?
All landscapes and all weathers freeze with fear,
But none have ever thought, the legends say,
The time allowed made it impossible;
For even the most pessimistic set
The limit of their errors at a year.
What friends could there be left then to betray,
What joy take longer to atone for; yet
Who could complete without the extra day
The journey that should take no time at all?

IV The Traveller

No window in his suburb lights that bedroom where
A little fever heard large afternoons at play:
His meadows multiply; that mill, though, is not there
Which went on grinding at the back of love all day.
Nor all his weeping ways through weary
wastes have found
The castle where his Greater Hallows are interned;
For broken bridges halt him, and dark thickets round
Some ruin where an evil heritage was burned.
Could he forget a child's ambition to be old
And institutions where it learned to wash and lie,
He'd tell the truth for which he thinks himself too young,
That everywhere on his horizon, all the sky,
Is now, as always, only waiting to be told

To be his father's house and speak his mother tongue.

V The City

In villages from which their childhoods came
Seeking Necessity, they had been taught
Necessity by nature is the same
No matter how or by whom it be sought.
The city, though, assumed no such belief,
But welcomed each as if he came alone,
The nature of Necessity like grief
Exactly corresponding to his own.
And offered them so many, every one
Found some temptation fit to govern him,
And settled down to master the whole craft
Of being nobody; sat in the sun
During the lunch-hour round the fountain rim,
And watched the country kids arrive, and laughed.
VI. The First Temptation
Ashamed to be the darling of his grief,
He joined a gang of rowdy stories where
His gift for magic quickly made him chief
Of all these boyish powers of the air;
Who turned his hungers into Roman food,
The town's asymmetry into a park;
All hours took taxis; any solitude
Became his flattered duchess in the dark.
But, if he wished for anything less grand,
The nights came padding after him like wild
Beasts that meant harm, and all the doors cried Thief;
And when Truth had met him and put out her hand,
He clung in panic to his tall belief
And shrank away like an ill-treated child.

VII The Second Temptation

His library annoyed him with its look
Of calm belief in being really there;
He threw away a rival's boring book,
And clattered panting up the spiral stair.
Swaying upon the parapet he cried:

"O Uncreated Nothing, set me free,
Now let Thy perfect be identified,
Unending passion of the Night, with Thee."
And his long-suffering flesh, that all the time
Had felt the simple cravings of the stone
And hoped to be rewarded for her climb,
Took it to be a promise when he spoke
That now at last she would be left alone,
And plunged into the college quad, and broke.

VIII *The Third Temptation*

He watched with all his organs of concern
How princes walk, what wives and children say,
Re-opened old graves in his heart to learn
What laws the dead had died to disobey,
And came reluctantly to his conclusion:
"All the arm-chair philosophies are false;
To love another adds to the confusion;
The song of mercy is the Devil's Waltz."
All that he put his hand to prospered so
That soon he was the very King of creatures,
Yet, in an autumn nightmare trembled, for,
Approaching down a ruined corridor,
Strode someone with his own distorted features
Who wept, and grew enormous, and cried Woe.

IX *The Tower*

This is an architecture for the old;
Thus heaven was attacked by the afraid,
So once, unconsciously, a virgin made
Her maidenhead conspicuous to a god.
Here on dark nights while worlds of triumph sleep
Lost Love in abstract speculation burns,
And exiled Will to politics returns
In epic verse that makes its traitors weep.
Yet many come to wish their tower a well;
For those who dread to drown, of thirst may die,
Those who see all become invisible:
Here great magicians, caught in their own spell,

Long for a natural climate as they sigh
"Beware of Magic" to the passer-by.

X *The Presumptuous*

They noticed that virginity was needed
To trap the unicorn in every case,
But not that, of those virgins who succeeded,
A high percentage had an ugly face.
The hero was as daring as they thought him,
But his peculiar boyhood missed them all;
The angel of a broken leg had taught him
The right precautions to avoid a fall.
So in presumption they set forth alone
On what, for them, was not compulsory,
And stuck half-way to settle in some cave
With desert lions to domesticity,
Or turned aside to be absurdly brave,
And met the ogre and were turned to stone.

XI *The Average*

His peasant parents killed themselves with toil
To let their darling leave a stingy soil
For any of those fine professions which
Encourage shallow breathing, and grow rich.
The pressure of their fond ambition made
Their shy and country-loving child afraid
No sensible career was good enough,
Only a hero could deserve such love.
So here he was without maps or supplies,
A hundred miles from any decent town;
The desert glared into his blood-shot eyes,
The silence roared displeasure:
looking down,
He saw the shadow of an Average Man
Attempting the exceptional, and ran.

XII *Vocation*

Incredulous, he stared at the amused
Official writing down his name among

Those whose request to suffer was refused.
The pen ceased scratching: though he came too late
To join the martyrs, there was still a place
Among the tempters for a caustic tongue
To test the resolution of the young
With tales of the small failings of the great,
And shame the eager with ironic praise.
Though mirrors might be hateful for a while,
Women and books would teach his middle age
The fencing wit of an informal style,
To keep the silences at bay and cage
His pacing manias in a worldly smile.

XIII The Useful

The over-logical fell for the witch
Whose argument converted him to stone,
Thieves rapidly absorbed the over-rich,
The over-popular went mad alone,
And kisses brutalised the over-male.
As agents their importance quickly ceased;
Yet, in proportion as they seemed to fail,
Their instrumental value was increased
For one predestined to attain their wish.
By standing stones the blind can feel their way,
Wild dogs compel the cowardly to fight,
Beggars assist the slow to travel light,
And even madmen manage to convey
Unwelcome truths in lonely gibberish.

XIV The Way

Fresh addenda are published every day
To the encyclopedia of the Way,
Linguistic notes and scientific explanations,
And texts for schools with modernised
spelling and illustrations.
Now everyone knows the hero must choose the old horse,
Abstain from liquor and sexual intercourse,
And look out for a stranded fish to be kind to:
Now everyone thinks he could find, had he a mind to,

The way through the waste to the chapel in the rock
For a vision of the Triple Rainbow or the Astral Clock,
Forgetting his information comes mostly from
married men
Who liked fishing and a flutter on the
horses now and then.
And how reliable can any truth be that is got
By observing oneself and then just inserting a Not?

XV *The Lucky*

Suppose he'd listened to the erudite committee,
He would have only found where not to look;
Suppose his terrier when he whistled had obeyed,
It would not have unearthed the buried city;
Suppose he had dismissed the careless maid,
The cryptogram would not have fluttered from the book.
"It was not I," he cried as, healthy and astounded,
He stepped across a predecessor's skull;
"A nonsense jingle simply came into my head
And left the intellectual Sphinx dumbfounded;
I won the Queen because my hair was red;
The terrible adventure is a little dull."
Hence Failure's torment: "Was I doomed in any case,
Or would I not have failed had I believed in Grace?"

XVI *The Hero*

He parried every question that they hurled:
"What did the Emperor tell you?" "Not to push."
"What is the greatest wonder of the world?"
"The bare man Nothing in the Beggar's Bush."
Some muttered: "He is cagey for effect.
A hero owes a duty to his fame.
He looks too like a grocer for respect."
Soon they slipped back into his Christian name.
The only difference that could be seen
From those who'd never risked their lives at all
Was his delight in details and routine:
For he was always glad to mow the grass,
Pour liquids from large bottles into small,

Or look at clouds through bits of coloured glass.

XVII *Adventure*

Others had found it prudent to withdraw
Before official pressure was applied,
Embittered robbers outlawed by the Law,
Lepers in terror of the terrified.
But no one else accused these of a crime;
They did not look ill: old friends, overcome,
Stared as they rolled away from talk and time
Like marbles out into the blank and dumb.
The crowd clung all the closer to convention,
Sunshine and horses, for the sane know why
The even numbers should ignore the odd:
The Nameless is what no free people mention;
Successful men know better than to try
To see the face of their Absconded God.

XVIII *The Adventurers*

Spinning upon their central thirst like tops,
They went the Negative Way towards the Dry;
By empty caves beneath an empty sky
They emptied out their memories like slops,
Which made a foul marsh as they dried to death,
Where monsters bred who forced them to forget
The lovelies their consent avoided; yet,
Still praising the Absurd with their last breath,
They seeded out into their miracles:
The images of each grotesque temptation
Became some painter's happiest inspiration,
And barren wives and burning virgins came
To drink the pure cold water of their wells,
And wish for beaux and children in their name.

XIX *The Waters*

Poet, oracle, and wit
Like unsuccessful anglers by
The ponds of apperception sit,
Baiting with the wrong request

The vectors of their interest,
At nightfall tell the angler's lie.
With time in tempest everywhere,
To rafts of frail assumption cling
The saintly and the insincere;
Enraged phenomena bear down
In overwhelming waves to drown
Both sufferer and suffering.
The waters long to hear our question put
Which would release their longed-for answer, but.

XX *The Garden*

Within these gates all opening begins:
White shouts and flickers through its green and red,
Where children play at seven earnest sins
And dogs believe their tall conditions dead.
Here adolescence into number breaks
The perfect circle time can draw on stone,
And flesh forgives division as it makes
Another's moment of consent its own.
All journeys die here: wish and weight are lifted:
Where often round some old maid's desolation
Roses have flung their glory like a cloak,
The gaunt and great, the famed for conversation
Blushed in the stare of evening as they spoke
And felt their centre of volition shifted.

The Riddle

Underneath the leaves of life,
Green on the prodigious tree,
In a trance of grief
Stand the fallen man and wife:
Far away the single stag
Banished to a lonely crag
Gazes placid out to sea,
And from thickets round about
Breeding animals look in
On Duality,
And the birds fly in and out

Of the world of man.
Down in order from the ridge,
Bayonets glittering in the sun,
Soldiers who will judge
Wind towards the little bridge:
Even politicians speak
Truths of value to the weak,
Necessary acts are done
By the ill and the unjust;
But the Judgment and the Smile,
Though these two-in-one
See creation as they must,
None shall reconcile.
Bordering our middle earth
Kingdoms of the Short and Tall,
Rivals for our faith,
Stir up envy from our birth:
So the giant who storms the sky
In an angry wish to die
Wakes the hero in us all,
While the tiny with their power
To divide and hide and flee,
When our fortunes fall
Tempt to a belief in our
Immortality.
Lovers running each to each
Feel such timid dreams catch fire
Blazing as they touch,
Learn what love alone can teach:
Happy on a tousled bed
Praise Blake's acumen who said:
"One thing only we require
Of each other; we must see
In another's lineaments
Gratified desire";
This is our humanity;
Nothing else contents.
Nowhere else could I have known
Than, beloved, in your eyes

What we have to learn,
That we love ourselves alone:
All our terrors burned away
We can learn at last to say:
"All our knowledge comes to this,
That existence is enough,
That in savage solitude
Or the play of love
Every living creature is
Woman, Man, and Child."

The Two

You are the town and we are the clock.
We are the guardians of the gate in the rock.
The Two.
On your left and on your right
In the day and in the night,
We are watching you.
Wiser not to ask just what has occurred
To them who disobeyed our word;
To those
We were the whirlpool, we were the reef,
We were the formal nightmare, grief
And the unlucky rose.
Climb up the crane, learn the sailor's words
When the ships from the islands laden with birds
Come in.
Tell your stories of fishing and other men's wives:
The expansive moments of constricted lives
In the lighted inn.
But do not imagine we do not know
Nor that what you hide with such care won't show
At a glance.
Nothing is done, nothing is said,
But don't make the mistake of believing us dead:
I shouldn't dance.
We're afraid in that case you'll have a fall.
We've been watching you over the garden wall
For hours.

The sky is darkening like a stain,
Something is going to fall like rain
And it won't be flowers.
When the green field comes off like a lid
Revealing what was much better hid:
Unpleasant.
And look, behind you without a sound
The woods have come up and are standing round
In deadly crescent.
The bolt is sliding in its groove,
Outside the window is the black removers' van.
And now with sudden swift emergence
Come the woman in dark glasses and
humpbacked surgeons
And the scissors man.
This might happen any day
So be careful what you say
Or do.
Be clean, be tidy, oil the lock,
Trim the garden, wind the clock,
Remember the Two.

They Wondered Why the Fruit had Been Forbidden

They wondered why the fruit had been forbidden:
It taught them nothing new. They hid their pride,
But did not listen much when they were chidden:
They knew exactly what to do outside.
They left. Immediately the memory faded
Of all they known: they could not understand
The dogs now who before had always aided;
The stream was dumb with whom they'd always planned.
They wept and quarrelled: freedom was so wild.
In front maturity as he ascended
Retired like a horizon from the child,
The dangers and the punishments grew greater,
And the way back by angels was defended
Against the poet and the legislator.

This Lunar Beauty

This lunar beauty

Has no history
Is complete and early,
If beauty later
Bear any feature
It had a lover
And is another.
This like a dream
Keeps other time
And daytime is
The loss of this,
For time is inches
And the heart's changes
Where ghost has haunted
Lost and wanted.
But this was never
A ghost's endeavor
Nor finished this,
Was ghost at ease,
And till it pass
Love shall not near
The sweetness here
Nor sorrow take
His endless look.

Twelve Songs

I

Song of the Beggars
"O for doors to be open and an invite with gilded edges
To dine with Lord Lobcock and Count
Asthma on the platinum benches
With somersaults and fireworks,
the roast and the smacking kisses"
Cried the crippies to the silent statue,
The six beggared cripples.
"And Garbo's and Cleopatra's wits to go astraying,
In a feather ocean with me to go fishing and playing,
Still jolly when the cock has burst himself with crowing"
Cried the cripples to the silent statue,

The six beggared cripples.
"And to stand on green turf among the
craning yellow faces
Dependent on the chestnut, the sable, the Arabian horses,
And me with a magic crystal to foresee their places"
Cried the cripples to the silent statue,
The six beggared cripples.
"And this square to be a deck and these
pigeons canvas to rig,
And to follow the delicious breeze like a tantony pig
To the shaded feverless islands where the melons are big"
Cried the cripples to the silent statue,
The six beggared cripples.
"And these shops to be turned to tulips in a garden bed,
And me with my crutch to thrash each merchant dead
As he pokes from a flower his bald and wicked head"
Cried the cripples to the silent statue,
The six beggared cripples.
"And a hole in the bottom of heaven, and Peter and Paul
And each smug surprised saint like parachutes to fall,
And every one-legged beggar to have no legs at all"
Cried the cripples to the silent statue,
The six beggared cripples.
Spring 1935

II

O lurcher-loving collier, black as night,
Follow your love across the smokeless hill;
Your lamp is out, the cages are all still;
Course for heart and do not miss,
For Sunday soon is past and, Kate, fly not so fast,
For Monday comes when none may kiss:
Be marble to his soot, and to his black be white.
June 1935

III

Let a florid music praise,
The flute and the trumpet,
Beauty's conquest of your face:

In that land of flesh and bone,
Where from citadels on high
Her imperial standards fly,
Let the hot sun
Shine on, shine on.
O but the unloved have had power,
The weeping and striking,
Always: time will bring their hour;
Their secretive children walk
Through your vigilance of breath
To unpardonable Death,
And my vows break
Before his look.
February 1936

IV

Dear, though the night is gone,
Its dream still haunts today,
That brought us to a room
Cavernous, lofty as
A railway terminus,
And crowded in that gloom
Were beds, and we in one
In a far corner lay.
Our whisper woke no clocks,
We kissed and I was glad
At everything you did,
Indifferent to those
Who sat with hostile eyes
In pairs on every bed,
Arms round each other's necks
Inert and vaguely sad.
What hidden worm of guilt
Or what malignant doubt
Am I the victim of,
That you then, unabashed,
Did what I never wished,
Confessed another love;
And I, submissive, felt

Unwanted and went out.
March 1936

V

Fish in the unruffled lakes
Their swarming colors wear,
Swans in the winter air
A white perfection have,
And the great lion walks
Through his innocent grove;
Lion, fish and swan
Act, and are gone
Upon Time's toppling wave.
We, till shadowed days are done,
We must weep and sing
Duty's conscious wrong,
The Devil in the clock,
The goodness carefully worn
For atonement or for luck;
We must lose our loves,
On each beast and bird that moves
Turn an envious look.
Sighs for folly done and said
Twist our narrow days,
But I must bless, I must praise
That you, my swan, who have
All the gifts that to the swan
Impulsive Nature gave,
The majesty and pride,
Last night should add
Your voluntary love.
March 1936

VI

Autumn Song
Now the leaves are falling fast,
Nurse's flowers will not last,
Nurses to their graves are gone,
But the prams go rolling on.

Whispering neighbors left and right
Daunt us from our true delight,
Able hands are forced to freeze
Derelict on lonely knees.
Close behind us on our track,
Dead in hundreds cry Alack,
Arms raised stiffly to reprove
In false attitudes of love.
Scrawny through a plundered wood,
Trolls run scolding for their food,
Owl and nightingale are dumb,
And the angel will not come.
Clear, unscalable, ahead
Rise the Mountains of Instead,
From whose cold, cascading streams
None may drink except in dreams.
March 1936

VII

Underneath an abject willow,
Lover, sulk no more:
Act from thought should quickly follow.
What is thinking for?
Your unique and moping station
Proves you cold;
Stand up and fold
Your map of desolation.
Bells that toll across the meadows
From the sombre spire
Toll for these unloving shadows
Love does not require.
All that lives may love; why longer
Bow to loss
With arms across?
Strike and you shall conquer.
Geese in flocks above you flying.
Their direction know,
Icy brooks beneath you flowing,
To their ocean go.

Dark and dull is your distraction:
Walk then, come,
No longer numb
Into your satisfaction.
March 1936

VIII

At last the secret is out, as it always must come in the end, The delicious story is ripe to tell the intimate friend; Over the tea-cups and in the square the tongue has its desire; Still waters run deep, my friend, there's never smoke without fire. Behind the corpse in the reservoir, behind the ghost on the links,
Behind the lady who dances and the man who madly drinks, Under the look of fatigue, the attack of the migraine and the sigh There is always another story, there is more than meets the eye.
For the clear voice suddenly singing, high up in the convent wall, The scent of the elder bushes, the sporting prints in the hall, The croquet matches in summer, the handshake, the cough, the kiss, There is always a wicked secret, a private reason for this.
April 1936

IX

Stop all the clocks, cut off the telephone,
Prevent the dog from barking with a juicy bone,
Silence the pianos and with muffled drum
Bring out the coffin, let the mourners come.
Let aeroplanes circle moaning overhead
Scribbling on the sky the message He Is Dead,
Put crêpe bows round the white necks of the public doves,
Let the traffic policemen wear black cotton gloves.
He was my North, my South, my East and West,
My working week and Sunday rest,
My noon, my midnight, my talk, my song;
I thought that love would last forever: I was wrong.
The stars are not wanted now: put out every one;
Pack up the moon and dismantle the sun;

Pour away the ocean and sweep up the wood;
For nothing now can ever come to any good.
April 1936

X

O the valley in the summer where I and my John
Beside the deep river would walk on and on
While the flowers at our feet and the birds up above
Argued so sweetly on reciprocal love,
And I leaned on his shoulder; "O Johnny, let's play":
But he frowned like thunder and he went away.
O that Friday near Christmas as I well recall
When we went to the Matinee Charity Ball,
The floor was so smooth and the band was so loud
And Johnny so handsome I felt so proud;
"Squeeze me tighter, dear Johnny, let's dance till it's day":
But he frowned like thunder and he went away.
Shall I ever forget at the Grand Opera
When music poured out of each wonderful star?
Diamonds and pearls they hung dazzling down
Over each silver or golden silk gown;
"O John I'm in heaven," I whispered to say:
But he frowned like thunder and he went away.
O but he was fair as a garden in flower,
As slender and tall as the great Eiffel Tower,
When the waltz throbbed out on the long promenade
O his eyes and his smile they went straight to my heart;
"O marry me, Johnny, I'll love and obey":
But he frowned like thunder and he went away.
O last night I dreamed of you, Johnny, my lover,
You'd the sun on one arm and the moon on the other,
The sea it was blue and the grass it was green,
Every star rattled a round tambourine;
Ten thousand miles deep in a pit there I lay:
But you frowned like thunder and you went away.
April 1937

XI

Roman Wall Blues

Over the heather the wet wind blows,
I've lice in my tunic and a cold in my nose.
The rain comes pattering out of the sky,
I'm a Wall soldier, I don't know why.
The mist creeps over the hard grey stone,
My girl's in Tungria; I sleep alone.
Aulus goes hanging around her place,
I don't like his manners, I don't like his face.
Piso's a Christian, he worships a fish;
There'd be no kissing if he had his wish.
She gave me a ring but I diced it away;
I want my girl and I want my pay.
When I'm a veteran with only one eye
I shall do nothing but look at the sky.
October 1937

XII

Some say that love's a little boy,
And some say it's a bird,
Some say it makes the world round,
And some say that's absurd,
And when I asked the man next-door,
Who looked as if he knew,
His wife got very cross indeed,
And said it wouldn't do.
Does it look like a pair of pyjamas,
Or the ham in a temperance hotel?
Does its odour remind one of llamas,
Or has it a comforting smell?
Is it prickly to touch as a hedge is,
Or soft as eiderdown fluff?
Is it sharp or quite smooth at the edges?
O tell me the truth about love.
Our history books refer to it
In cryptic little notes,
It's quite a common topic on
The Transatlantic boats;
I've found the subject mentioned in
Accounts of suicides,

And even seen it scribbled on
The backs of railway-guides.
Does it howl like a hungry Alsatian,
Or boom like a military band?
Could one give a first-rate imitation
On a saw or a Steinway Grand?
Is its singing at parties a riot?
Does it only like classical stuff?
Does it stop when one wants to quiet?
O tell me the truth about love.
I looked inside the summer-house;
It wasn't ever there:
I tried the Thames at Maidenhead,
And Brighton's bracing air.
I don't know what the blackbird sang,
Or what the tulip said;
But it wasn' in the chicken-run,
Or underneath the bed.
Can it pull extraordinary faces?
Is it usually sick on a swing?
Does it spend all its time at the races,
Or fiddling with pieces of string?
Has it views of its own about money?
Does it think Patriotism enough?
Are its stories vulgar but funny?
O tell me the truth about love.
When it comes, will it come without warning
Just as I'm picking my nose?
Will it knock on the door in the morning,
Or tread in the bus on my toes?
Will it come like a change in the weather?
Will its greeting be courteous or rough?
Will it alter my life altogether?
O tell me the truth about love.
January 1938

Victor

Victor was a little baby,

Into this world he came;
His father took him on his knee and said:
'Don't dishonour the family name.'
Victor looked up at his father
Looked up with big round eyes:
His father said; 'Victor, my only son,
Don't you ever ever tell lies.'
Victor and his father went riding
Out in a little dog-cart;
His father took a Bible from his pocket and read;
'Blessed are the pure in heart.'
It was a frosty December
Victor was only eighteen,
But his figures were neat and his margins were straight
And his cuffs were always clean.
He took a room at the Peveril,
A respectable boarding-house;
And Time watched Victor day after day
As a cat will watch a mouse.
The clerks slapped Victor on the shoulder;
'Have you ever had woman?' they said,
'Come down town with us on Saturday night.'
Victor smiled and shook his head.
The manager sat in his office,
Smoked a Corona cigar:
Said; 'Victor's a decent fellow but
He's too mousy to go far.'
Victor went up the his bedroom,
Set the alarum bell;
Climbed into bed, took his Bible and read
Of what happened to Jezebel.
It was the First of April,
Anna to the Peveril came;
Her eyes, her lips, her breasts, her hips
And her smile set men aflame,
She looked as pure as a schoolgirl
On her First Communion day,
But her kisses were like the best champagne

When she gave herself away.
It was the Second of April.
She was wearing a coat of fur;
Victor met her upon the stair
And he fell in love with her.
The first time he made his proposal,
She laughed, said; 'I'll never wed;
The second time there was a pause;
Then she smiled and shook her head.
Anna looked into her mirror,
Pouted and gave a frown:
Said 'Victor's as dull as a wet afternoon
But I've got to settle down.'
The third time he made his proposal,
As they walked by the Reservoir:
She gave him a kiss like a blow on the head,
Said; 'You are my heart's desire.'
They were married early in August,
She said; 'Kiss me, you funny boy';
Victor took her in his arms and said;
'O my Helen of Troy.'
It was the middle of September,
Victor came to the office one day;
He was wearing a flower in his buttonhole,
He was late but he was gay.
The clerks were talking of Anna,
The door was just ajar:
One said, 'Poor old Victor, but where ignorance
Is bliss, et cetera.'
Victor stood still as a statue,
The door was just ajar:
One said, 'God, what fun I had with her
In that Baby Austin car.'
Victor walked out into the High Street,
He walked to the edge of town:
He came to the allotments and the rubbish heap
And his tears came tumbling down.
Victor looked up at the sunset
As he stood there all alone;

Cried; 'Are you in Heaven, Father?'
But the sky said 'Address not known'.
Victor looked at the mountains,
The mountains all covered in snow
Cried; 'Are you pleased with me, Father?'
And the answer came back, No.
Victor came to the forest,
Cried: 'Father, will she ever be true?'
And the oaks and the beeches shook their heads
And they answered: 'Not to you.'
Victor came to the meadow
Where the wind went sweeping by:
Cried; 'O Father, I love her so',
But the wind said, 'She must die'.
Victor came to the river
Running so deep and so still:
Crying; 'O Father, what shall I do?'
And the river answered, 'Kill'.
Anna was sitting at table,
Drawing cards from a pack;
Anna was sitting at table
Waiting for her husband to come back.
It wasn't the Jack of Diamonds
Nor the Joker she drew first;
It wasn't the King or the Queen of Hearts
But the Ace of Spades reversed.
Victor stood in the doorway,
He didn't utter a word:
She said; 'What's the matter, darling?'
He behaved as if he hadn't heard.
There was a voice in his left ear,
There was a voice in his right,
There was a voice at the base of his skull
Saying, 'She must die tonight.'
Victor picked up a carving-knife,
His features were set and drawn,
Said; 'Anna it would have been better for you
If you had not been born.'
Anna jumped up from the table,

Anna started to scream,
But Victor came slowly after her
Like a horror in a dream.
She dodged behind the sofa,
She tore down a curtain rod,
But Victor came slowly after her:
Said; 'Prepare to meet thy God.'
She managed to wrench the door open,
She ran and she didn't stop.
But Victor followed her up the stairs
And he caught her at the top.
He stood there above the body,
He stood there holding the knife;
And the blood ran down the stairs and sang,
'I'm the Resurrection and the Life'.
They tapped Victor on the shoulder,
They took him away in a van;
He sat as quiet as a lump of moss
Saying, 'I am the Son of Man'.
Victor sat in a corner
Making a woman of clay:
Saying; 'I am Alpha and Omega, I shall come
To judge the earth some day.'

Villanelle

Time can say nothing but I told you so,
Time only knows the price we have to pay;
If I could tell you, I would let you know.
If we should weep when clowns put on their show,
If we should stumble when musicians play,
Time can say nothing but I told you so.
There are no fortunes to be told, although
Because I love you more than I can say,
If I could tell you, I would let you know.
The winds must come from somewhere when they blow,
There must be reasons why the leaves decay;
Time can say nothing but I told you so.
Perhaps the roses really want to grow,
The vision seriously intends to stay;

If I could tell you, I would let you know.
Suppose the lions all get up and go,
And all the brooks and soldiers run away?
Time can say nothing but I told you so.
If I could tell you, I would let you know.

Voltaire At Ferney

Almost happy now, he looked at his estate.
An exile making watches glanced up as he passed,
And went on working; where a hospital was rising fast
A joiner touched his cap; an agent came to tell Some of
the trees he'd planted were progressing well.
The white alps glittered. It was summer. He
was very great.
Far off in Paris, where his enemies
Whispered that he was wicked, in an upright chair
A blind old woman longed for death and letters. He
would write "Nothing is better than life." But was it?
Yes, the fight Against the false and the unfair
Was always worth it. So was gardening. Civilise.
Cajoling, scolding, screaming, cleverest of them all,
He'd had the other children in a holy war
Against the infamous grown-ups, and, like a child, been
sly and humble, when there was occasion for
The two-faced answer or the plain protective lie,
But, patient like a peasant, waited for their fall.
And never doubted, like D'Alembert, he would win:
Only Pascal was a great enemy, the rest
Were rats already poisoned; there was much, though, to
be done, And only himself to count upon.
Dear Diderot was dull but did his best;
Rousseau, he'd always known, would blubber and give
in. So, like a sentinel, he could not sleep. The night was
full of wrong,
Earthquakes and executions. Soon he would be dead,
And still all over Europe stood the horrible nurses
Itching to boil their children. Only his verses
Perhaps could stop them: He must go on working:
Overhead The uncomplaining stars composed their lucid

song.

We Too Had Known Golden Hours

We, too, had known golden hours
When body and soul were in tune,
Had danced with our true loves
By the light of a full moon,
And sat with the wise and good
As tongues grew witty and gay
Over some noble dish
Out of Escoffier;
Had felt the intrusive glory
Which tears reserve apart,
And would in the old grand manner
Have sung from a resonant heart.
But, pawed-at and gossiped-over
By the promiscuous crowd,
Concocted by editors
Into spells to befuddle the crowd,
All words like Peace and Love,
All sane affirmative speech,
Had been soiled, profaned, debased
To a horrid mechanical screech.
No civil style survived
That pandaemonioum
But the wry, the sotto-voce,
Ironic and monochrome:
And where should we find shelter
For joy or mere content
When little was left standing
But the suburb of dissent?

We're Late

Clocks cannot tell our time of day
For what event to pray
Because we have no time, because
We have no time until
We know what time we fill,
Why time is other than time was.

Nor can our question satisfy
The answer in the statue's eye:
Only the living ask whose brow
May wear the Roman laurel now;
The dead say only how.
What happens to the living when we die?
Death is not understood by Death; nor You, nor I.

Who's Who

A shilling life will give you all the facts:
How Father beat him, how he ran away,
What were the struggles of his youth, what acts
Made him the greatest figure of his day;
Of how he fought, fished, hunted, worked all night,
Though giddy, climbed new mountains; named a sea;
Some of the last researchers even write
Love made him weep his pints like you and me.
With all his honours on, he sighed for one
Who, say astonished critics, lived at home;
Did little jobs about the house with skill
And nothing else; could whistle; would sit still
Or potter round the garden; answered some
Of his long marvellous letters but kept none.

Chapter 7

Critical Reception

Auden is widely regarded as one of the greatest poets of the twentieth century. Though a decidedly modern poet in terms of his radical politics and bold experimentation with accepted literary forms, Auden's idiosyncratic virtuosity and protean ethical perspective distinguishes him from his contemporaries. As many critics note, Auden's striking originality stems from his counterrevolutionary appropriation of traditional poetic forms, unabashed Christian faith, and mistrust of irrationalism, all seemingly at odds with the tenets of both modernism and romanticism from which his poetry derives. While most critics view Auden's poetry from the 193s and early 194s as his best, especially as found in *The Orators, Another Time,* and the poems "Spain," "In Time of War," and "New Year Letter," controversy surrounds evaluation of the middle and later periods of his career.

"New Year Letter" continues to receive much critical attention, as does the relevance of Auden's self-imposed exile in America. Some critics believe that Auden's poetry lost much of its imaginative power and vitality after his emigration to the United States. However, others contend that the contemplative Christianity and Horatian intellectualism of Auden's American period represents the apogee of his disciplined style and sensibility, particularly as evident in *The Age of Anxiety,* "The Sea and the Mirror" from *For the Time Being,* and "In Praise of Limestone" from *Nones.* Many critics note a tendency toward obscurity in much of Auden's poetry throughout his career, variously attributed to his liberating genius, private satire, and cloaked references to his homosexuality. Despite Auden's significant contributions to contemporary musical theater, he remains largely unstudied as a dramatist and librettist, mainly due to the fact that the forms in which he worked have either fallen out of favor or never fully developed popular appreciation. A prolific poet of extraordinary technical dexterity, intellectual domain, engaging perspicacity, and epigrammatic wit, Auden forged a rare poetic voice that reconciled the opposing forces of tradition and modernism, for which he is hailed as a towering figure of twentieth-century literature.

Critical Appreciation of Auden's Funeral Blues:

Although it is not seen at first, Funeral blues can be portrayed and understood in many different ways.

Auden could be writing about the death of a public figure, as he writes about 'white necks of the public doves' and the 'traffic policemen'. Another interpretation is that Auden wrote this poem about his loss of faith in God. This would explain the use of a capital H is ?He Is Dead?. A reference to God could also be found in the line 'my Sunday rest' (Sunday being the Sabbath day).

Although these ideas could be equally argued, I still believe that Auden wrote this poem while mourning the loss of his lover. It carries a sad and heartbreaking tone that puts Auden as the speaker. Being a homosexual would explain why the subject of his poem is a man. The title of the poem includes the word ?funeral?, immediately indicating death or loss. In the first stanza Auden makes use of works like stop, cut, prevent and silence ? these words all signify ending.

Stop all the clocks, cut off the telephones?, this describes how Auden wanted to be excluded from the world while he was mourning his loss. Let aeroplanes circle moaning overhead / Scribbling on the sky the message He Is Dead?. Auden uses personification in these first two lines of the second stanza by giving the aeroplanes human characteristics to inform everyone that ?He Is Dead?. This man meant so much to Auden that he wanted his death to be recognized and written in the sky for all to see. In the third stanza, Auden writes: 'He was my North, my South, my East and West'. This man was everything to Auden, he was Auden's world. It is written in the third stanza: ?I thought love would last for ever: I was wrong?. This demonstrates that even though love is meant to last forever, it can only be carried to the grave and no farther.

Whatever the true meaning of the poem, it was about someone who meant a lot to Auden and made a huge impact on him when they were gone. I believe my interpretation to be that of many, and although analysing poetry comes with diverse ideas, Auden wrote this poem to express something he felt strongly about, that is what truly matters.

Chapter 8

Themes of W.H. Auden's "The Unknown Citizen"

Conformity and Anonymity in the Modern World

"Social Security Number? Birthdate? Nine digit telephone number starting with area code? Mother's Maiden Name?" In many ways, we are simply faceless numbers to modern society, not individuals with feelings and emotions and dreams. W.H. Auden, a well-known English poet and dramatist, discusses this important theme in his poem "An Unknown Soldier." Auden, being a modernist, is concerned with this modern idea of people losing their identities in the face of the changing, technological world. In the poem "An Unknown Soldier," Auden speaks of the dangers of modern society to the individual including anonymity, conformity, and government control.

The anonymity of the unknown citizen is shown in Auden's repeated use of metaphor. Auden shows the reader everything the unknown citizen was and was not-"a saint", "wasn't odd in his views", "normal in every way", "was insured", "had everything necessary to the Modern man", "held proper opinions for the time of year", and added the right number of children to the population . While it seems as though the unknown citizen is praised for these qualities, Auden is mocking how anonymous the man has become. This citizen is completely defined by his statistics, not by any of his qualities or feelings. He isn't even given a name but is referred to by a number.

Conformity is the virtue in most in demand by society as

Emerson pointed out many years before. Auden's unknown citizen is a model of conformity in a society where everyone must follow the rules if things are to run smoothly. He does all the right things. The government can produce reports to show that he did all the right things. He had the right opinions, owned the right products, and even had the correct number of kids. In this poem, people have become noting more than commodities that must fulfill their roles for the wheel to turn. Conformity has created apathetic and obedient citizens which is exactly what the government

"Social Security Number? Birthdate? Nine digit telephone number starting with area code? Mother's Maiden Name?" In many ways, we are simply faceless numbers to modern society, not individuals with feelings and emotions and dreams. W.H. Auden, a well-known English poet and dramatist, discusses this important theme in his poem "An Unknown Soldier." Auden, being a modernist, is concerned with this modern idea of people losing their identities in the face of the changing, technological world. In the poem "An Unknown Soldier," Auden speaks of the dangers of modern society to the individual including anonymity, conformity, and government control.

The anonymity of the unknown citizen is shown in Auden's repeated use of metaphor. Auden shows the reader everything the unknown citizen was and was not-"a saint", "wasn't odd in his views", "normal in every way", "was insured", "had everything necessary to the Modern man", "held proper opinions for the time of year", and added the right number of children to the population . While it seems as though the unknown citizen is praised for these qualities, Auden is mocking how anonymous the man has become. This citizen is completely defined by his statistics, not by any of his qualities or feelings. He isn't even given a name but is referred to by a number.

Conformity is the virtue in most in demand by society as Emerson pointed out many years before. Auden's unknown citizen is a model of conformity in a society where everyone must follow the rules if things are to run smoothly. He does all the right things. The government can produce reports to show that he did all the right things. He had the right opinions, owned the right products, and even had the correct number of kids. In this poem, people have become noting more than commodities that must fulfill their roles for the wheel to turn. Conformity has created apathetic and obedient citizens which is exactly what the government wants. wants.

Chapter 9

An Analysis of W.H. Auden's, "The Unknown Citizen"

In 1939 W.H. Auden and his companion Christopher Isherwood arrived in New York City after traveling much of Europe. Auden was born in York, North Yorkshire in 1970 to a prominent physician and his wife. He was educated at boarding schools throughout his youth, and obtained a degree from Oxford University. Although he had chosen poetry as a profession at the age of fifteen, it was not until the age of twenty one that his first work was published. This collection was entitled Poems, and it quickly gained Auden fame. His work was "versatile and inventive" (Auden par. 1), and until his death in 1973, he completed more than 3, lines of verse and wrote several plays.

In 1940 Auden wrote "The Unknown Citizen", a poem depicting the plight of modern man as he struggles through life and death in a faceless society. The poem makes a statement against technology and it's ability to allow the government to view each individual citizen as nothing more than a complement to a statistic. "The Unknown Citizen" is Auden's satirical portrayal of a man living in a society which views each person as a number, and rewards conformity.

Although the unknown citizen, was important enough to erect a marble statue in his honour, his name is withheld, replaced by government issued numbers. From the opening of this poem, readers grasp the dehumanizing way the government has treated this citizen. The cold marble statue erected in his honour is "as cold and lifeless as his existence was" and symbolic of the cold lifeless way the government has honored this man. In the first line of the poem, we are greeted by the Bureau of Statistics and their findings. The incorporation of the Bureau of Statistics into this poem immediately envelopes the reader in the flat, formal tone of the poem. The poem then goes on to say statistically, this man is found to be normal.

He was the perfect statistic of a man of his age and era. The poem then states that "all the reports on his conduct agree that, in the modern sense of an old-fashioned word, he was a saint/ For in everything he did he served the Greater Community." From these lines we can assume that the modern day definition of saint is someone who conforms completely to society's expectations, behaving in every way to fit the statistic. The fact that he served the "Greater Community" may imply the government itself, as this man has behaved in exactly the way the government has desired.

The capitalization of the term "Greater Community" may imply the government attributing godlike qualities to themselves, reinforcing the belief that each citizen should conform to their expectations.

The poem continues with this man's work history. He worked for a major corporation which most likely also influenced this man's behaviour, as a large and powerful motor company can "dictate social norms in a significant way". The time which he did not work for Fudge Motors Inc. he served in the armed forces, which further reinforces the statistical ideals this man lives out. Both the armed forces as well as major corporations view their underlings in a similar way that the government views its' citizens.

He was a member of the Union, who reports he paid his dues and never caused a disturbance. This man had friends and enjoyed a drink now and again. The capitalization of the term Union shows that it too was a powerful entity similar to the government in its' dehumanizing of its' members. The fact that this man likes a drink furthers his normalcy as the practice of workers visiting a pub on their way back from a long day at the factory was a popular pastime during this era. The use of the word "popular" strengthens this citizen's overwhelming compliance with the expected, as this citizen lives adhering to the popular method of behaving.

The Press report that he reacted to advertisements in the way a normal man should, and bought a paper everyday. This man reacted to expectations perfectly; he complied with the norm in every aspect. This is beneficial to advertisers, who form statistics of their own and cater their messages to the reports they form. Since this man conformed perfectly to every statistic, advertisers could easily attract his attention and sell him their products.

The poem goes on to say "Policies taken out in his name prove that he was fully insured, and his Health-card shows he was once in a hospital but left it cured." These lines further the normalcy of this man, who had an illness so normal it was not important enough to mention. The fact that he even had an illness equates more normalcy, as we all get sick with unnamed colds and illnesses in our lifetimes.

More government agencies report, Producers Research and High-Grade Living state that he took advantage of the Installment Plan, and obtained all the material possessions that a normal man of his era should. He had a "phonograph, radio, a car, and a frigidaire.", the frigidaire being the most popular refrigerator brand at the time. By capitalizing the phrase "Modern Man", perhaps Auden is commenting on the government equating divine qualities to citizens who conform to their standards.

In the next few lines, more researchers indicate that the opinions he held corresponded with those the government deemed to be correct, "when there was peace, he was for peace, when there was war, he went." This man never questioned anything for himself, he went along with the crowd, never stepping outside the norm and thinking. He went to war, "not questioning or challenging it any way", simply conforming and blindly believing his government was justified in going to war.

The next three lines speak of his family. He was married and had five children, which the Eugenist declares is the correct amount. The fact that Auden used the term Eugenist perhaps implies a connection between the governments' treatment of this citizen with that of Nazi Germanys' treatment of its' citizens. Eugenics is "selective breeding as proposed human improvement". It is well known that Nazi Germany favored the practice of eugenics in the effort to create a perfect, uniform society. Perhaps Auden is making the statement that with conformity comes chaos, as was the case with Nazi Germany. If every citizen's life fit the statistic, conformity will ultimately lead to the downfall of society.

The final rhyming couplet asks a question, then answers it from the governments' perspective. "Was he free? Was he happy? The question is absurd: Had anything been wrong, we certainly should have heard." This man was in no way free, a person who conforms to society's standards his whole life is certainly not free. As for his happiness, there is never mention that he is happy, and no government report can tell whether or not someone is happy. Auden intentionally wrote this poem in a very clinical way to make a point about the flawed government that judges people based on reports and documents, and what they believe to be correct and normal. The poem's uneven lines further contribute to its purpose as it reads more like a government report than a poem. It's flat, matter of fact tone enhance the poem's irony as this man's life seems as boring and cold as the reports written about him. Auden's use of rhyme help to exaggerate the uneasy feeling the poem gives the reader. Rhymes vary through the poem, for instance as Carol Pippen writes "Auden uses rhyming lines, but he varies the rhyme so the reader is slightly off balance. The first few lines begin an abab pattern, but by the sixth line Auden fails to supply a b to complement the a rhyme in the fifth line. From then on, Auden rhymes in short spurts." "Just as the reader is expecting rhymes, Auden puts off the rhyme for a few lines." .

Auden comments on human nature and our struggle to fit into our society. It is human nature to want to belong, but where does belonging end and denial begin? Auden was himself homosexual, in an era where homosexuality was shunned, and in some countries illegal. In his autobiography Auden writes " We were the tail, a sort of poor relation/To that debauched, eccentric generation/ That grew up with their fathers at the war,/ and made new glosses on the noun Amor." Auden lived in a time where his lifestyle was irregular and looked down upon. Many homosexuals during this time were forced to live life as heterosexuals, or face the wrath of society. Auden tried to make sense of his sexuality by citing contributing factors such as "the eleven years he spent away from home and parents between the ages of seven and eighteen at boarding schools for boys, and also the fact that between his seventh and twelfth year, his father was absent on war service in France and Egypt." Perhaps during the time of this poem, he felt the need to fight against the society who had not accepted him, so this poem is enabling him to speak o the homosexuals of his era to break free of the society's expectations, and live their lives as they please. Why try to fit into a society where normalcy will bring you nothing more than being remembered as numbers and reports. Stepping outside the norm, your life perhaps would be remembered for your actions, beliefs, and thoughts.

Perhaps another reason why Auden wrote "The Unknown Citizen" is the outbreak of World War II. The unknown citizen served in the war, and the title itself is reminiscent of "The Unknown Soldier". Auden may have felt hurt and abandoned as a child, when his father was in the medical corps. Maybe this feeling of abandonment gave way to anger at a government that gave life or death commands to soldiers that are honored only as a faceless statistic by the government they fought to uphold. Perhaps Auden is speaking to the many soldiers deployed in World War II, telling them to question the authority that is sending them into harm's way.

W.H. Auden wrote this poem in 194, and although over sixty five years have passed, this poem rings truer than ever. As technology becomes faster, better, and more accurate, we are becoming less human and more of a statistic. We are "losing our personal identity and autonomy" (Pippen par.1) in a society where we are labeled, given a number, and are faceless citizens forming together like a sea of ants. Yet we still all want to fit into the society that dehumanizes us. We do not want to be labeled an outcast, or looked down upon as being different. But if all we achieve for all our efforts to be normal is to be part of a statistic, and remembered as a number, what is the point?

Chapter 10

Normal is Overrated

An entire population of people is difficult to control since chaos can be halted by keeping the mob content in their lives, yet everyone reaches happiness through different goals. It is the government's job to let us all fulfill our own pursuit of happiness as individuals and independent thinkers, but when our mirth clashes with another's, one of the contender's joy must surrender for the other to remain content. With these constant battles between beliefs, the only way to make life easier to govern is for the entire population to accept to same standard. A bureaucracy imagines all special interest groups as one person with all of the qualities and stereotypes that are in reality scattered among a collection of people.

Someone that radical is too extreme with which to negotiate easily, but one hundred different people who are not so radical are even harder to handle. This fallacy reveals how much the government wants us to be one person, since they can keep watch over one person. This is all especially true of the 194's when women were expected to be housewives, men were expected to be John Wayne, and W. H. Auden wrote "The Unknown Citizen", a fake eulogy to a man whose beliefs are created for him by the government after his death. Auden's poem is a scathing look at how the Cold War administration tried its hardest to keep tabs on its citizens by creating a homogenous culture in a nation of variation.

Auden's government begins by stripping this anonymous man of any individuality that he may have once had. Even if they had known what kind of person he was while living before writing the eulogy, they wouldn't care since they need to mold him into bait. He loses his name and becomes a series of statistics that are supposed to represent his personality, or what other's wanted his personality to be. He really becomes unknown in the sense that by describing his identity in such a shallow translation, he becomes hollow of emotions.

To succeed in this endeavor, he must be unrecognizable so that his family and friends can't contest to his new image, but since no one knows, and they can make this blank slate exactly what they want "normal" to be. And since he is dead, this man cannot fight back or contradict him as to what they say about him, so the writers of the memorial can insert qualities of life that he may have never had. The first line even states "He was found by the Bureau of Statistics to be", an outward admission that they are not taking facts from his life, but merely taking the majority traits that are present in all other men like him.

He is that one personification of a certain population, only he is only radical in the opinions that they want him to have. Represented by his perceived routine and possessions as if that is all a person is, the unknown citizen is reduced to a shell. When they describe what it is that makes him a good person, their evidence is based on hearsay. According to psychologists, he was "popular with his mates and liked a drink", yet what did his "mates" say? And who is to say that that is even what decency is? They manage to link "popular" and "value" as if they are similar, and in this way, the nation is encouraged to sink into superficiality.

Acting as if being able to hold "the proper opinions for the time of year", as if the only proper opinions are the ones that we are fed, demeans the worth of opinions. They don't want him to have different opinions because that will incite change, and the government never wants to have to change. They want to appear infallible, so their puppet must agree with them. The poem describes him as not being "odd in his views" implying that they have an idea of what his views are, and according to them, his views are their views, that is, the views that agree with all of their ethics. Auden's government propaganda projects a safe sense of identifying with this man, which is accomplished by going to "experts" and finding the normal statistics, and they are not subtle about their outside sources. When finally acknowledging if he had a soul, the question is brushed off as "absurd" since "Had anything been wrong, we should certainly have heard".

Who are they really protecting if the people who try and help them to change go unheard? Are they trying to tell us that the negative opinions being expressed are untrue, or will continue to be unanswered? Either way, Auden is trying to tell us that authority doesn't take us seriously if we disagree with them, and sometimes even if we do. Consider how little they must think of this person whose eulogy they are writing if they won't even allow him to have once been human. Whoever he really was, he probably didn't embody the image that was being sold, and if he did, it was only a façade. Auden sets up an air that authority only sees us as two dimensional, who, once dead, can represent whatever it is that they want us to represent.

When someone's life is being presented on the news, we never hear about the interesting qualities of that person. She is always a beautiful, and he is always brave. They never have any opinions. This is the problem with being dead: we cannot tell the nation how we want to be remembered. And no one actually cares that this man died, or that his identity is being sacrificed to cement images of normality that are supposed to be tempting and eventually adopted by the masses. He is a manikin who is being dressed up in a way to make us feel bad that we don't look like him, and that we should try and be someone else. The problem is that it is tempting, and people do try and change to suit a false ideal.

Saddest of all, the public would actually fall for this trick, and our government knows it. They know that if it is believed that he is happy, even when that question is never answered, others will want to adopt his secret to vivacity. People are often impatient and lazy and want someone else, someone with more power, to make them happy instead of going out and searching for it. It is in this way that we are trapped into thinking that if a strategy succeeded for someone else, then that is the absolute strategy. It is the easy way out, and it is on this that the government in Auden's poem is counting. Everything is passed off as "necessary" and his normality is mistaken for contentment.

They begin by calling him a saint which gives spiritual support to the case that is being made. It seems that somehow by living in a state where one gives up power of opinion and choice and surrenders to being like everyone else and making everyone happy, then that person deserves to be canonized. Where is the miracle to that? It seems more astonishing that "He worked in a factory and never got fired/ But satisfied his employers, Fudge Motors, Inc." is glorified as if people who are unfortunate enough to be laid off are delinquents to society. He is not happy because he works efficiently or is lucky enough to keep his job. No, this does not make him lucky, it makes him competent, but in order to keep people from despairing over their jobs, we must remind them that they should be happy that they have one.

Humans always seem to find joy in comparing themselves to the less fortunate. This sense of financial achievement is paralleled in the lines "And had everything necessary to the Modern Man/ A phonograph, a radio, a car, and a fridgidaire". We are once again lead to believe that material objects can satisfy any problem we have and make us who we are, but it is who we are that makes up what we choose to buy. One person may never need a phonograph, yet the advertisers that are looking to link "normal" and "modern" to "pleasure" want us to believe that all people need appliances. Auden's government is now reaching out to the companies who want the public to buy all of these useless objects because not only does it make those companies rich, but it also gives outsiders that impression that America is a country lacking poverty. It is a distraction to show how the middle class' insecurities can lead to a booming economy and cover up the impoverished people hiding behind them.

The next point that "And our teachers report that he never interfered with their [his children's] education". Apparently, we are expected to send our children to school and not inquire about what they are learning. Should we be blind to their education and be satisfied since it is a government run facility and they can do no wrong? Had no one interfered with their children's education, there would have been no end to segregation, and who would be willing to pay taxes to make it better let alone know that it needs to be better? Not only does the government want us to be all one person, but they also want that person to vote them into office and let them make the rest of the decisions uninterrupted.

And many of us allow them to run us. We don't always realise that we have the right and the duty to check up on what our government is doing for the country, but at the same time, we want them to make us happy. A government will only become too powerful if we become lazy and let them make the decisions about how we live our lives and how we choose our goals. Auden is trying to tell us that it's not all the governments fault: they didn't get the taste for power until we gave it to them.

Auden displaying how the government is deciding what should make us happy, and he is also showing us how we fed this belief. A democracy is led by its people, and America's people were beginning to be slothful about their rights. They could have found pleasure in their life if they had only chose to search for it. This poem is based in the reality of people who were too exhausted to be different. Commercialism in America had created in people a need for "A phonograph, a radio, a car, and a fridgidaire", as if these were really necessary to living. Actually, it was able to bring people together and create a sense of unity and brotherhood. Linking the population together, these objects were identifiable to everyone, which gave the impression that a housewife in Arizona is the same as one in Vermont because they have the same refrigerator.

The problem was that these objects were becoming an identity for some who were unable to distinguish products that showed personality from products that made an identity. No object can create character, but this was a lost idea. "The Unknown Citizen" was written in 194, at the end of the Great Depression, when having money was becoming easier as jobs became more prevalent, so people were more money conscious and would look up to someone who was able to have and keep these appliances. They came to symbolize achievement and success throughout the difficult era since the ability to buy them gave a sense of no worries.

A nice house and nice commodities were essential to provide an end to fears that poverty was just around the corner. It gave back a solid foundation after Black Tuesday had destroyed so many others. Increasingly, people felt that they needed to be safer with their finances, which to some meant more money, so they must be " fully sensible to the advantages of the Installment Plan". The Great Depression had taken wealth, but it did not take away family. While, it did not smash dreams, it is commonly believed that to live out dreams, one needs money. For men, this loss was a great emasculator since it took away a man's ability to provide for his family, but it didn't take away his family. When people lost these things, they saw them as the only way to return to the sublime times in the past, and once they were able to return to it, they grappled to become happy again through luxury. And who had returned us to this state?

The government, or more specifically Franklin Roosevelt, and there inlaid our newly developed trust that our administration could bail us out of any problem. They·had given us the means to work and create a better life, therefore they must be able to do this in many other ways. And so, "When there was peace, he was for peace; when there was war, he went" because we believed that they were " the proper opinions for the time of year". Opinions shouldn't change with the way the government takes action, and one person is not more patriotic than another just because he believes that everything the government does is right; however, we should have opinions that we believe in because they will be beneficiary to the country. Auden, who was an Englishman with American citizenship, saw from an outsider's point of view the uselessness of this way of thinking, and with his poem, he attempted to show us how absurd it was.

Whether he was accentuating how propaganda was taking

advantage of our emotions, or how we were allowing it to, Auden's poem is eerily precise. He was able to see that we all wanted to live happily, even if it meant that someone else was unhappy, but we didn't want to do anything about it. These demands to make the government give us mirth instead of pursuing it ourselves strained them, and to make it easier, they began to create an image of delight that would benefit them by making us all the same.

Normal is only helpful for statistics, and we should not yearn for it, but we did. We handed over the power that we had to find what makes us happy for something that was supposed to make us happy, and in his death, Auden's unknown citizen cemented this is our minds. Beneath the surface, this could have been an embittered man, but the way he was presented forced us to only think him happy, and we wanted it too. Though we knew nothing about him, the unknown citizen made us believe that in normality there is joy.

Chapter 11

Analysis of Auden's Poem "In Memory of W.B. Yeats"

The Desolation Without Sun: an Analysis of Auden's Line Each line of a poem represents a carefully crafted piece of artistry that supports the whole work. Via intentionally placed words, punctuation, and sounds, a poem moves forward with athletic quickness or slow realization. In the first stanza of W.H. Auden's *In Memory of W.B. Yeats*, all of these tools help to produce a poem that captures the weight of Yeats' life, with lines that stand and bear the powerful weight of that man's life and influence, as well as the conditions present at his death.

The punctuation of the poem produces a clear structure that urges the reader on with the energy of the thought structure it supports. In the first section of the poem, Auden notes that "He disappeared in the dead of winter:" and uses a colon at the end to produce a brief pause that trips to the next line, as well as for an emphasis that produces the urge to read more. In the next lines, "The brooks were frozen, the air-ports almost deserted/And snow disfigured the public statues;" a series of images separated by commas, and ended with the briefest pause - a pause designed only for a moment's worth of reflection before the stanza rushes onward.

The narrator's voice goes on to the end-stop, the first full thought at the end of these rushing lines, by saying, "The mercury sank in the mouth of the dying day." This stop effectively slows the current of the words in order to set up the lament "O all the instruments agree / The day of his death was a dark cold day." Important here is the lack of stop between these two lines, as if the narrator had to force them out through grief.

To continue with this stanza, the language of each line constructs the full thoughts outlined briefly above, but also introduces strong images that stand on their own. "He disappeared in the dead of winter:" introduces a strong image of Yeats walking out alone into the darkness of winter. The power of this line is its representation of a highly dramatic scene, an epic scene large enough to fill Yeats' life, and his leaving it, with the grandeur required for one of the greatest poets of the twentieth century.

The line sets the tone of the stanza, and the poem, as one of epic loneliness. This loneliness is reinforced by the images recurring in the stanza, "The brooks were frozen, the air-ports almost deserted, / And snow disfigured the public statues;" The desolation of the scene becomes stronger with each successive image. The subtext connects the loss of Yeats with the absence of warmth, the absence of the sun.

The last three lines "The mercury sank in the mouth of the dying day. / O all the instruments agree / The day of his death was a dark cold day." close the stanza with the image of the thermometer - "mercury" and "instruments" - agreeing that the day of Yeats' death was unusually cold. Not only nature, but the cold and mechanical works of man felt the passing of Yeats, and the lines thrust the reader step by step into the cold shock of the described day.

Finally, as each line and its punctuation form and unify the thoughts of the poem, the sounds of the words themselves propel those thoughts. While the first line begins with speed, "He disappeared in the...", using plosive consonants like 'd' 'p' and short monosyllables, the last part of the line elongates and slows like taffy in the mouth as the reader reaches the colon, "dead of winter:". The vowels slow the line to the partial stop of the colon, and help to allow for the moment of reflection on the image.

The lines after this begin with the chewy 'brook' and 'snow' but end with words filled with plosives like "deserted" and "statues". The impetus of these lines forces us to struggle to the emphasized plosive words that give the images their cold sting. This impetus begins to slow as the reader reaches "day" but the final two lines that make up the lament of the stanza slow to a brutal crawl with "O" and "agree," "day" and "day." The struggle through this cold time becomes clearer, and one can even visualize a person struggling with the shock of cold grief, struggling desperately to speak and eulogize with precision.

This poem, and this particular stanza, shows the very particular consciousness of the poet at work. Auden's grandiloquent imagery saves no expense, but superbly reaches the reader with the desolation of a world losing one of the greatest expressers of the human condition. In this way Yeats' becomes immortal, and the desolation of his passing lives on. As Auden writes "A few thousand will think of this day / As one thinks of a day when one did something slightly unusual." The poem, like all good eulogies (and poems perhaps?), touches both the intellect as well as inspiring a visceral connection to language that few people can create, much less inhabit.

Chapter 12

An Analysis of W.H. Auden's September 1, 1939

The invasion of Poland by the German-Nazi forces commenced upon September 1, 1939 yet it is not the hallmark of W.H. Auden's intention in his poem "September 1, 1939." No, this work is far more than a description or criticism of the German-Nazi decision to invade an innocent country; this work, these words, this plea comes from the heart of a man who is living in a society filled with an oppressive nature towards those they deem less human or unfitting to society. Despite such risk of oppression Auden went ahead and published this gorgeous piece of poetry in 194 with conscious thought to mask his true intentions because unbeknownst to his public Wystan Hugh Auden was "homosexual" . By use of allusion, symbolism, and straight out diction Auden suggests truly mind-expanding concepts and a criticism of something rather unexpected.

"September 1, 1939" is split into nine, eleven lined, stanzas with no set rhyme scheme or exact meter. For the most part shifts occur randomly although one can group them to certain degrees though it would be best, in one's opinion, to absorb the allusion-based meanings individually for yes they are ever-so deep. The first two stanzas seem to make reference to the German invasion of Poland; the third and forth stanzas takes a shot at democratically industrialized man; stanzas five and six touch on the concept of sin; surprisingly the seventh, eighth and ninth stanzas bring out the strongest messages which are rather hopeful if not optimistic. Occasionally one meets a rhyme but they are inconsistent in one's eyes and not truly compelling if one suggested they pushed the overall meaning of the work.

In the first two stanzas one finds the speaker in "one of the dives on Fifty-second Street" where he is both "Uncertain and afraid". At first glance one could conclude that Auden or the speaker is merely in a small club, but with thought towards his sexual orientation it may in fact suggest that he is avoiding a crowded area where he would normally be uncomfortable. In the second stanza there is a strong reference to Germany by means of Luther (an anti-Semitic) being that which has pushed the German society to their status quo. After such Auden then makes a reference to Linz and a psychopathic god in lines 16 and 18 which seems to make an allusion to Hitler due to the fact that Hitler was born in Linz and could easily be thought of as a sort of psychopathic god . Auden then tosses in the phrase "Those to whom evil is done do evil in return" which makes one possibly consider that this may be an allusion, though not directly, to the Treaty of Versailles which in 2/2 hindsight clearly sets those who made the treaty as doers of evil.

In stanzas three and four one is shown a more anti-American concept. Auden first makes a reference in line 23 to Thucydides who was one of the first people to suggest that history should always be recorded for what it is and not for the glory of the country that records it; because of such a statement, Thucydides was exiled from his home. Towards America this may reference things such as the old propaganda movies our military used to show which were filled with lies and stereotypes to make us think in a more pro-American way. Stanza four then takes focus upon the boasts of "The strength of Collective Man". Effectually Auden starts to write this idea that the buildings we make show our greatness as a "vain competitive excuse" which when considered is justifiably true. To make clear his meaning Auden adds "Out of the mirror they stare, imperialism's face and the international wrong". These lines suggest a great deal much of which pushes a thought that perhaps America is imperialistic as opposed to democratic and all good. Maybe some of our policies bring about an international wrong; although one should note that this is not applied to the wars of today but to a pre-U.S. involvement with WWII.

Stanzas five and six bring about evoking thoughts. Five suggests that the average person never wants to escape their norm; instead everything must always be same. If things changed those people would finally see what's going on around them. They would be "lost in a haunted wood, children afraid of the night who have never been happy or good" which symbolizes that they are stuck in a bad or unjust place where they've never really been right or happy. The sixth stanza takes a shot at the unimportant things important people shout. There is then an allusion to Nijinsky, a dance student to Diaghilev, who was driven insane by his teacher's pressure. Auden then makes a reference to natural sin in line 62 and follows it by the concept that the sinful heart wants "not universal love but to be loved alone" which deeply suggests it that people are exceedingly selfish.

The last three stanzas set each other up to deliver the message Auden intends to plainly give. Stanza seven focuses upon the concept of not being able to reach the average person for they are deaf and dumb to the message. Specifically Auden sets up the deaf-dumb bit in lines 75-77 with a keen literary device known as a parallel which adds a more dramatic push by means of repetition. In stanza eight Auden goes on to suggest that the speaker is one person set to tell the truth about authority and its corruption. Auden even dares to say that "there is no such thing as the state" and that people are controlled by human necessity. More importantly this stanza ends with a beautiful phrase: "We must love one another or die". The final stanza encapsulates a real sense of hope. It stands that though our world is not always understanding or right there is still hope. Hope can be found in those who believe in goodness. Auden then alludes that he is composed "of Eros and of dust" in line 96 which suggests that he is made of love, for Eros is the god of love, and dust which references the creation of man according to scripture. Though Auden feels the same "negation and despair" as others, he still hopes to stand true to his good ideals.

Overall the poem makes a slight comparison between the fascist Nazi oppression and our own U.S. oppression. The Nazis persecuted the Jews; the U.S. persecuted homosexuals. In his own time period Auden could never allow his audience to know that he was indeed a homosexual for the repercussions would not be gentle. Americans did not approve of homosexuals in this time period and if one looks closely at the text one sees that Auden is wishing people could understand or just see that their way is not necessarily the right way. By Auden's use of allusions, symbols, and phrases one sees his real message: the world is forever condemned if people cannot learn to accept and love others for their differences.

Chapter 13

The Process of Grieving and Dealing with Death in W.H. Auden's Famous Poem "Stop All the Clocks, Cut Off the Telephone"

Dealing with Death: The Speaker Wants to Stop Living & Stop Everyone Else from Living While He's at it

W. H. Auden has written an unusual response to death in "Stop All the Clocks, Cut Off the Telephone." The title itself demands that seemingly unreasonable actions be carried out. Why should all the clocks be stopped? Why should the telephone be cut off? The normal events of daily life, such as clocks ticking, telephones ringing, dogs barking, and pianos playing are for some reason not allowed. We do not yet know what this reason is. The imperative verbs in the first three lines of the first stanza are all controlling, forbidding words: 'stop,' 'prevent,' and 'silence.' Only with the first mention of death do the verbs become permitting: 'bring,' 'let,' 'put,' and yet another 'let.' A coffin and mourners are both allowed to be present. In fact, the more public happenings that do not ordinarily have anything to do with death must be made undeniably representative of it. Aeroplanes can make "moaning" noises as they fly, "public doves" must wear black bows as they take wing. Policemen are allowed to "wear black cotton gloves" as they direct traffic.

The less stern, more lenient verbs present with the mention of death suggest that a choice is possible. By giving the normally life-affirming entities a choice to represent death, the speaker is implying that they, or, in the case of the aeroplanes and doves, those who may manipulate them, would do so in the favor of death without a second thought. If they do not choose to, however, they are allowed this breach of expected conduct – it seems as if the speaker does not truly care either way. With a limp, shooing hand movement, the speaker implies that whatever happens to transform itself to represent death can or not; it is in his mind as changed already. Only the normal, private activities of life *must* be repressed, as the speaker's grief has presumably interrupted the normalcy of his own life.

Calling the deceased man "my North, my South, my East and West" in line 9 implies he was the speaker's compass; perhaps the speaker's moral compass, or reason for traveling in any direction with his life. This brings up the question of the speaker's relationship to the dead man: friend, relative, lover? Whichever the connection, the reader can assume the speaker loved the man dearly. Declaring the dead man "my working week and my Sunday rest" suggests that the latter was the speaker's entire life, since work and 'Sunday rest,' or relaxation/time spent not working, usually comprise the overarching categories of adult life. The following concepts the speaker insists the man embodies, his 'noon,' 'midnight,' 'talk,' and 'song,' fall into the more complex realms within 'rest.' 'Noon' could stand for the playful heat and relaxation commonly associated with noon; 'midnight' a solemn, mysterious, bewitched time - the parts of a human relationship that are mysterious and never truly understood. 'Talk' implies discussion of serious subjects, whereas 'song' suggests merriment and fun. The four terms cover a complex and diverse swathe of human life, suggesting that the dead man was a large part of the speaker's life.

In the last line of the third stanza, the speaker says that he was wrong in thinking "that love would last for ever". This brings up the possibility that the poem is not about death at all. The speaker could be suggesting that death has ended the love between himself and the man, but could also be insinuating that the entire poem is an exaggerated outpouring of emotions loosed by the end of a relationship.

In the last stanza, the heavenly bodies that create noon and midnight are ordered to be destroyed, with the harsh finality of the imperatives in the first three lines of the poem. The most constant bodies that have been around since the birth of man and helped sustain him, as the speaker must feel the 'deceased' man has been, must be disposed of. The speaker's audience is ordered to "pack up the moon," "dismantle the sun," "pour away the ocean," and "sweep up the wood." In this case, 'wood' might stand for the trees of forests, which create oxygen, equally as essential for human survival as the light of the sun and water, and as the speaker feels the dead man was to his continued existence. Even the stars, the last glimmers of hope lighting up the dark, unfathomable sky of human life, must be "put out."

The last line, a depressing assertion that "nothing now can ever come to any good," reaffirms the possibility that the poem may be about an ended relationship. With a true removed from the speaker's life in some way, but still alive, he may feel that his life is hopeless until the man is persuaded to enter the relationship again with the speaker. With a true love dead, the man may feel that any chance for happiness and genuine connection with another in his life is dashed for good. Every time he attempts to engage in the daily activities that form the backbone of his life, he will be alone, his true love destroyed like the poem demands of the ocean and stars, and feel hopeless. Auden has taken the universal, inarticulate despair everyone feels when somehow losing a loved one, and successfully articulated it.

Chapter 14

Study Questions and Answers

Q. Thank you, fog: W. H. Auden as presiding genius. Discuss

Or

Q. How does the poetry of Auden explore only "irreality".

-Is there... any figure traditionally associated with the stage who could be made to stand for this imaginative faculty? Yes, there is: the actor. "Genius & Apostle" Grown used to New York weather, all too familiar with Smog, You, Her unsullied Sister, I'd quite forgotten and what You bring to British winters now native knowledge returns. (Collected Poems 886) H. Auden's apostrophe to the fog might be taken as a willful demonstration of all that is self-consciously poetic about poetry. If, as Jonathan Culler argues, any use of apostrophe demonstrates a "fiction which knows its own fictive nature", then it seems as if Auden is deliberately writing a poem that foregrounds its fictional devices in order to undermine the experience presented in the poem, thus achieving what Lucy McDiarmid has called his deliberate undermining of poetry's "frivolity, vanity, and guilt". Accentuating the apostrophe with an ongoing capitalization of, among other words, every pronoun referring to the fog, Auden writes a poem that seemingly reflects Paul de Man's argument that the loss of the representational function in poetry goes hand in hand with the loss of self, the poet-as a result being left to explore only "irreality".

Auden's apostrophe to the fog employs what Geoffrey Hartman has called one of poetry's most self-conscious, founding superstitions, the belief in the spirit of place, the genius loci. Focusing on the time period between Gray and Wordsworth, Hartman explores the revaluation of this phenomenon and finds that in their effort to challenge their vocation's "darker graces," poets in this period continue Milton's "grand march of intellect," thus contributing to the "humanization of the mind". The predominant sign of the success of such a de-sublimation process is the mute epiphany: the transcendent, presiding genius or Other not speaking in response to the poet's appeal to it for renewed vision. As a result of becoming familiar with this silence, the poet's address-or apostrophe-to the presiding genius becomes "purely rhetorical".

Rather than insist on simply a linear progression of such revaluating, however, Hartman observes a cyclical progression: that is, there are also times during which poets return to their vocation's "superstitious" roots, to the "allegorical or mythological" mode. Such times are characterized by the self-consciousness of persona (when "self-identification becomes a more than personal, indeed a prophetic decision"), which happens "when the poet feels himself alien to the genius of country or age and destined to assume an adversary role". As the ages become increasingly secular, the poet who sees the sacred would feel himself or herself at odds with the age and assume this role of adversary. Cyclical or not, however, Hartman argues that moments in which the "burden of the mystery" is lifted are short-lived, and eventually, in spite of these returns to vocational roots, the span between Wordsworth and Wallace Stevens demonstrates a progressive demystification, a de-evolution of the imagination that reflects the imagination's dwindling ability to experience the sublime: as Thomas Weiskel tests it, that epiphanic experience in which by encountering some transcendent entity, human beings transcend, in feeling and in speech, their culturally and biologically determined human existence.

Thus, even though Hartman argues that the road to demystification takes occasional circuits back to superstitious belief, that belief is only superstitious. His theory, focused as it is on explaining the genesis of the Romantics, assumes that the poet's relationship to any "Other" is always the same: that the poet's task is always to represent such an encounter, which, given poets' increasing awareness of even the fictional aspects of language, is doomed to fail.

To return to the idea that Auden is willfully demonstrative about all that is self-conscious in poetry, then, it is possible to see that his talking to the fog is a sign of one who feels at odds with his age and, as a result, selfconscious about his persona-one, who, as the age's adversary, confronts it with what his age would feel is a complete fiction: in this case a "ThouThou" relationship to nature as if it were a second self.' Auden compounds this adversarial role, however, by using fictional devices in a way that undermines the fictionality. That is, he writes in the quiet tone of one who is supremely at home with such fictionality-with no self-consciousness about his persona at all.

There is nothing in Hartman's argument to explain this anomalous variation: Auden is not simply returning to superstitious belief (that is, using an abundance of devices only to draw attention to the fictionality of such belief); nor is he struggling to represent what the Romantics find out is impossible to represent without undermining it. As I will argue, Auden's poem attests to a movement from Wordsworth to Auden that shows us not a demystification and not a mute epiphany but a re-sublimation in the vocation of poetry: by enacting the role of the "Other," the poet speaks for the "Other," thus breaking its silence.

Q. Auden is an indispensable poet of our time. Discuss

When W. H. Auden died, in 1973, no one would have imagined that thirty years later he would come back as the poet of another age, our own. He seemed miserable and seedy then, having made a failed return to Oxford after two decades on St. Marks Place in the East Village and become the model of a modern poet who had lost his way and got stranded on an island of his own pet phrases. The obituaries, though large, mostly quoted his lyrics from the thirties: "As I Walked Out One Evening" or "Lullaby" ("Lay your sleeping head, my love,

/ Human on my faithless arm...") or, more brazenly, the line from "September 1, 1939"—"We must love one another or die"—which he had pointedly cut from his own canon. The body of poetry that he produced after his emigration to America, in 1939, was pretty poorly regarded—Philip Larkin, once a disciple, had written a brisk, common-sense dismissal of it as "a rambling intellectual stew," while the greatest American reviewer, Randall Jarrell, another apostate, referred to the later Auden manner as one of a man "who has turned into a rhetoric mill grinding away at the bottom of Limbo."

Yet, at the beginning of the new century, he is an indispensable poet. Even people who don't read poems often turn to poetry at moments when it matters, and Auden matters now. In the eighties, his lyric "Stop All the Clocks" became the elegy of the AIDS era, sold on bookstore counters, by the registers. In the nineties, Robert Hughes led off his memorable polemic against postmodernism "The Culture of Complaint" with a long, marvelling quote from Auden's Christmas oratorio, "For the Time Being," where the liberal King Herod mourns the loss of rational consensus in the face of feckless sectarianism. In the past year, Auden has been everywhere, by the sheer force of popular will. Two of his lyrics about suffering and confusion—"Musée des Beaux Arts" and "September 1, 1939"—sprang to renewed life after last September 11th as the embodiments of our mood, posted on Web sites and subway walls. Even fashion models, and not just fashion models, now name their sons Auden, as they might ten years ago have called them Dylan, and pose with them on the cover of Vogue.

The odd thing is that Auden's poems are often saying the reverse of what we have now decided to hear. "Stop All the Clocks" was written as a jaunty, Noël Coward-like ironic pastiche of a mourning song, unmoored from grief—no more meant to be taken seriously as an elegy ("Prevent the dog from barking with a juicy bone"?) than "You're the Top" is to be taken seriously as a love poem. The quote from "For the Time Being" that Hughes used so effectively to warn against the mess the world can become in the absence of rationality was first meant to demonstrate the opposite—the rational voice, after all, is Herod's as he orders the massacre of the innocents. And "September 1, 1939," far from being a call to renewed conscience after a period of drift, is actually a call to irony and apolitical retreat, a call not to answer any call.

from the issuecartoon banke-mail thisBut, past a certain point, poets can't be misread, not by an entire time, no more than an entire family can misread a father: the homecoming noises in the hallway are the man; the accumulated impression is the poet. What matters is the sound he makes. Auden's emotional tone is our tone, even if his meanings are not always our meanings.

That Auden tone, the one that matters most now, was made in New York between 1939 and 1948, when Auden came to this city and made it his home. In those nine years, he underwent an extraordinary transformation, which implicated every line on his face. He entered as the smooth-faced mysterious druid of the English industrial landscape, the Marxist lyricist who spellbound a generation, and he emerged as the boozy, creased, garrulous Auden who lasted. He taught, loved, wrote more journalism than seems quite possible, and produced the four long poems that remain the astounding heart of his work: "For the Time Being," a Nativity oratorio in modern dress; "New Year Letter," an abstract philosophical poem in Swiftian couplets; "The Age of Anxiety," a pastoral eclogue set in a New York bar and written in alliterative verse; and "The Sea and the Mirror," a commentary on Shakespeare's "The Tempest." At last, we have a big book in which we can step into the quarry of the ideas, good and bad, from which he mined those four poems, and that is the second volume of Princeton's complete edition of Auden's prose, edited by Edward Mendelson.

The essays are overwhelming in the number and variety of the subjects addressed, ideas aired, capital letters employed, and systems invented to prove a small point. When one recalls that they are merely the garden wall on which the ivy of the decade's poems grew, and that not even the whole wall is there—for instance, the recently collected lectures on

Shakespeare and the long lecture series of 1948 on the imagery of the sea in Romantic poetry, "The Enchafèd Flood," are not included—they seem as lasting a monument to poetic energy allied to intellectual purpose as we possess. The essays are also a reminder of how many more places a poet could work out his worries in public fifty years ago. There are the now impossible to imagine short essays for Mademoiselle and Harper's Bazaar and Vogue; there are medium-length, middlebrow essays in the Times Book Review; there are long, chewy pieces for small magazines. There are lots of brief reviews for The Nation, and there are fine original essays on Tennyson and Kipling in particular, but for the most part these are review-essays. The reviewer is given a book on a subject—Baudelaire, Tennyson—by the editor, and gives back an essay not just, in the time-honored manner, on what the author should have thought about the subject, had he been as wise as the reviewer, but on what the subject should have thought about his own experience, had he understood it as well as the poet does. Not only is the biographer told what he should have thought about Tennyson and the Victorian age; Tennyson is told what he should have thought about the Queen.

Q. Write a note on Auden's various residences and travels.

Or

Q. How can you say Auden's poetry emerged from an existence - a career - in movement, a life with multiple foci?

It is easy to see that the cultural and philosophical co-ordinates of Auden's poetry range widely across space and time. But it is also very much of its own time, particularly in its restless, vagrant, sometimes harried, note of unsettlement. In 1939 in an "Ode" in praise of a Manhattan hotel where he was temporarily based, Auden wrote that: "I've stayed in hotels in most places | Where my passport permits me to go/ (Excluding the British Dominions/And Turkey and U.S.S.R.)". The tone is light, but the claim contains a significant figurative truth, one that most critics have not taken seriously enough, or have not thought through in detail. The claim goes to the heart of the kind of poet that Auden was. It points to the role of the displaced, cosmopolitan poet which history forced Auden to take on and which, when he did take it on, made him such a historically representative figure.

But just how "cosmopolitan," how "international" was Auden? What precisely were the historical conditions from which his uprooted vantagepoint emerged? How much travelling did he in reality do? How much of his life was spent away from his residence of the moment (whether that was in England, Germany, the United States, Italy, or Austria)? What were the journeys and choices that produced his own complicatedly transnational literary identity and his ideal of "a sort of world, quite other/altogether different from this one | with its envies and passports"? This note attempts to supply some basic details out of which satisfying answers to these questions might be built.

In a note to himself late in life Auden roundly declared that "Behaviour that can be statistically expressed, is the behaviour of the enslaved". My first impulse on reading this sentence is to agree cravenly. Striving to be more honest, though, I find that in gauging the extent of Auden's boundary-spanning cultural profile, a few figures and statistics are actually helpful.

They make clear that the restlessness and eclecticism of Auden's poetry emerged not just from a cerebral internationalism of the desk and study but from an existence - a career - in movement, a life with multiple foci. Auden's cosmopolitanism was not just an ethical notion but a reflection of specific cultural and social experiences during a period in which almost no-one expected life to go on unchanged, a period which one historian (Eric Hobsbawm) has called "an era of havoc.".

So... some facts. During his lifetime Auden held two different passports (British and American) at different times. Although he was finally "naturalized" as an American citizen in May 1946, apparently he did not receive an American passport until Feb 1948, shortly before he travelled to Italy. This presumably means that he travelled to Europe with the USSBS in 1945 on some kind of temporary, military-issued pass rather than an ordinary American passport. At various points Auden had long-term homes in five countries: UK, Germany, USA, Italy, and Austria (these are places where he lived at least once for six-months or more at a stretch). He made no - or practically no - journeys abroad from the place which was at the time his de facto home during 26 years out of the 67 or so years of his life (197-1924, 1933 [bar a few days in Germany during January 1933], 194-44, 1946-47). However, if we subtract his years of childhood from this total, we see that Auden made no - or practically no - journeys abroad in only eight out of his 49 adult years, and five of those eight years were a direct result of wartime restrictions. In other words, when Auden was an adult and could have travelled abroad, he did so during roughly 94% of the possible years, frequently for quite substantial stretches of time. For him, then, travelling was a norm.

Vaguely defined plans to travel to Australia in 1935 and Mexico in 1938 fell through, meaning that Auden visited or lived in four of the world's seven continents (Asia, Africa, Europe and North America). In all he visited 27 countries at some point in his life (leaving aside Britain, the place of his birth, which of course later, technically became a foreign country for him). Those countries (and colonies) are: Austria, Belgium, Canada, Ceylon, China, Czechoslovakia, Denmark, Djibouti, Egypt, France, Germany, Greece, Hong Kong, Hungary, Iceland, India, Israel (is there any other important English-language poet with a reputation established before the Second World War who travelled to Israel, I wonder?), Italy, Japan, Macao, Norway, Portugal, Spain, Sweden, Switzerland, USA, and Yugoslavia.

We have already seen that Auden claimed by the age of 32 he had "stayed in most places" where he was allowed to go, "Excluding the British Dominions I And Turkey and U.S.S.R." Perhaps the most noticeable and significant places that Auden did not visit are Russia (an especially meaningful omission for a supposed poet of the 193s Left), Central and South America: "I... have never been to Mexico nor wish to go there" Auden wrote rather camply in his 1956 introduction to

John Ashbery's Some Trees. (The tentative plan for Auden and Isherwood to meet Spender in Mexico in the summer 1938, after their trip to China, was apparently abandoned.) Closer to "home", we note he never set foot in the country that, in his elegy for W. B. Yeats, he aggressively describes - based on no first-hand knowledge - as "mad Ireland."

In judging the substance of Auden's travels, I count 29 separate journeys that each lasted more than two months. Indeed, 26 of those 29 journeys lasted more than five months, blurring remarkably the notion that, especially in Auden's later years, there were for him clear definitions of what "at home" and "abroad," "domestic" and "foreign," "here" and "there," meant.

In a manner that helps us to sharpen our sense of specificity about Auden's travel-dominated life, the extent of his movement contrasts starkly and suggestively with those of two major poets of the generations before and after his own. First, the older poet. In 1946 Eliot wrote of Ezra Pound that "I have never known a man, of any nationality, to live so long out of his native country without seeming to settle anywhere else." Yet in spite of Ezra Pound's cultivation of an intensely cosmopolitan, mobile poetic persona and in spite of his bookish fascination with the ancient cultures of Egypt and China, he seems only ever to have set foot in seven countries (the United States, Spain [Gibraltar], the United Kingdom, France, Italy, Germany, and at the very end of his life, seeking medical treatment, Switzerland), all of them, bar his native land, in the heart of Western Europe. Together these were essentially the countries that produced the literature covered in his MA in Romance languages at Penn as long ago as 195-6.

(Besides comparing Pound's mobility to Auden's, it is also interesting to compare it in passing to William Carlos Williams's. Pound travelled less widely and less often than Auden. He even travelled less widely than Williams. In the 191s and 192s, Pound often cast his internationalist purview against Williams's nativist stance. Yet Williams actually saw a more diverse group of cultures than Pound - he travelled at various times to France, Switzerland, Belgium, Germany,

Holland, the United Kingdom, Italy, Spain, Austria and the Commonwealth of Puerto Rico. This suggests that being identified, by oneself or by others, as a rooted or a deracinated artist has as much to do with the stories that writers tell about themselves as it does with actual experience. I am reminded that in A Colder Eye Hugh Kenner calculated Yeats, the poet of Irish nationalism, spent more time out of Ireland than James Joyce, the professional exile. Yet in 1948, the Irish government actively sought to have the body of the nationalist Yeats returned to Ireland while discreetly rejecting the idea of repatriating Joyce's remains.)

Of course, the duration and intensity of a person's immersion in a culture counts for far more in the shaping of an identity than the number of places visited for brief holidays. The Cantos is impossible to imagine without Pound's confrontation with avant-garde ideas and poetic techniques in London and Paris during the 1910s and 1920s, or with his immersion in Italian politics in the 1920s and 1930s. Quite why some literary historians persist in seeing Pound's poem as simply "American" and Pound as an "American" poet is a mystery to me: surely it and he are as much products of Europe as they are anything else? Still, the degree of diversity that a writer experiences surely also matters and in this respect Williams was more widely-travelled than Pound.

But if Pound's personal experience of the world seems limited compared with Auden's, then the self-proclaimed introspective isolatedness of the most important poet of a younger generation of English poets, Philip Larkin, seems even more distinct and contrasting. In spite of Larkin's enthusiasm for the works of Isherwood (that prototypical 193s wanderer), Larkin himself made only a tiny number of excursions away from English territory. He made trips to Germany in 1936 and 1937 with his father and to Belgium in 1939 with his school. But subsequently he seems to have travelled abroad only twice in his entire adult life in journeys that together amounted to no more a few days' duration (a short trip Paris with Bruce Montgomery in 1952, and a reluctant flying visit to Hamburg in 1976 to collect the Shakespeare Prize). In other words, while

Auden travelled abroad in 94% of the years of his adult life, Larkin travelled similarly in about 5% of the years of his maturity. And, given the brevity of Larkin's forays and the usual lengthiness of Auden's, such a stark numerical comparison actually understates the degree of disparity between their experiences of the wider world. In later years Larkin's carefully cultivated dislike of foreignness and of travel became widely known, and it was from this vantagepoint that the parochial weight of his sarcasm in his 1960 review of Homage to Clio can best be felt. Bemoaning Auden's disappearance from the English scene in 1939, Larkin castigated the "individual and cosmopolitan path" that the later Auden had followed.

What follows is a summary list of Auden's main foreign journeys, together with dates, the approximate length of the journey being given in months (side trips and brief stops are indicated in square brackets). The order of the countries listed here is, in the simplest sense, the order in which Auden visited the countries during his travel for that year. But each country is listed only once for each journey even if Auden visited the country several times during that journey. This was often the case with his trips to Britain, Germany, Italy and Austria after 1948. Short of a day by day itinerary, which would be beyond my powers to compile and anyone else's to read through, it is impossible to represent the frequent complexities the circlings, lateral movements, hiatuses, forays, and repetitions of Auden's journeys, especially in the post-World War 2 period. For example, in 1956-57, Auden made several journeys back and forth from Italy to Britain. I list each country only once in each journey, indicating merely the order in which he first visited them during the trip. Note too that the dating of the journey refers only to the months in which all or part of the journey was made. It does not necessarily mean that Auden was away for the whole of the month in question.

With a British passport:
Aug 1925: Austria
Dec 1925: Jan 1926: Austria
Dec 1926: Jan 1927: Austria

July - Aug 1927: Yugoslavia
July-Aug 1928: Belgium
Oct 1928 - July 1929: Germany
June-July 193: Germany
Dec 193: Germany
July 1931: Germany
Dec 1932 - Jan 1933: Germany
Aug - Sept 1934: (motoring tour through) Belgium, Germany, Czechoslovakia, Hungary, Austria, Switzerland
Jan 1935: Denmark
Oct 1935: Switzerland [possible visit to Greece?]
Oct 1935: Belgium
March - April 1936: Portugal
May 1936: Belgium
June - Sept 1936: Iceland
Jan - March 1937: [France], Spain
April 1937: France
Jan - July 1938: [France, Egypt, Djibouti, Ceylon, Hong Kong, Macao], China, [Japan, Canada, USA]
Aug - Sept 1938: Belgium
Dec 1938 - Jan 1939: [France], Belgium, [Germany]
Jan 1939 -: USA
With an American military pass:
April - Aug 1945: [Britain], Germany
With an American passport:
April - Sept 1948: [Britain, France], Italy, [Austria]
April - Sept 1949: Italy
March - Sept 195: Italy
March - Sept 1951: India, Italy
March - Sept 1952: [France], Italy, [Austria]
May - Nov 1953: Italy, [Britain, Austria]
April - Sept 1954: [France], Italy, [Britain, Austria]
April - Sept 1955: [Britain], Italy, [Germany]
April 1956 - Nov 1957: Italy, Britain, [Austria]
April - Oct 1958: Britain, Austria, Italy
April - Oct 1959: Britain, Austria, [France]
Feb 196: Britain
April - Nov 196: Britain, Austria, [Germany]

April - Oct 1961: Austria, [Germany, Norway, Britain]
April - Oct 1962: Austria, [Britain, ?Germany]
April - Oct 1963: [Britain, Germany], Austria
April 1964 - Oct 1965: Iceland, [Sweden], Austria, [Britain, USA, Greece, Yugoslavia], Germany, [Hungary, Italy]
April - Oct 1966: Britain, Austria, [Germany]
April - Oct 1967: Austria, Britain, [France]
Feb - 1968: Austria
April - Oct 1968: Austria, [Italy, Britain]
March - Oct 1969: [?Greece], Austria, Britain, [Sweden]
April - Nov 197: Israel, [Greece], Austria, Britain
April - Oct 1971: [Italy], Austria, Britain, [Macedonia]
April 1972 - Sept 1973: Austria, Britain, [USA, Belgium]

Clearly Auden's travels are not without cultural foci or biases: they predominantly, though not exclusively, involve journeys around and between Europe and the United States. Such intensive journeying was far less typical or easy than it is today. After he had flown on a US military plane from the United States to Britain on his way to Germany in April 1945, Auden presciently announced to friends waiting to greet him, "I'm the first major poet to fly the Atlantic." (Pound's flight to the United States in November 1945 also seems to have been made on a US military plane.)

But before long in the post-war period, flying writers were becoming less anomalous. Isherwood flew to Britain in January 1947; E M Forster flew to the United States in April 1947; Eliot flew from the States to Britain in November 1948. So Auden was not the first "major poet" to cross the Atlantic ocean on a commercial flight when, in September 1949, when he flew TWA from Italy to the United States.

Auden's history of geographical mobility - the Christmas of 1937, the year in which he suffered a laying on of patriotic hands when the George VI personally awarded him a Gold Medal for Poetry, was the last Christmas he spent in England until the Christmas of 1972, his last - while telling and pronounced is hardly unique within the culture of Auden's place and time. And of course it does not count as one of the innumerable histories of tragic journeying involuntarily lived out around the planet in the 193s and 194s. But then that is the point. During Auden's life, travel was becoming not so much a rarefied class privilege as a more general condition. Raymond Williams identified exilic, modernist writing and experimentation as occurring within the "general processes of mobility, dislocation and para-national communication."

Reflecting on Williams's words and commenting on this idea of "mobility" as a key to modernism both as a literary and a social formation, Michael North considers the endlessly peripatetic careers of just three British subjects, Charlie Chaplin, Claude McKay and D H Lawrence, and comments that they share and "experience of restless travel so relentless that citizenship ceases to have any meaning."

Such was also Auden's case. Auden's status as a writer almost always "in transit" derives from a particular historical moment, and endows his work with a certain very modern cultural representativeness. These are facets of his writing which are still too infrequently analyzed, or even noticed. It was not as if Auden was unaware of this motif of displacement in his writing and his life. Some of his most telling self-definitions (whether in his poetry, prose, letters or conversations) involve ideas of dislocation or displacement. Thus, at various times after 1940, Auden refers to himself as "the Wandering Jew," as an "alien," a "déraciné," a "metic."

In 1941 Auden looked back to the exemplary writing of another heroic member of the first generation of modernists (just as he would do in his 1946 address to the Grolier Club on the expatriated Henry James), when he sought to define why the disaffiliated or nationless writer had become such an important symbol of the fate imposed on everyone by modernity. "Kafka is important to us," Auden the New World émigré claimed, "because the predicament of his hero is the predicament of the contemporary man.... It was fit and proper that Kafka should have been a Jew, for the Jews have long been placed in the position in which we are all now to be, of having no home."

The place where a person is born has a symbolic value in the story of their life. So too does the place of their death. As we noted at the start of this essay, in 1939 Auden announced that he had "stayed in hotels in most places | Where my passport permits me to go." By 1947 he had begun to believe that he would not only keep staying in hotels. He told a friend mournfully: "I shall probably die in a hotel." In September 1973, Auden, on his last evening as himself, gave a poetry reading and then, during the ensuing night, died alone in the Altenburgerhof in Vienna. Chester Kallman wrote that the following morning he found Auden "Turning icy-blue on a hotel bed."

Note: During a visit to Athens in 1965, Auden appears to have mentioned that he had visited the city thirty years before. See David Jackson, "Three Pictures of W. H. Auden," Christopher Street, 2.4, 42. October 1935 seems to me the likeliest date for a short, otherwise unrecorded visit by Auden to Greece at this period. Contemporary accounts suggest that, factoring in stops and changes of aircraft, it took approximately three days to travel from London to Athens by plane in the mid-1930s.

Special thanks are due to Edward Mendelson who offered essential help with the compilation and tabulation of data about Auden's travel as well as several important memory-joggers. I would be grateful to readers for any corrections and/ or additions they can offer.

Q. WH Auden's first poems, rooted in guilt and desire. Explain

Or

Q. Is it right to say for Auden "Just under his skin lies the 'indolent ulcer'."

They were the most brilliant bunch of boys English literature has ever seen, those writers who came to fame in the Thirties. And as this volume of the poems he wrote at school and university brings home, the most brilliantly precocious of them all was Wystan Hugh Auden.

Katherine Bucknell's collection, WH Auden: Juvenilia as loving and meticulous and informing an edition as any writer, young or old, could wish for leaves off as Auden, just down from Oxford, armed with a poor third-class degree in English, departs for Berlin in the early autumn of 1928. His first, tiny, volume was about to appear, hand-printed by Stephen Spender, Poems , an astonishing achievement, egotistical, cranky, fiendishly allusive and stacked with talent. It was the tip of an immense iceberg. In the mere six or so years since he decided as a schoolboy of 15 to become a poet, he'd produced more than 2 poems. Most of them are here, an extraordinary ransacking of modes, a trying on and swift discarding of voices, a confident striding towards a poetic mind and voice of his own. He was only 21.

What's going on here in Katherine Bucknell's tellingly assembled collection (drafts, notes, cross-checked allusions, forward pointings, and all) is Auden's quest for a way of combining in verse his various loves. He's nothing if not a lover. 'This world is full of lovely things.' He meant the scarred, bird-haunted landscape of northern England, with its sadly derelict traces of the early industrial revolution, the shafts of worked-out mines, pumping sheds and winding gear: Alston Moor, Allendale, Rookhope. He also meant the men who worked up there.

'Doth it not welcome thee? This land? With all its splendid men, its loveliness?' And not just men, engineers, farmers, shepherds, and their like, with their magnetically efficient, work-nicked hands, but boys, sexual partners his own age, like the glorious two Auden observes bathing in 'The Tarn' when he's 17, 'splendid of limb,/ Ruddy and beautiful'. Of such were his moments of youthful vision: 'life's great doxology', as he put it.

Dr George Auden and his High Anglican wife could hardly be expected to endorse their clever son's sexual drift. There was close questioning of Auden and a schoolfriend after some swimming-pool verses were found. Fathers and Mothers and 'doddering Jehovah' come into these early texts as fearful prohibitionists. Much of this writing is about the roping in of alternative, surrogate fathers. The more prolific the young Auden becomes, the more avidly he devours useful assistants and inspiring ancestors.

Thomas Hardy, he who 'used to notice such things', is

acquired as a great model of post-Christian regard for an earth 'lovely beyond belief'. Edward Thomas teaches Auden how to learn from agricultural labourers' talk in a poem. Thomas Stearns Eliot quite staggers the cocky Christ Church undergraduate with a besotting blend of sexy worldliness and an austere investment in the tropes and modes of the highest Western culture. At every stage of his development, this amazing young pasticheur becomes what he is currently admiring: 'I, Thomas', now this Thomas, now that.

The impediment to voicing his passion was the illegal and transgressive nature of his homosexual feelings. Intense guilt over forbidden erotic fruit racks these early poems. There are many frustrated nights in beds with heterosexual friends when only cold toes tangle.

Auden fantasised, the wonderfully informative Katherine Bucknell informs us, about being rogered by his father. Watching Auden invent the Audenesque in a wrestle with boshed desires and unsatisfactory partings - 'The glabrous suction of goodbye', 'The ragged ends of overdrawn farewells' - is one of the many great joys of this volume. But it is still dismaying to note the persistence of the sadness and the guilt, and to watch the poet settling for a life in the furtive sexual underground which parents, school and the law are imposing as his dismal future lot.

The trawler's lusts - the 'pressure of strange knees at cinemas' - can be sweet, but cottaging, like the pathetic schoolmasterly maulers of pupils in these verses, is a degraded option. Auden 'sniffs with distaste', but keeps nosing up to the 'whiff' of the damned. Between his palms, perturbingly, the loved one is said to have 'viced'. Repeatedly the poet feels himself slipping and falling in moral 'slush'. Just under his skin lies the 'indolent ulcer'.

Particularly moving in this volume is to see the whole tragic future already unfolding - a vista of rough trade, sexual wounding, perpetual unease, protracted dissatisfaction in loving while not being really loved in turn. There's a repeated, magical encounter with a kindly engineer, who shows the young poet how some old bit of machinery works, or worked, in an upland engine house. But already it's a bad dream, a fearful anticipation of 'the padded room, the clinic and the hangman's little shed'. Auden craves the sort of male bonding he found in Anglo-Saxon texts - ly ng down beside the lord you loved. But these were dead men, defeated in battle.

Little consolation to be had there. Far more pleasurable was thinking back, as the collection ends with Auden doing, fantasising about school adventures, boyish crushes, the erotic lure of smelly kit in mouldy lockers. The 15-year-old Auden made himself sound like a little old man, Hardy in short pants. Headed for Berlin and the adult world, the graduate Auden's verse has lapsed into prep-school giggling. It was the very odd matrix from which the best English poetry of the Thirties was to come.

Q. How Auden settled for the wrong blond?

Or

Q. Discuss Auden's agony on "not being loved by anyone

The lives of all great poets are a part of their poetry and cannot be separated from it. This would be as true of Homer, of whom we know nothing, as it is of Milton or Goethe, Byron or Mandelstam, about whom we know a great deal, some would say far too much. 'One life, one writing,' wrote Robert Lowell, and recent poets, like he and John Berryman, have sought to present the two together, an independent whole, the life as art and the art as life.

Too conscious the process may have become and yet it seems natural enough. Auden, however, would have strongly disapproved. Old fashioned in this as in other ways he would have felt with Jane Austen and Henry James that the writer's life was in no case the reader's concern. He wished for no biography; attempted to leave instructions against one.

His reasons may have been less straighforward than he would have admitted. His life had no figure in the carpet, no unexpected twists or intriguing skeletons, none of the reserved sacrament, as it were, which makes the profane so inquisitive about Eliot's personality and history. It was just an amiable mess, in which anything went, everything hung out.

Not that Auden had the instincts or morals of a Bohemian

- far from it - but his being had nothing mysterious about it, no hidden clue for the biographical sleuth to get after. Perhaps, as many of us would, he feared the nothing that might be revealed rather than the too much.

Humphrey Carpenter and Edward Mendelson have already gone over the ground biographically in a conscientious way and revealed at some length what might in any case have been guessed. Auden in Love is an amiable title, provided we do not expect new revelations, and do not take it as adding anything of significance to our image of the poet.

'He became his admirers,' Auden wrote of the moment the poet died, in his elegy for Yeats; and Valery celebrated in his poem on Poe's tomb the louche figure changed at last by eternity into himself as he really is. Dead poets do not change, but anything further we hear about them has the interest that belongs to a special relationship.

Dorothy Farman's shrewd and good-nature memoir begins from the evening of April 6, 1939, with Auden reading that elegy for Yeats from manuscript at an evening organised by the League of American Writers, a left-wing organisation popular in the thirties. He himself was 32 and had just arrived in New York with Christopher Isherwood. Among the admiring audience were a group of students from Brooklyn College, who afterwards managed to get into conversation. Chester Kallman was one of them. The following day he called at Auden's apartment.

Auden had written in his facetious poem about love the year before. It did; though at the instant of meeting, Auden stepped next door into the room where Isherwood was writing letters and remarked tersely: 'It's the wrong blonde.' By the evening it was clearly very much the right one, however, and a marriage began which ended only with Auden's death in 1973.

In a sense with Kallman's too, less than two years later. Although he caused the poet years of grief and jealousy he could not survive on his own, without his 'criterion,' as he rather strangely referred to Auden. To adapt earlier poetic epitaph admired by Auden:

Auden's agape had sheltered Kallman like the wings of the dove and its removal was the end of him. Though he had the same faults of envy and destructiveness, Kallman was the opposite of that archetypal diabolic boyfriend, Lord Alfred Douglas. He needed to be loved, and the older man needed to love him.

Kallman refused any permanent sexual relations with Auden and disclaimed any notion of possession of fidelity, although Auden paid for and looked after him and found him his jobs. Auden suffered much, and seemed at one point at the end of the war to be thinking seriously of a permanent sexual relation with Roan Jaffe, an attractive, merry but humourless girl whose one absorbing interest was in psychologising herself and her friends.

On this basis, and also apparently in bed, she had Auden got on very well. They remained great friends, but Auden afterwards said it had not affected him at all, that it was a 'sin' and felt like 'cheating.'

Girls in the offing would be likely to have a difficult time. Chester had met Dorothy and Mary Valentine in Ann Arbor and adopted the pair when they came to New York. 'My Mary and Dorothy period,' as he referred to it, certainly changed their lives. Chester found them jobs and looked after them like a brother. Mary fell in love with him, as girls tended to do, and eventually married his father, a big, clever, ebullient Jewish dentist. Auden was a benevolent presence.

The shy pair from religious homes in the middle west blossomed in New York, and Dorothy's memoir conveys very well the heady atmosphere of those post-war days, the parties, the summer shack on Fire Island, Auden at the opera immaculate in hired tuxedo but still wearing his bedroom slippers.

Dorothy remarks that Auden's tragedy was that 'nobody ever loved him the way he wanted to be loved.' The impression rather is that like many dominant men of powerful organising capability, he was not interested in being loved, other than through the receipt of mere sexual gratification, but extremely obsessed with loving. This was not all agape: he would have liked to own Kallman, who refused to be owned. But whatever was tragic in the relationship was also suited to it and to both men, and Auden always compared their meeting with the recognition scene between Siegmund and Sieglinde in the first act of Die Walkure. Before that moment, 'All that I had ever seen was strange, I never found a friend near me.'

Auden's greatest poetry was perhaps already written when they met, but Kallman was probably the muse who kept him a poet till his last day.

Q. Discuss the poetic stature of Auden?

"It's such a pity Wystan never grows up."

—W. H. Auden, Letter to Lord Byron

"I shall only ask you to apply to the work of the deceased a very simple test. How many of his lines can you remember?"

—W. H. Auden, "The Public v. the Late Mr. W. B. Yeats"

In June 1994, shortly before Princeton University Press brought out its edition of W. H. Auden's juvenilia, The New Criterion published a handful of those apprentice poems from the mid-to-late 192s. While working on a brief introduction to accompany the selection, I happened to have a conversation with a visiting English critic whose work I admire. I told him I was writing something about Auden's juvenilia. Without missing a beat he said, "It's all juvenilia, isn't it?"

I joined him in a laugh. But his comment did take me aback. W. H. Auden, perhaps the most accomplished poetic craftsman since Yeats—the man who once claimed to have written poems exemplifying every form discussed in George Saintsbury's History of English Prosody (three volumes)—a lifelong purveyor of juvenilia? Surely not. Auden was one of the most urbane and insightful essayists of the twentieth century. That much is indisputable. But his poetic stature?

There seem to be two main schools of thought. No one denies the prodigious skill, the cleverness, the wide if quirky erudition on display in Auden's poetry. And very few would deny the strength of many—well, anyway several—poems published between 193, when his first volume appeared, and around 194, the year after he emigrated (his enemies said "fled") to the United States. These were the years of most of

Auden's anthology pieces: "The Secret Agent," "Lullaby," "As I Walked Out One Evening," "Musée des Beaux Arts," "In Memory of W. B. Yeats," "September 1, 1939," "In Memory of Sigmund Freud," and one or two others. Opinion has long been divided about Auden's later work, especially his work after 1945. And since 1973, when Auden died at the age of sixty-six, opinion has also been increasingly divided about the larger question of what his poetic achievement really adds up to. Does it rival or even surpass that of Yeats or Eliot, say? Or has the discipline of posterity made it seem less capacious, less vital, less necessary?

Auden's champions include many distinguished and articulate figures: poets like Joseph Brodsky, Richard Wilbur, and John Fuller, whose recent reference work, W. H. Auden: A Commentary,1 is a meticulous labour of love and scholarship. A much-expanded and revised version of his 197 Reader's Guide to Auden's poems, the new Commentary attempts "to say something useful about every original poem, play, or libretto of his written in English that has so far reached print (with the exception of most of the juvenilia...)." Among Auden's other commentators, the palm must go to Edward Mendelson, the poet's literary executor, chief editor, bibliographer, and most devoted critic.

In Early Auden , Professor Mendelson distinguished between the traditions of "civil poetry" and "vatic poetry," locating Auden firmly in the former. "He had no wish to achieve an imaginative triumph over common reality," Professor Mendelson wrote in his introduction. "His poems were not visionary autonomous objects, exempt from the practical and ethical standards appropriate to all other human works. They were made to be judged both for their art and their truth." What Auden wanted, Professor Mendelson wrote later in the book, was "poetry that reflected the formal and linguistic lessons of modernism yet could still serve the public good. The art he wished to create was intent less on autonomy and stasis than on enlightenment and action."

Early Auden followed its subject's career through the eve of his emigration to the United States, in January 1939, with his friend, sometime lover, and occasional collaborator Christopher Isherwood. Later Auden2 picks up the story from there, providing a history and interpretation of Auden's work from 1939 through his death in 1973.

Later Auden is a scrupulous and inviting piece of literary-critical scholarship, crisply written and full of the quiet authority that comes with intimate mastery of a subject. Indeed, I doubt whether anyone can claim greater mastery of the Auden corpus than Professor Mendelson. He began with a doctoral dissertation on Auden. In 197, when Auden was thinking about putting together a collection of his book reviews and review essays, he found he was unable to remember exactly what he'd written or where.

But Professor Mendelson, who had met Auden while working on his thesis, had amassed photocopies of virtually everything. Auden—who was spectacularly disorganized himself—was duly impressed by this display of order (and doubtless by the homage it implied) and entrusted the selection of the volume that became Forewords and Afterwords to him. In 1972, Professor Mendelson was appointed Auden's literary executor (joining William Meredith and Monroe K. Spears), and he has devoted himself to Audeniana ever since.

In addition to his critical studies, he is a founding member of the Auden Society. He has also edited almost all of Auden's posthumous works:3 the last collection of poems, entitled Thank You, Fog , Collected Poems , The English Auden: Poems, Essays, and Dramatic Writings 1927–1939 , and the ongoing Complete Works of W. H. Auden of which three volumes (plays, libretti, and prose to 1938) have thus far appeared from Princeton University Press. All of which is to say that there is precious little about Auden's work that Professor Mendelson doesn't know.

Although it is half again as long as its predecessor, Later Auden does not come with the same kind of interpretative scaffolding. In Early Auden, by arguing for the merits of what he called the "civil tradition" of poetry, Professor Mendelson challenged the prevailing critical climate that gave precedence to the Romantic-Modernist tradition with its emphasis on the isolated individual and the autonomy of the work of art. His detailed discussion of Auden's early development was at the same time a brief for the view of poetry—and by implication, the view of society and man's place in it—that Auden came to represent.

At bottom, it is an eighteenth-century view, according to which the purpose of art is to delight and instruct. In Later Auden, such larger arguments are more implicit than explicit. In his introduction, Professor Mendelson lays out various oppositions—between myth and parable, between "the Ariel-dominated poet and the Prospero-dominated poet," between the poem as "verbal contraption" (Auden's phrase) and moral artifact—with which Auden's poetry contended. But the text proper is a tightly focused, sometimes almost abrupt, tour of Auden's work from the elegy for Yeats, which was written a few weeks after he arrived in New York, to the "concluding carnival" of his last, chatty poems.

As in his earlier volume, Professor Mendelson quietly punctuates his critical narrative with aptly chosen biographical details. While no substitute for a full-fledged biography, this procedure does provide readers with a kind of precis of Auden's movements, activities, and infatuations. Those interested in a fuller account of Auden's life may consult the excellent biography by Humphrey Carpenter and the briefer, more thematic life by Richard Davenport-Hines.

Early Auden argued for Auden's surpassing greatness ("the most inclusive poet of the twentieth century, its most technically skilled, and its most truthful"); Later Auden assumes it. It is revisionist in that it places Auden's later work on a par with, or even ahead of, his early work. Professor Mendelson is far from uncritical; about some poems from the early Forties, for example, he writes that "the contemplative saints briefly but disastrously took over much of his work, and they ruined every poem they touched." But such local criticisms occur in the context of presumed greatness. They tend to underscore the boldness of Professor Mendelson's arresting claim that "much of [Auden's] most profound and personal work was written in the last fifteen years of his life," that is from 1958 on. "Personal" of course it may be; any doodle might be personal. And in fact Auden, who famously declared that he did not want a biography written about him, often noted that his poems were full of coded autobiographical references. "For a poet like myself," he wrote, "an autobiography would be redundant since anything of importance that happens to one is immediately incorporated, however obscurely, in a poem."

The task of identifying such references has kept scholars busy for years and is one of the things that makes John Fuller's Commentary so valuable. Among other things, he is almost always able to provide the relevant biographical correlative: "Auden wrote this poem while staying at the new Pennsylvania home of Caroline Newman, his patron," "Auden spent the night of 19 January in Paris, en route with Isherwood for Marseilles," "The circumstances of this early poem to [his lover, Chester] Kallman are," etc.

But by "profound" Professor Mendelson means artistically significant: not only technically accomplished but also (given Auden's understanding of art) morally wise and aesthetically compelling. Professor Mendelson argues this case passionately and intelligently; whether he argues it convincingly is another matter. There are many ways in which one can trace Auden's poetic development. The road from existential bafflement to religious affirmation charts one course (in 1940, at the age of thirty-three, Auden began "in a tentative and experimental way" to return to the Anglo-Catholic faith of his youth). The movement from lyric isolation to deliberate didacticism marks another. A third path has to do with what we might call diminishing poetic tautness.

I do not mean a loss of prosodic virtuosity. Auden's astonishing technical mastery never left him; if anything, he became more facile with age. His stupendous example helped make us more aware of the ways in which technical facility can be the precondition of poetic achievement. It may also have encouraged us to neglect the fact that technique, uncatalyzed by sensibility and subject matter, can be the enemy of poetic achievement. In any event, for Auden technical fluency sometimes resulted in poetry that seemed to proceed on verbal autopilot. Auden often remarked on his fondness for the Oxford English Dictionary. In later life, it provided some of his favourite reading matter and indeed was the source of many of the lexical curiosities that—increasingly—bedizened his poetry. Humphrey Carpenter notes that the most prominent object in the workroom of Auden's house in Kirchstetten, Austria (where he summered from 1958 to the end of his life), was the OED.

The set, Carpenter writes, would always be "missing one volume, which was downstairs, Auden invariably using it as a cushion to sit on when at table—as if (a friend observed) he were a child not quite big enough for the nursery furniture." Auden's raids on the lexicon resulted in some bewildering rarities. In a review of Epistle to a Godson , one critic lists "blouts, pirries, stolchy, glunch, sloomy, snudge, snoachy, scaddle, cagmag, hoasting, drumbles," among others.

How many do you know? How many were chosen because the poet felt he had stumbled upon the one absolutely right word for the thought or feeling he was trying to express? How many did he adopt because he happened to pick them up from yesterday's trip through the dictionary and they filled a metrical hole? Auden regularly described poetry as a verbal puzzle, akin to a crossword. Well, it is and it isn't. Not all poems are verbal puzzles—not even all good ones—and it should go without saying that not all verbal puzzles are poems. These are distinctions that some of Auden's later poetry elides.

In 1936, Auden said that "the first, second and third thing in... art is subject. Technique follows from and is governed by subject." Possibly he later changed his mind; he certainly changed his practice. Auden's love of complicated verse forms and unusual words was doubtless partly an expression of a poet's delight in the resources of language and his ability to manipulate it skillfully. It may also have been an attempt to compensate for the diminishing tautness I mentioned: an effort to inject arbitrary verbal complexity to distract readers—and even, perhaps, himself—from the lack of genuine poetic density that characterizes so many of his later poems. In this regard, it seems significant that the word "cosy" came to loom large in Auden's vocabulary in later years.

These features of Auden's poetry have not gone unremarked. Already in 194, reviewing Another Time, Randall Jarrell complained that, unlike Auden's early "oracular" verse, the present poems seemed "moral, rational, manufactured, written by the top of the head for the top of the head." Although he was full of generalized compliments about Auden's talent, Jarrell also wrote that "the poems say often now, 'Be good.' They ascend through moral abstractions, gnomic chestnuts, to a vaguish humanitarian mysticism." And this was only 194. By 1955, when he reviewed The Shield of Achilles, Jarrell was resorting to sarcasm: "non-Euclidean needlepoint, a man sitting on a chaise longue juggling four cups, four saucers, four sugar lumps, and the round-square: this is what great and good poets do when they don't bother even to try to write great and good poems."

One of the most devastating reflections on Auden's development—or decline—was Philip Larkin's review of Homage to Clio in 196. Entitled "What's become of Wystan?" (a play on Anthony Powell's novel What's Become of Waring), Larkin begins by praising Auden's pre-194 poetry and proceeds to describe his later verse as "too verbose to be memorable and too intellectual to be moving." Larkin readily acknowledges Auden's large ambition and poetic virtues—"the wide-angled rhetoric, the seamless lyricism, the sudden gripping dramatisations"—but he insists that "almost all we value is still confined to the first ten years" of his career. Auden, he wrote, had "become a reader rather than a writer" with the result that his poetry suffered a "loss of vividness" and "a certain abstract windiness."

The "rambling intellectual stew of 'New Year Letter,' " Larkin wrote, "was hardly more than a vamp-till-ready." The poems in Homage to Clio were "agreeable and ingenious" but their "poetic pressure is not high." Too often, he mused, readers find "a wilful jumble of Age-of-Plastic nursery rhyme, ballet folk-lore, and Hollywood Lemprière served up with a lisping archness that sets the teeth on edge." As an example, Larkin quotes this bit from "Plains" , part of Auden's sequence Bucolics:

Romance? Not in this weather. Ovid's charmer
Who leads in quadrilles in Arcady, boy-lord Of hearts who can call their Yes and No their own.
Would, madcap that he is, soon die of cold or sunstroke:
Their lives are in firmer hands; that old grim She
Who makes the blind dates for the hatless genera Creates their country matters.

Tough as Larkin's review was, it exhibited disappointment as much as hostility. It was with sadness, not malice, that Larkin concluded that Auden, "never a pompous poet, has now become an unserious one" who "no longer touches our imaginations." It speaks extremely well of Auden that, a few months after this review appeared, he wrote about Larkin's first book The Less Deceived and, as Professor Mendelson notes, "praised it without reservation."

The tweeness that Larkin discerned in Auden's verse was always a temptation for Auden; it was a temptation he gave into more and more as the years went by. Hence the increasing levity and campiness of Auden's poetry. This was something that Christopher Ricks registered with deadly precision in his review of About the House . Professor Ricks begins by describing the "disarming" quality that much of Auden's poetry displays; he then goes on to note that it is "harder to pinpoint the moment at which such a word has to be said accusingly rather than thankfully."

Consider, for example, the prominence of the word "silly" in Auden's poetic vocabulary (e.g., from the elegy on Yeats: "You were silly like us.") As Professor Ricks points out, Auden doubtless expected his readers to recall the etymology of "silly" ("blessed," "fortunate"), but the line depends mostly on the word's deflationary effect: a confidential, homey effect that can easily be overplayed. Increasingly, Auden did overplay it. Consider the lines that Professor Ricks quotes from "Grub First, Then Ethics" :

surely those in whose creed

God is edible may call a fine
omelette a Christian deed.

At best, this is silly in the modern sense: "showing a lack of good sense," "frivolous." The fact that Auden wrote not to ridicule but out of professed commitment to Christian doctrine makes the poem in even more questionable taste.

Taste is the lodestar of art, the inner principle that accounts for the decorum of the appropriately said. Increasingly, Auden's faculty of taste functioned accurately only in a risible or mocking mode. Given the right subject and the right form, he could be very funny. He was, for example, a master of the clerihew: "No one could ever inveigle/ Georg Wilhelm Friedrich Hegel/ Into offering the slightest apology/ For his Phenomenology." Or: "Mallarmé /Had too much to say: / He could never quite/ Leave the paper white." But he had difficulty purging his poetry of that superciliousness. As Professor Ricks points out, this shows itself with lamentable consequences in his habit of irregular capitalization: "A Major Prophet taken Short," "a Perfect social Number," etc. The effect is unsettling, and ultimately unserious. Exactly how, Professor Ricks asks, does it differ from A. A. Milne's procedure with Winnie the Pooh: "A Good Hum, such as is Hummed Hopefully to Others"?

This family of criticisms is broached even by some of Auden's most stalwart admirers. In the 194s and 195s, Edmund Wilson became a staunch booster of Auden. He concluded his long tribute, "W. H. Auden in America" , by describing him as "a great English poet who is also... one of the great English men of the world." Nearly twenty years earlier, however, Wilson put his finger on another dimension of Auden's sensibility: "W. H. Auden has presented the curious spectacle of a poet with an original language... whose development has seemed to be arrested at the mentality of an adolescent schoolboy." There is no doubt that Auden's poetry developed; the question is whether it can really be said to have matured. The quality that, in their different ways, Wilson, Jarrell, Larkin, and Ricks dilate on has to do with a precociousness that never outgrew itself. In later years, Auden took to referring to himself as "mother," especially in relation to the monumentally irresponsible Chester Kallman. (Although they were lovers only briefly, Auden supported Kallman for the rest of his life and the two periodically lived together.) More telling and finally more appropriate was the nickname Auden acquired at Oxford: "The Child." The coyness and prolixity that characterize Auden's later poetry are emblematic of what happens when the desire for perpetual adolescence fails to outgrow itself: it becomes seedy. It is shocking, as one looks back over Auden's poetic oeuvre, to note how early the seediness set in.

Auden memorably defined poetry as "memorable speech." How well does his own poetry do by this criterion? Auden certainly said and wrote some memorable things. His comment that Rilke was "the greatest lesbian poet since Sappho" may be described as unforgettable. Likewise his comment that his face, which in later years was ravaged by the thick furrows of Touraine-Solents-Gole syndrome, was "like a wedding cake left out in the rain." The widely memorable lines from his poetry are almost exclusively from poems written, as Larkin observed, from the first decade of his career. They also tend to be fragmentary: a line here, two or three lines there. "Lay your sleeping head my love/ Human on my faithless arm" from "Lullaby" ; "About suffering they were never wrong,/ The Old Masters" from "Musée des Beaux Arts" ; "In the prison of his days/ Teach the free man how to praise" from the Yeats elegy , which also appears as the epitaph on Auden's memorial stone in Westminster Abbey; "sad is Eros, builder of cities,/ And weeping anarchic Aphrodite" from the elegy for Freud.

It is ironical that what is probably Auden's single most famous poem, "September 1, 1939," was one that he disavowed and even, as he put in 1957, came to "loathe." Nevertheless, the poem contains some of Auden's most memorable poetry, from the ominous opening lines,

I sit in one of the dives
On Fifty-Second Street
Uncertain and afraid

As the clever hopes expire
Of a low dishonest decade

to the famous end of the eighth stanza: "We must love one another or die." As Professor Mendelson points out, "this line was more widely quoted and admired than perhaps anything else" in Auden's work. E. M. Forster said that because Auden had written it, "he can command me to follow him." Which doubtless tells us a lot about Forster.

In any event, Auden soon had misgivings about the poem. In 1944, he abandoned the celebrated eighth stanza partly because he believed that in the context of the poem ("Hunger allows no choice/ To the citizen or the police") the line about love reduced what should be a voluntary act to an instinctual drive like hunger. In 1964, Auden's dislike of the poem hardened into revulsion when an advertising consultant for Lyndon Johnson misappropriated the line in an infamous campaign commercial.

As Richard Davenport-Hines reports in his biography, the commercial featured a little girl counting the petals of a flower; suddenly, she is interrupted by a stern male voice counting down from ten to zero, at which point the girl is replaced by the flash of an explosion and a mushroom cloud. Then Johnson's voice intoned: "These are the stakes: to make a world in which all of God's children can live, or go into the dark. We must love each other or we must die." Auden bitterly responded, "I pray to God that I shall never be memorable like that again." When he prepared his Collected Shorter Poems for publication the following year, he omitted the poem and later gave instructions that it was not to be reprinted in his lifetime.

Most readers will be able to cite a few other lines or poems—"At the Grave of Henry James" , for example, with the beginning of its stern last stanza: "All will be judged." But after around 194, most readers will find that the gems are fewer and farther between. It is sad that among Auden's later poems, one of the most memorable is the last verse he ever wrote, an often-reproduced haiku:

He still loves life

but O O O O how he wishes
the Good Lord would take him.

(As Professor Mendelson points out, the "O"s need to be elided to keep the haiku to the requisite seventeen syllables; but should they be read as three syllables, as he says, or two, as I suspect?) In the end, Auden's poetry has produced relatively faint echoes. He was a remarkable mimic; he did marvelous impersonations of seriousness; but his continual worries about the authenticity of his poems show that even in his own mind he did not transcend impersonation. In comparison, say, to the poetry of T. S. Eliot, Auden's poetry lacks density. His example has meant a great deal to several poets who came after him; his techniques are preserved in the practice of some of the best. But Auden's poetry has left indifferent traces on the sensibility of our epoch. It is accomplished, not ineluctable. Reverberations from "Prufrock," The Wasteland, "Gerontion," and The Four Quartets are everywhere: the meter and the matter of those poems are part of the poetic metabolism of the age. Auden wrote nothing that has entered our pulses so thoroughly.

The permanent Auden is found elsewhere, above all in the scintillating and companionable essays of The Dyer's Hand , Forewords and Afterwords, and some of his lectures, especially The Enchafèd Flood and parts of Secondary Worlds . He was always penetrating on literary subjects. His essay on Trollope in Forewords and Afterwords is a masterpiece. So is his essay on Shakespeare's sonnets. As in the scenario he described in "Musée des Beaux Arts," his essays hail the triumph and consolation of the ordinary in the face of the extraordinary. In the poem, "the expensive delicate ship" saw "something amazing, a boy falling out of the sky," but it had somewhere to go and "sailed calmly on." One of Auden's most salutary services was to remind us of the importance of sailing calmly on.

Auden wrote often and well about the contradictory desire to find in art both an escape from and a revelation of reality. In an essay on Robert Frost, he observed that

we want a poem to be beautiful, that is to say, a verbal

earthly paradise, a timeless world of pure play, which gives us delight precisely because of its contrast to our historical existence with all its insoluble problems and inescapable suffering; at the same time we want a poem to be true, that is to say, to provide us with some kind of revelation about our life which will show us what life is really like and free us from self-enchantment and deception, and a poet cannot bring us any truth without introducing into his poetry the problematic, the painful, the disorderly, the ugly.

Auden was especially effective in his admonitory mode, warning about the hubris of art absolutized. In a prose passage of "The Sea and the Mirror" , a character observes that "if the intrusion of the real has disconcerted and incommoded the poetic, that is a mere bagatelle compared to the damage which the poetic would inflict if it ever succeeded in intruding upon the real." This admonition is a leitmotif in Auden's work. "Poetry," he wrote in The Dyer's Hand, "is not magic. In so far as poetry, or any other of the arts, can be said to have an ulterior purpose, it is, by telling the truth, to disenchant and disintoxicate." Later on in that volume, he expands on this thought. The effect of formal beauty, he writes, is "evil to the degree that beauty is taken, not as analogous to, but identical with goodness, so that the artist regards himself or is regarded by others as God, the pleasure of beauty being taken for the joy of Paradise, and the conclusion drawn that, since all is well in the work of art, all is well in history." And again: "Orpheus who moved stones is the archetype, not of the poet, but of Goebbels." Poetry, Auden said in the elegy for Yeats, "makes nothing happen." Many of his essays expatiate on the mischief of trying to have it otherwise.

Auden's essays are rich and endlessly rewarding. Yet in them, too, there is a large element of impersonation. In "Reading," the opening essay of The Dyer's Hand, Auden remarks that "in literature, as in life, affectation, passionately adopted and loyally persevered in, is one of the chief forms of self-discipline by which mankind has raised itself by its own bootstraps." This is undoubtedly true, though not necessarily reassuring. It is also true, as Auden remarks a few pages later, that "some writers confuse authenticity, which they ought always to aim at, with originality, which they should never bother about." Authenticity and affectation are not opposites, exactly, but if they can co-exist, they must do so uneasily. Auden never really resolved such tensions; he exploited them. The beguiling urbanity of Auden's essays depends partly on his native brilliance and erudition, partly on what we might call his air of easygoing religious seriousness. He never simply reviewed a book, he made it part of an existential project. He managed to do this whether he was writing about Kierkegaard, migraines, or M. F. K. Fisher's The Art of Eating.

Auden was fond of quoting Yeats's line about being forced to choose between perfection of the life and perfection of the work. He early on chose the latter. "Charade" is too strong a word. But there is a startling disjunction in Auden between the avuncular moralist who has such remarkable things to say about art, pride, sin, self-deception, etc., and the disheveled, lickerish narcissist who habitually besotted himself with horrifying quantities of alcohol, benzedrine, and some fifteen-thousand cigarettes yearly, who talked about being "married" to the disreputable Chester Kallman and then diverted himself with a steady procession of call-boys.

George Orwell retracted his description of Auden as "a sort of gutless Kipling," but not, I believe, his comment from 194 (soon after Auden absented himself from the perils of war-threatened England) that "Mr. Auden's brand of amoralism is only possible if you are the kind of person who is always somewhere else when the trigger is pulled." Auden later wrote to the British embassy offering to do "anything when and if the Government ask me," but he oughtn't have been surprised to find his offer rebuffed. Auden mounted a campaign against an overly aestheticized view of the world, but he did so while remaining within the orbit of aestheticism. His anguish was no doubt genuine, but his solution always had something of a performance about it. This is not to say that it lacked pathos. In a sermon he delivered in Westminster Abbey in 1966, Auden poignantly observed that.

those of us who have the nerve to call ourselves Christians

will do well to be extremely reticent on the subject. Indeed, it is almost the definition of a Christian that he is somebody who knows he isn't one, either in faith or morals. Where faith is concerned, very few of us have the right to say more than—to vary a saying of Simone Weil's—"I believe in a God who is like the True God in everything except that he does not exist, for I have not yet reached the point where God exists." As for loving and forgiving our enemies, the less we say about that the better. Our lack of faith and love are facts we have to acknowledge, but we shall not improve either by a morbid and essentially narcissistic moaning over our deficiencies. Let us rather ask, with caution and humour—given our time and place and talents, what, if our faith and love were perfect, would we be glad to find it obvious to do?

Referring to Christianity, G. K. Chesterton once said that anything worth doing is worth doing badly. It is a witty statement, partly true. But only partly. In both his art and his life, W. H. Auden leaned heavily on the resources of the subjunctive, even as he entertained his readers with dreams of indicative truth. When he was eight years old, his mother taught him the love duet from Tristan.. Auden played Isolde. It is not clear that he ever ceased giving that performance.

Q. Analysis of Auden's The Age of Anxiety.

Or

Q. Write a brief passage on the Age of Anxiety.

In Auden's lengthy poem, The Age of Anxiety, he follows the actions and thoughts of four characters who happen to meet in a bar during a war. Their interactions with one another lead them on an imaginary quest in their minds in which they attempt, without success, to discover themselves. The themes and ideas that Auden's The Age of Anxiety conveys reflect his belief that man's quest for self-actualization is in vain.

W. H. Auden was born in York, England, in 197, the third and youngest son of Constance and George Auden. His poetry in the 193's reflected the world of his era, a world of depression, Fascism, and war. His works adopt a prose of a "clinical diagrostician [sic] anatomizing society" and interpret social and spiritual acts as failures of communication. They also put forth a diagnosis of the industrial English society among economic and moral decay in the 193's. Conflicts common in his works are those between war and peace, corruption of modern society, and the "dichotor ιy between the rich and the poor". The Age of Anxiety is, in general, a quest poem.

Unlike the ideal quest, however, this quest accomplishes nothing. The characters search for the meaning of self and, in essence, the meaning of life, but because their search is triggered by intoxication due to alchohol, the quest is doomed from the start. Throughout the quest, the characters believe themselves to be in a form of Purgatory when they are allegorically in Hell. They fail to realise this due to "the modern human condition which denies possibility but refuses to call it impossible".

In The Age of Anxiety, there are four characters of significance. Quant, the first to be introduced, addresses himself in a mirror, an action typical to a drunken man. He is an aging homosexual widower who finds refuge in the mirror because it offers him the easiest way of facing himself -118).

Malin, the most dominant character overall, is a medical intelligence officer on leave from the Canadian Air Force. His background labels him as the "would-be doctor and leader" in the world of The Age of Anxiety. His name is reminiscent, in relation to the war, of a malingerer, and the composition of his personality hints at the evil within him.

Rosetta, the most human of the characters, is a department store buyer, and comes closer to self-actualization than any of the other characters in the poem. Emble is a young sailor and would-be prince whose wish is to have sex with Rosetta. Ironically, his failure to do so is the primary composition of the climax of the work. Part I of The Age of Anxiety, the "Prologue" as it is commonly called, introduces the scene and characters. The characters each think aloud in monologue so as to reveal their true nature to the reader. Quant views himself with false admiration, and Malin questions the natue of man. Rosetta constructs an imaginary past to compensate for a less than adequate one. Emble, with youthful tact, passes judgment on the others' follies. The first act of Part II, "The Seven Ages," is dominated by Malin, acting as a guide. He controls the actions of the characters through his introductions to each age. The other characters support his theories by drawing from their past, present, and potential future experiences).

The first age begins with Malin asking the reader to "Behold the infant" as though he is observing us as the infant while his own infancy fails to exist. The child is "helpless in cradle and / Righteous still" but already has a "Dread in his dreams." By this, Auden means that even when we are most innocent, we are still imperfect.

The second age is youth, as Malin describes it. It is at this age at which man realizes "his life-bet with a lying self." Despite this, man's naive belief in self and place in life is boundless. It is in this age that the belief in the future is possible). The third age is termed by Malin as the age of sexual awakening. It is in this age that the distinction between dream and reality begins to surface in the mind of man. With this distinction comes the discovery that love, as it was thought to be, is a sharp contrast to love in the bounds of reality.

The fourth age presents circus imagery "as a form of art too close to life to have any purgative effect on the audience." It is reinforced by Rosetta's definitions of life as an "impertinent appetitive flux," and the world as a "clown's cosmos". Malin conveys the image of man as "an astonished victor" in the fifth age. Man in this age feel as though he has made peace with the meaning of life. The anxiety of life declines as "He [man] learns to speak / Softer and slower, not to seem so eager." Here, man discovers he is no longer confined in a prison of prisimatic colour, but free in the dull, bland place that is the world

Emble, being the youngest of the four, refuses to drift into the middle age of the fifth age willingly. Instead, he demands to know why man must "Leave out the worst / Pang of youth." He is unlike the others in that he is still young enough to have an influence on his future).

Quant is more dominant in this age than any other for it is this age that he represents. In it, he attempts to eliminate all hope for a future. He feels that "if man cannot adjust to mediocrity, it is too bad... If man asks for more, the world only gets worse". The sixth age is attributed to man's "scars of time," to man's aging. "Impotent, aged, and successful," Malin portrays man to be indifferent to the world.

"Hypothetical man" is exhausted when "His last illusions have lost patience / With the human enterprise" in the seventh age. Malin greets this age with preparedness, but the other characters feel reluctance in greeting death.

The second act of Part II of The Age of Anxiety, "The Seven Stages," is different from "The Seven Ages" in that the first act is based on experiences and the second act consists entirely of a dream. The purpose of "The Seven Stages" is to determine the ideal time of life for man in which he can reside for eternity. The first stage begins like all quests begin, with all characters alone. They are each "isolated with his own thoughts." Their journey ends in the same fashion, with each of them alone, which labels this as a false quest for nothing is accomplished.

The second stage is initiated by the pairing of the characters. This pairing represents the possibility of hope with the two youngest, Emble and Rosetta, and it also symbolizes the futility of hope with the two eldest, Quant and Malin.

The third stage begins as the couples begin to head inland. Emble and Rosetta travel via plane, which symbolizes the useless attempt to escape life by flying above it. Quant and Malin, on the other hand, travel by train, which represents the same inability to escape life, although this time the method is through immersion into life (.

In the fourth stage, Malin speaks for the group in his derogatory statements about the city. Malin also passes judgment on the people of the city not on the basis of personality content, but on that of the surroundings of which he thinks so lowly.

The fifth stage is reached when the group sights "the big house" while riding on a trolley. Rosetta, with her false past as an outline, references the house to one in which she was imaginarily reared, and to which she shall return. During her visitation to the house, Quant and the others analyze the house's exterior. Quant comments on the house's appearance: "The facade has a lifeless look." The house is compared to a human being, with its "book-lined rooms" serving as the brain and "the guards at the front gate [who] / Change with the seasons" serving as the senses. Rosetta finds her life within the house no better than before.

The sixth stage takes place in a "forgotten graveyard." It is observed as a "still / Museum [exhibiting] / The results of life," which could either be death or the life that results from death as the "Flittermice, finches / And flies restore / Their lost milieu".

The seventh stage begins as each character plunges deep into a dense forest where they are confronted by a vast desert. Here, Quant asks the question, "Do I love this world so well / That I have to know how it ends?" The four take heed of the question and realise that their quest has no meaning, and as they do so, their dream world drifts upwards into the realm of consciousness and the vast desert makes the transition to reality. The remaining three parts follow each of the characters from the bar to their respective homes. They each remember the despair of the conclusion of "The Seven Stages," but have no recollection of the journey itself.

Auden has effectively portrayed the flaw of man in his fruitless quest for the meaning of self. His representations of Quant and Malin as the elders whose future is bleak counters the bright and cheery illusion that Emble and Rosetta may possibly have a future, though, in reality, the only sure future is death.

Q. Write a brief biography of W. H. AUDEN.

Born: February 21, 197
York, England
Died: September 28, 1973
Vienna, Austria
English-born American poet

The English-born American poet W. H. Auden was one of the greatest poets of the twentieth century. His works centre on moral issues and show strong political, social, and psychological (involving the study of the mind) orientations.

Early Life

Wystan Hugh Auden was born on February 21, 197, in York, England. He was the last of three sons born to George and Constance Auden. His father was the medical officer for the city of Birmingham, England, and a psychologist (a person who studies the mind). His mother was a devoted Anglican (a member of the Church of England). The combination of religious and scientific themes are buried throughout Auden's work. The industrial area where he grew up shows up often in his adult poetry. Like many young boys in his city, he was interested in machines, mining, and metals and wanted to be a mining engineer. With both grandfathers being Anglican ministers, Auden once commented that if he had not become a poet he might have ended up as an Anglican bishop.

Another influential childhood experience was his time served as a choirboy. He states in his autobiographical sketch, A Certain World, "it was there that I acquired a sensitivity to language which I could not have acquired in any other way." He was educated at St. Edmund's preparatory school and at Oxford University. At Oxford fellow undergraduates Cecil Day Lewis, Louis MacNeice, and Stephen Spender, with Auden, formed the group called the Oxford Group or the "Auden Generation."

At school Auden was interested in science, but at Oxford he studied English. He disliked the Romantic (nineteenth-century emotional style of writing) poets Percy Bysshe Shelley and John Keats , whom he was inclined to refer to as "Kelly and Sheets." This break with the English post-Romantic tradition was important for his contemporaries. It is perhaps still more important that Auden was the first poet in English to use the imagery (language that creates a specific image) and sometimes the terminology (terms that are specific to a field) of clinical psychoanalysis (analysis and treatment of emotional disorders).

Early Publications and Travels

In 1928, when Auden was twenty-one, a small volume of his poems was privately printed by a school friend. Poems was published a year later by Faber and Faber (of which T. S. Eliot [1888–1965] was a director). The Orators was a volume consisting of odes (poems focused on extreme feelings), parodies of school speeches, and sermons that criticized England. It set the mood for a generation of public school boys who were in revolt against the empire of Great Britain and fox hunting.

After completing school Auden traveled with friends in Germany, Iceland, and China. He then worked with them to write Letters

Reproduced by permission of the Corbis Corporation. from Iceland and Journey To A War . In 1939 Auden took up residence in the United States, supporting himself by teaching at various universities. In 1946 he became a U.S. citizen, by which time his literary career had become a series of well-recognized successes. He received the Pulitzer Prize and the Bollingen Award and enjoyed his standing as one of the most distinguished poets of his generation. From 1956 to 1961 he was professor of poetry at Oxford University.

Poetic Themes and Techniques

Auden's early poetry, influenced by his interest in the Anglo-Saxon language as well as in psychoanalysis, was sometimes riddle-like and clinical. It also contained private references that most readers did not understand. At the same time it had a mystery that would disappear in his later poetry.

In the 193s W. H. Auden became famous when literary journalists described him as the leader of the so-called "Oxford Group," a circle of young English poets influenced by literary Modernism, in particular by the artistic principles adopted by T. S. Eliot. Rejecting the traditional poetic forms favored by their Victorian predecessors, the Modernist poets favored concrete imagery and free verse. In his work Auden applied concepts and science to traditional verse forms and metrical (having a measured rhythm) patterns while including the industrial countryside of his youth. Coming to the United States was seen by some as the start of a new phase of his work. World War II (1939–45; a war in which France, Great Britain, the Soviet Union, and the United States fought against Germany, Italy, and Japan) had soured him to politics and warmed him to morality and spirituality. Among Auden's highly regarded skills was the ability to think in terms of both symbols and reality at the same time, so that intellectual ideas were transformed. He rooted ideas through creatures of his imagining for whom the reader could often feel affection while appreciating the stern and cold outline of the ideas themselves. He nearly always used language that was interesting in texture as well as brilliant verbally. He employed a great variety of intricate and extremely difficult technical forms. Throughout his career he often wrote pure lyrics of grave beauty, such as "Lay Your Sleeping Head, My Love" and "Look Stranger." His literary contributions include librettos (opera texts) and motion picture documentaries. He worked with Chester Kallmann on the librettos, the most important of which was T. S. Eliot's The Rakes Progress. Auden was well educated and intelligent, a genius of form and technique. In his poetry he realized a lifelong search for a philosophical and religious position from which to analyze and comprehend the individual life in relation to society and to the human condition in general. He was able to express his dislike for a difficult government, his suspicion of science without human feeling, and his belief in a Christian God.

Later Works

In his final years Auden wrote the volumes City without Walls, and Many Other Poems , Epistle to a Godson, and Other Poems , and Thank You, Fog: Last Poems , which was published posthumously (after his death). All three works are noted for their lexical (word and vocabulary relationship) range and humanitarian (compassionate) content. Auden's tendency to alter and discard poems has prompted publication of several anthologies (collected works) in the decades since his death on September 28, 1973, in Vienna, Austria. The multivolume Complete Works of W. H. Auden was published in 1989. Auden is now considered one of the greatest poets of the English language.

Chapter 15

From Love to Lightness: Defining Auden's Light Verse

Light Verse as Chorus

Contained in Auden's introduction to the 1938 Oxford Book of Light Verse, beneath its Eliotic thesis on the relative conditions for difficulty and for clarity in poetry, there is a series of telling remarks. These remarks encourage the inference that for Auden, the prospect of imagining an audience - one congenial to every aspect of his work, in all its tensions and contrary impulses - was especially fraught. Principally, this prospect is seen to rest upon the viability of "closeness"; that is, the proximity of the poet to his audience, the features common to their lives, the similarity of their experiences, or in Auden's words, their "intimate relation".[234] The role of the voice in Auden's lyric comprises the aesthetic manifestation of this fraught imagining. Monody describes our encounter with the speaker of Auden's work in which closeness is achieved through the illustration - and at times, the activation - of those difficulties of poetic communication attendant on the rise of mass society. But what other possibilities of expression did Auden instinctively render in his lyric modes?

Before we consider these possibilities, as realised in Auden's light verse, and before we broach a more useful definition of lightness as it applies to his work in the crucial aspect of voice, a brief discussion of the preparatory ground for Auden's lightness is needed. I have already argued that a fully theorised account of Auden's range is the crux of understanding the nature and value of his lyric poetry. It is the light works which complicate the positioning of Auden as an experimental high modernist, and I aim to resist the comfortable division of Auden's work into the popular and the arcane. Instead I seek to explain both tendencies, as part of Auden's manifold inherited sources and subsequent trajectories. The central issue might be put thus: what kind of opportunities did Auden glean from lightness? What kind of imaginative space does light verse open for the reader, and how might that space be related to, but go beyond, its historical conditions? Walter Benjamin's seminal study Charles Baudelaire-A Lyric Poet in the Era of High Capitalism contains a neat account of the perceived problems for lyric poetry as they were seen to apply in the modern age. Light verse is noticeable for its absence here; Benjamin seems tacitly to distinguish it from lyric proper:

That the climate for lyric poetry has become increasingly inhospitable, is attested to, among other things, by three factors. In the first place, the lyric poet has ceased to represent the poet per se. He is no longer a "minstrel", as Lamartine still was; he has become a representative of a genre.... Secondly, there has been no success on a mass scale in lyric poetry since Baudelaire...As a result, a third factor was the greater coolness of the public even towards the lyric poetry that has been handed down as part of its cultural heritage.

It is reasonable to assume that only in rare instances is lyric poetry in rapport with the experience of its readers. This may be due to a change in the structure of their experience.

The presentation of the communicative freedoms tapped by Auden's monodic poetry demonstrated that a modified kind of rapport between the poet and his audience was in fact generated within the conditions of mass media. To Benjamin's first point, we might give qualified assent: certainly the notoriety of Pound's Cantos, and Eliot's The Waste Land, for instance, displaced the idea of lyric as a synecdoche for all poetry amongst the cognoscenti at least, yet it must be added that the allotted roles of poets, or their assumed titles, may indeed have lost all fixity. The two subsequent points also need to be qualified with reference to AngloAmerican poetry; Yeats clearly had some degree of success in lyric poetry, whether defined in artistic or commercial terms, and the English poetry reading public remained relatively immune to the appeal of experimental modernist verse, as the continued popularity of Hardy, Housman and the Georgian poets illustrated.

Yet, as we have discussed in other contexts, Benjamin's central premise that the climate for lyric poetry has undergone radical changes in the modern age is indisputable. Benjamin is working with a distinctive understanding of lyric, one which, with Baudelaire as its avatar, configures the form more appreciably in line with what I have called monody. This is to say, he focuses on the solo voice and records, with Baudelaire taking centre stage, the incursions of mass society inflicted on the version of the individual underpinning that voice. But we can argue that light verse warrants inclusion in this thesis of hostile modernity; and furthermore, the lyrical features of light verse record a different experience available within this historical paradigm, and so make possible a new way of thinking. The question occurs, then; in what sense are light poems lyrics, if we understand the lyric as the form which modulates our encounter with the page by bringing forth our own speaking voice, as the basis of a critical moment? The light poem, we would reply, invokes a choral model of encounter and involvement. It carries a different set of presumptions about communication and commonality than the monodicsolo poem. It can be deemed lyrical in the more traditional, ancient sense: the notion of singing and performance is raised from the implicit to the explicit. In Auden's case many of the light lyrics first emerged as songs as parts of dramatic performances so the connection with literal speaking and singing is manifest, as in "What's in your mind, my dove, my coney" (November 1930) which first appeared in the lost play The Fronny: What's in your mind, my dove, my coney;

Do thoughts grow like feathers, the dead end of life; Is it making of love or counting of money, Or raid on the jewels, the plans of a thief?

The term lyric has a conventional generic application to such works in the sense that they are songlyrics. But this straightforward offering of lyric's bases in song dovetails in light verse with a historically vital manner of access, which possesses a vitality that I have attributed to the lyric form in the revised sense.

Auden's light verse requires inclusion as a strain of modern revised lyric on this basis. Through the choral voice of light verse we are aware of the immediate and unqualified notion of clear placement within a collective, even when the subject matter of the poem may not possess a discursive or polemic force (though we will see that it can). In short, we can call Auden's light verse lyrics in the revised sense as well as the traditional because how we read is as important as what we read.

Considering the importance of this ease of access we find in light verse, we note that a number of Auden's light lyrics comprise the fulfilment of certain wishes of earlier modernism, as well as the refutation of its hidebound assumptions and tactical exclusions.

Following the apex of early modernism, held in works such as the Cantos and The Waste Land, there is an acknowledgement amongst serious discursive poets sometimes tacit, sometimes, as we saw with Eliot, quite open that the territory of the lyric has been curtailed by other media. But in the thirties the levelling of discourse, which paradoxically increases the scope for lyric address, clears many of the avenues assumed blocked by the preceding generation.

More specifically, the increasing saturation of the poetic consciousness by the influences of mass media lends a greater significance to light verse, and it is in this context that Auden's work (and the political tone of his introduction to the Oxford volume) needs to be understood. We have seen previously how Auden's generation responded to increased media exposure, to the curious pressures of public selfexposition determined by political barometers.

Another fairly obvious, but no less vital factor is the prominence of entertainment, shaped by the growth of cinema and radio. Entertainment or the intention to entertain according to the example of the more immediate, collective, forms of film and spoken word becomes the lever which decreases the distance between artist and audience, and this need not entail an attenuation of artistic value. We are more concerned with the space and shape of poetic communication in the thirties; once again, it is the contiguity of industrialised mass culture with lyric poetry that informs and supports Auden's light verse.

Perhaps the bifurcation of difficult and light we see in Auden's poetry has its prose analogue in the works of his contemporary, Graham Greene, who calculatedly divided his output in terms of "entertainments" and serious novels. For the poet Auden, this situation was personally congenial because of his familiarity with the heritage of light verse, which lent to him the modes and stances required to communicate at an impersonal, accessible level. And yet the modified gravity of that communication its historical significance in the context of thirties culture - intensified its importance.

Where Greene openly declared his interest in the remunerative potential of entertainment, for a poet such potential did not exist to the same degree. However, just as with difficult poetry, the paradigm of mass production profitcentrism undoubtedly coloured the creation of modern light verse, in the sense that within this paradigm an audience might cohere in the mind of the artist: vexatious questions about the dislocation of poet from reader could be put aside. With its unquestioning assumption of a readership bound by a common collection of cultural reference points, light verse finds the conditions to evolve in twentieth century modernity in a way that can be clearly plotted. Those unquestioning assumptions are vivified in the confined imaginative spaces of mass society, encouraged by the unclear distinction between public and private realms and the new sense of cultural and geographical proximity characterising mass communication. In the mid thirties Auden produces light verse songs whose debt to American songwriters such as Cole Porter has been amply acknowledged:

Some talk of Alexander
And some of Fred Astaire,
Some like their heroes hairy
Some like them debonair,
Some prefer a curate
And some an A. D. C.,
Some like a tough to treat 'em rough,
But you're my cup of tea.
"The Soldier loves his rifle": March 1936

Rather than becoming mired in points of conditions, influences and classifications, it is preferable to remain with the poetry itself and consider how the voices and poetics of Auden's light lyrics work with this assumption of commonality. We begin to observe that the importance of light verse lies in its exemption from the interminable debates of the modernist period regarding aesthetics. Reference was made earlier to the staunchly oppositional tendencies of the preceding generation of modernists such as those belonging to the Bloomsbury group, to whom aesthetics, in contrast to the spiritually corrupt principle of objectifiable profit, was necessarily exclusive. In contrast Auden's light verse, as Stan Smith has recently argued, carries a "democratic, levelling impetus"; and the energy powering this impetus is the lyric voice, freed to encompass the localparticular and the historicalgeneral in the same stanza. The comic treatment of reality, which forms the lifeblood of light verse, is premised on the mutuality of all experiences. The attraction of the voice of a poem like "Letter to Lord Byron", which will be examined in greater depth later in this chapter, lies in the manner that Auden balances this mutuality with promiscuous references to the personal or recondite:

I read that there's a boomlet on in Birmingham,
But what I hear is not so reassuring;
Rumours of War, the B.B.C confirming 'em,
The prospects for the future aren't alluring;
Noone believes Prosperity enduring,

Not even the Wykehamists, whose golden mean
Maintains the All Souls Parish Magazine.

Even at such (autobiographical) times the reader's experience can be described as choral on account of its mutual involvement with the speaking voice. That which, as present day readers, we do not share with the speaker in terms of precise history, we partake of the worldview that he makes available. The choral lyric is defined not primarily by its first person plural, but by the way that its voice ensures its utterances are speakable, and that the worldview is readily adoptable. As such, Auden's choral lyrics present a vision of the civic life unfettered by division and irreconcilably particular experiences. The monodic lyric voice reclaims, with the speaking reader, the modern private realm from subjective isolation by demonstrating the anteriority of interrelationships, or the prior conditions of collective involvement the underpin all expressions of individuality.

In monody this recognition, presented to us more forcibly through actual speech, counterbalances the distance from the experience related in the lyric; the colloquy of voices brings this collective involvement into focus. The choral counterpart is simpler; it annexes a version of the public realm from the confusion of the social, in which the individual voice speaks the general experience alongside the particular.

How is this so? Moreover, if we bestow a philosophical weight onto light verse, do we jeopardise its value? Certainly Auden's own thoughts on this matter throughout his career would argue against freighting his light verse with concerns exterior to its own poetics, which, he contended, should be "simple, clear, and gay". But there is a balance we can strike between recognising the spirit of light verse and putting that spirit into a significant context: something which Auden's introduction to the Oxford Book attempts to do with its potted history of the form and the sociological theory that runs alongside it. To explain the spirit of light verse we need to explain in more detail how we respond to it as readers. In contrast to the monodic lyric, light verse presents a closed circuit of meaning, in a way that prefigures (and, in the twentieth century, converges with) the innovations of mass society entertainments. It is, so far as a poem can be, nonnegotiable: its intent is writ large in its techniques, its ironies are inclusive (even where, as in many of these examples, the poem could be called "gay" in the modern sense); and as readers we chime with it to produce the choral moment:

Some say that Love's a little boy
And some say he's a bird,
Some say he makes the world go round
And some say that's absurd:
But when I asked the man next door
Who looked as if he knew,
His wife was very cross indeed
And said it wouldn't do.
"Some say that Love's a little boy": January 1938

This simplicity is essential to the public qualities of light verse, something so obvious as to appear unremarkable, but which has not been properly addressed in critical accounts of Auden. In the specific context of the thirties such simplicity has increased force. Accessible but not disposable, inclusive rather than exclusive, Auden's light verse possesses a vitality that fulfils Ford Madox Ford's 1919 vision of what Michael Levenson calls "civic realism", where "the artist assumes…the responsibilities of citizenship in the modern world,…the artist's goal is to reflect contemporaneity,".[245] Less a manner of avoiding the claims of responsibility in the thirties, light verse is more a way of reconfiguring the notion of responsibility by invoking the choral voice.

Here we remember from the previous chapter the fundamental question about historical existence asked by Heidegger - that of "mitsein": who am I with, at this time, in this place, and how am I with them? The choral voice assumes that the speaker is one among many, and that the speaking reader shares in the experience of common placement among others. In this sense Auden's work confirms that the collapse of strongly demarcated public and private realms can offer a tonic to light verse. The choral voice is inspired by the dynamics of mass communication, but such that it challenges notions of atomism and deracination. A shared experience is utterable, and Auden's light lyrics use the conventional touchstones of light verse - humour, ease of access, a heightened speed of reading and comprehension - in the context of twentieth century modernity. Auden's sensitivity to this context meant that such techniques frequently bled into his more discursive lyrics, creating, as Anthony Hecht has it, hybrid lyric of redoubled significance.[246] Hence we can use the term "lightness" to describe features and effects of many lyrics, rather than restrict discussion to dry classifications.

The evidence presented by his own work would seem to undermine Auden's arguments in the Oxford book. His inclusions in that volume, and by extension his working understanding of the genre of light verse, are classified thus;

- Poetry written for performance, to be spoken or sung before an audience (e.g. folk songs, the poems of Tom Moore)
- Poetry intended to be read, but having for its subject matter the everyday social life of its period or the experiences of the poet as ordinary human being (e.g. Chaucer, Pope, Byron)
- Such nonsense poetry as, through its properties and techniques, has a general appeal (Nursery Rhymes, the poems of Edward Lear.

In 1937, the year preceding his editorship of the volume, Auden had written a number of lyrics in which the implied element of performance is paramount. That they can be deemed examples of a new kind of light verse will be demonstrated by close readings: later in this chapter I will discuss two prominent examples, "As I Walked Out One Evening" and "It's farewell to the drawing room's civilised cry", in isolation.

Auden's editorship of the volume compounded a pivotal aspect of his poetic identity, ever present since his juvenilia, but which comes to full artistic significance in the mid thirties. Emerging from the choral experiments of early works such as "It's no use raising a shout" is a poetry of a different kind of pace and address. Steeped in the tradition of light verse, it is attuned to the standing of modern subjects toward each other in the inchoate space of twentieth century public life. As such it will be predicated upon "closeness" and proximity, but will take these conditions for granted rather than, as in its monodic counterpart, interrogating them. In an unpremeditated way, Auden's first point given above, detailing a poetry written for performance becomes the basis for his own poetics, with the quality of performance recalibrated to minimise the distance between poetic utterance and interpretation.

Remaining with the Oxford book briefly, we can observe the sound Eliotic principles underpinning Auden's conception of light verse sitting rather uneasily alongside his avowed leftism; but, more significantly, we can discern an account of his own anxieties as a light poet. Those anxieties seem to prefigure Adorno's wariness of false immediacy, which is, superficially, precisely what light verse offers:

Lightness is a great virtue, but light verse tends to be conventional, to accept the attitudes of the society in which it is written. The more homogeneous a society, the closer the artist is to the everyday life of his time, the easier it is for him to communicate what he perceives, but the harder for him to see honestly and truthfully, unbiased by the conventional responses of his time.

We could say that Auden effectively seeks to harness this antithesis in his own work, with the caveat that the introduction cannot be taken as a watertight selfaccount. We recall the new social imperatives fostered by the thirties poets: their polemical thrust, their emphasis on clarity of vision with regard to the functioning of the social body. In Auden's introduction he is palpably suspicious, good socialist that he was, of any ease of expression which may bespeak the "conventional", which may be paying lip service to the status quo. Politically (and this is important because it bears on the nature of some of his light verse directly, at the level of polemical intent) Auden could never have pronounced the England of the thirties a homogeneous society in the sense of being "both integrated and free". We noted previously how the blossoming of mass media brought the iniquities of English life into focus, and how literary life was increasingly drawn along lines determined by this cultural shift (in 1937, for example, Victor Gollancz had published Orwell's The Road to Wigan Pier, a high watermark of polemical socialism). But perhaps we have to demur from Auden's politicocritical judgement here in order to properly establish the context for his poetry (Edward Mendelson contends that in any case, Auden "did not entirely believe his own argument" in the Oxford Book).

Auden's critical equation is simple: light verse in the purest sense is only possible for poets fully integrated and comfortable in their society, and no poet of conscience could declare himself such in the thirties, ergo, the conditions for light verse are presently unfavourable. Yet Auden's most significant work of the mid thirties can be called light, as distinguished from his earlier difficult works, because of the different kind of immediacy of its address, often but not exclusively marshalled to the service of polemical intent. Homogeneity, when we consider it from another angle, is more pliant than Auden's political usage of the term may permit. Defined as "of the same kind of nature, having the constituent elements similar throughout", the word "homogeneous" is best applied to a body politic advisedly; the structure of society need not be homogeneous in being politically secure (in, for instance, the way in which the feudal society of Chaucer or mercantile capitalist society of Byron were perceived to be by Auden) for there to exist a bedrock of common experience and perceptions which would support successful light verse. (It is debatable, of course, whether a society both integrated and free has ever existed in England at all, in the sense Auden implies.) Light verse involving humour, topical reference, an instinctual feel for the personality types of an age with their mores and quandaries can surely flourish when other factors engender other types of homogeneity.

In this case, the combination of mass media saturation and a political situation popularly understood, particularly from the mid thirties onwards, as one of impending disaster, supported just the kind of grounding from which a sense of commonality could be grasped. This sense of loss or, increasingly, of doom, grounds the expression of lightness to Auden. His light verse is manifestly post October 1929, made all the more palpable in a piece such as "O what is that sound which so thrills the ear", whose ominous portents are sharpened into a paradoxically contemporary shape by the traditional ballad quatrains:

O what is that sound which so thrills the ear
Down in the valley drumming, drumming?
Only the scarlet soldiers, dear,
The soldiers coming.

Doom and loss are the principles of commonality, the shared fate of the societies of the European Enlightenment. In this sense Auden's light lyric is conditioned in part by the emergence of totalitarianism, which sought to impose on its peoples a travestied version of the common experience, using behaviourism as its tool. Again, it is Orwell who offered the most urgent synopsis of this danger in Homage to Catalonia, which professedly aimed to expose the totalitarian destruction of the foundations of historical truth: to attack its clear agenda, in which the British left wing press were complicit, to destroy the grounds for mutual intelligibility. Similarly in Nineteen Eighty-Four, Winston Smith is given "the book": the last surviving account of history before Big Brother effectively eradicated it. The author of the book, (the possibly nonexistent) Emmanuel Goldstein, reflects on the death of the Enlightenment in the thirties: "The earthly paradise had been discredited at exactly the moment when it became realizable." From total possibility to total catastrophe: this is the nature of the loss which creates the homogeneity sustaining light lyrics such as "As I walked out this evening", over which lurks the spectre of conflict and state coercion.

Of course, Auden's concerns about the apolitical quality of traditional light verse are instructive. By invoking an idea of the collective experience, and not being bound to any imperatives of historical veracity, light verse could be symptomatic of a wider quietism, false immediacy, or worse, a refusal to be "responsible" in the face of the totalitarian threat. According to its thirties inflection, the word "community" is charged with potentially malign intent: the continual invocation of "volk" as an idealised racial community by the Nazis is the obvious example. Here we can discern the oppositional quality of light verse. When centred upon the recognition of mutuality light verse is an emblem of "human values". MacNeice's "Eclogue from Iceland", from Letters to Iceland coauthored with Auden, attests that such values became indispensable in the period. The ghost of Grettir speaks to Craven and Ryan, prefiguring MacNeice's comments in Modern Poetry regarding the "tiny measure" of contribution that poetry could make:

Ghost: Minute your gesture but it must be made -
Your hazard, your act of defiance and hymn of
hate,
Hatred of hatred, assertion of human values,
Which is now your only duty.

This project informs "As I walked out this evening" and other lyrics which merge a lightness of tone or form with an interrogative force, turning their attention to the because of the lack of nonpropagandist documents. I warn everyone against my bias, and I warn everyone against my mistakes. Still, I have done my best to be honest. But it will be seen that the account I have given is completely different from that which appeared in the foreign and especially the Communist press." versions of public life that persist in modernity, in which the choral speaker takes an active part. Light lyric is a living endorsement of the principle of mutual intelligibility: Auden's lyrics of the mid thirties recognise the need to restate this principle and to cherish the "simple, clear and gay", as a riposte to those who would impose the will of a bogus collective on a subject people.

This notion of partaking in the choral moment needs to stridently put. How does the reading experience become manifest as we encounter light verse? When we read and speak it, Auden's light verse has a pace that resides not in our interpretative process, as described in a difficult poem such as "Our hunting fathers", but which is patterned into the poetry itself, using prosodic features to offer an alternative stance toward the material of the poem. Consequently the experience of reading the lyric has an external quality: it invites the reader to partake in the lyric performance, completing the choral circuit. Auden himself would later offer another way of putting this in 1966, using the seriouscomic dyad, in his introduction to the Selected Poetry and Prose of Byron:

In serious poetry thought, emotion, event, must always appear to dictate the diction, meter, and rhyme in which they are embodied; vice versa, in comic poetry it is the words, meter and rhyme which must appear to create the thoughts, emotions and events they require.

This creation of "thoughts, emotions and events" by the prosodic features of the poem is imbued with new significance in the mid thirties. In the light lyric, just as in its difficult sibling, the reader helps define a singular event - what Auden will describe as "a way of happening" in 1939 - but here he or she is being openly invited into a performance where clarity is given in advance; it is not the vaunted end result of an interpretative process (as in "to make the need for action urgent, its nature clear"), but its precondition. The pace of the lyric exists independently of the reader, and is intuited as soon as he or she begins to engage with the lines which evoke this pace. The manic metrical waltz of "It's farewell to the drawing room's civilised cry" (January 1937), achieved through incantatory sequences of anapaests and end stresses, is a good example:

It's farewell to the drawingroom's civilised cry, The professor's sensible whereto and why,

The frockcoated diplomat's social aplomb,
Now matters are settled with gas and with bomb.

At such times the pace of light verse becomes directly mimetic, representing a sense of historical motion careening headon towards disaster. Put succinctly, light verse is easy, but as Auden himself ensures us, "Light verse can be serious." In the thirties, its seriousness - its importance in illuminating the terms of communication between people as a collective - is at a premium.

Intimately related to song, frequently presenting itself as

such, Auden's light verse is voiced as freely accessible, often precisely because it depends on impersonality. After the earlier excursions into difficult poetry, Auden's work of the mid thirties might be regarded as a consolidation of Eliotic principles, once more. Judged occasionally to escape his control, by F. R. Leavis among others, Auden's earlier work finds its counterpart in coolly arranged, necessarily precise light verse.

The doctrinaire impersonality advocated by Eliot in his famous essay "Tradition and the Individual Talent" of 1919 is, needless to say, angled towards the loftier heights of poetic expression, to what he calls "greatness" (the inverted commas are his). But the impersonality which can underscore light verse is equally adept at giving us "significant emotion" (Eliot's italics). The coda of the essay is salient here:

> The emotion of art is impersonal. And the poet cannot reach this impersonality without surrendering himself wholly to the work to be done. And he is not likely to know what is to be done unless he lives in what is not merely the present, but the present moment of the past, unless he is conscious, not of what is dead, but of what is already living.

Or, we might add with reference to the cultural situation in the thirties, unless he is conscious of what is in the process of dying. The chain of healthy artistic succession ("conformity") which constitutes "tradition" for Eliot, with its selfevident political preconditions, is by the mid thirties assumed to be in a state of entropy beyond rescue. But in such a context Auden's production of light verse stands not as an anachronistic diversion from what is present - as if the poet were burying his head in the sand - but as an inspired interpretation and vivification of it, through art. The impersonal utterance is fortified by Auden's light verse. These lyrics recognise their tradition, but instead of the secure ground of a (politically guaranteed) social milieu, they have as their basis three primary sources: the repository of received lightpoetic modes and forms; the modes of mass media address still in their relative infancy (newsprint, cinema, radio); and a cultural narrative of loss and impending disaster. Auden's light verse springs from these labile foundations. His lightness fulfils Eliot's prescription for "greatness" in his arrangement of material - the common experience exalted, elevated into "new art emotion" - and in the significance of the manner of reading light verse, as a counterclaim to the pretensions of totalitarianism to impose the general on the particular. Here the speaking "I" is not predicated upon or confined to personal experience and, furthermore, as a kind of communication now inevitably contiguous with mass media consciousness, it is primed to invoke the general experience with renewed power. Auden redeems the standardising tendencies of modern communication, building upon the sense of communicative reach (the common understandings, the shared experiences, the traffic of information) that support those standards. His light verse is not drawn into advertising its own significance; its significance lies in how uncomplicated it is to read, and what this lack of complication may reveal about the terms of modern communal life and the potential of the lyric within it.

Auden's Early Lightness

The variety of Auden's output from his juvenilia onward ought to teach the critic to be wary of arbitrary distinctions and speculative taxonomies. Nevertheless, we can observe a qualitative shift as we follow Auden's career as a poet of light verse, which reaches full maturity with lyrics written in 1936 and 1937. Prior to that, Auden had consistently turned to the principles of light verse to bolster his poetic selfidentity. His earliest efforts demonstrate not only the beginnings of his exceptional facility, but an intriguing sense of the farcical and the ridiculous too, employed as weapons in a generational conflict which he would go on to fight along psychological, artistic and political lines. One of his first light lyrics, "Proem" (its lyricism evident in the use of singable couplets and the straightforward invocation of the lyric "I") survives in manuscript:

I tried to raise them from the dead "Have you heard this one?" I said: It seems it gave them some surprise Here are some of their replies

"You go too far" -
" Ha ha ha ha!"
"But aren't you rather..."
"I'll tell my father"
"Teach me to fly"
"I want to cry"
"It's like James Joyce"
"I like your voice"
"Tell me another"
"You'd cure my mother"

And so it continues. The joke that cajoles and challenges; that provokes outrage and defeats apathy; as trifling as the lyric may be, it sheds interesting light on the young Auden's fantasies of literary power and the quality of his nascent ambition. There might be nothing exceptional in such ambition alone, but though the lyric is clearly too gauche to detain us for long, we might remark on its techniques: the rhyming couplets particularly, which Auden would come to master, luxuriate in their obviousness, and equally in their agile avoidance of the staid thought. More intriguing is the content: the lyric imagines a conversation which prompts an impassioned response, a joke which separates its listeners into the assenters and the dissenters. Its scenario is useful, then, as a type of blueprint for soughtafter immediacy: the utterance with immediate and decisive effect, which calls for no kind of reflection or interpretation.

It is a fantasy of instantaneity, of facetoface address. We will see that this imaginative motif recurs throughout Auden's mature light verse, and acquires a gravity that orientates its frivolity and deliberate excess. But, fundamentally, by imagining a conversation between the poet and his (in this case scandalised) audience, "Proem" prefigures the immediacy of the speaking voice that would come to maturity in the monodic and choral tendencies of Auden's later work. Also significant, it is Auden speaking qua poet. The thirties trend for anxious selfscrutiny, born of a high modernist inheritance and a partisan political climate among the young, found in cAuden the poet who responded to it most variously. Not simply in the wider, adumbrating division between light and difficult, but within the oeuvre of the light verse as a distinct poetic project, we see continual alteration of voices, tones and stances, each of which puts the lyric to a different kind of use. The kind of voice present in "Proem" - the seigniorial observer, the versifier piercing hackneyed thinking and convention - colours instances of tone in many poems, but is especially predominant in "Letter to Lord Byron". To gauge the richness of that piece and others from later in the decade, however, we must first look at their earlier sources.

In the attempt to get a stronger conceptual handle on the spectrum of voices and tones in Auden's early light verse we must bear two points in mind. First, the distinction between light and difficult only really obtains at the furthest extremities of Auden's output: "Letter to Lord Byron", for instance, is manifestly, programmatically light; "Our Hunting Fathers" is by contrast manifestly difficult: syntactically abstruse, thematically nebulous, selfconsciously discursive. The majority of Auden's early lyrics have a porosity of tone and imagery, making any gesture toward taxonomy a moot point. It is preferable, then, to understand Auden's lightness as a tendency - as capable of gathering itself through voice, tone, stance, or prosody - to whatever effect the poem wishes. This will allow us to include in our discussion some examples that may not obviously announce themselves as light verse, and to consider how these light elements colour our readings. Proceeding from this point, secondly we must prize clarity as a barometer of lightness.

Howsoever clarity may nourish the poem - for example in the character of its voice, in its prosodic regularity, in its marked satiric intent - it is the most salient aspect of the address of light verse. The kind of clarity we find in "We made all possible preparations", written in December 1928, is intriguing. Voiced in an inflectionless bureaucratese and apparently a post hoc report on some kind of apocalyptic catastrophe, it carries a clear satirical intent, but Auden loosens the strictures of satire so that the tone coalesces differently. In satire we have to know who we are mocking because, as

Auden put it in 1966, "The goal of satire is reform;". The Urvoice of this lyric is certainly familiar, but principally because of its neutrality. The first person plural that opens the lyric has a less coherent presence than the lyric language itself, such that its vocality strikes us first and foremost:

We made all possible preparations, Drew up a list of firms, Constantly revised our calculations And allotted the farms, Consequently the satiric value of the lyric is overmastered by a sense of pervasive foreboding: we look for the closed circuit of meaning which satire promises (what exactly is being criticised and needs reform?) only to find ourselves asking different questions. Who is signified by "we", how might "we" ourselves be implicated in this disaster? The rehearsals of concepts and discourses that the voice undertakes - rationalism ("preparations"), capital ("list of firms"), precedent ("Issued all the orders expedient"), executive violence ("Chiefly against our exercising/Our old right to abuse:" define an Enlightenment programme of civic rule. Formerly cherished as the bases of civilisation, here, in the shellshocked regularity of cross rhymed quatrains, alternating between full rhyme and pararhyme, that programme is reduced to a litany of selfimposed mystifications. So the effect is almost that of an anti chorus: we realise the trauma of our belonging to that opening "we" only after submitting to it. The voice continues, offering us the realisation that such mystifications are the foundations for all events and undertakings ("Others, still more astute/Point to the possibilities of error / At the very start"). Despair seeps into the collectedness of the voice: only oldfashioned "honour" and indispensable sanity are left to it. I would contend that the voice of "We made all possible preparations" has a vestigial aspect which we can understand in relation to the light verse heritage.

Tallying with this account of "We made all possible preparations", Kingsley Amis (the subsequent editor of the Oxford Book of Light Verse) remarked upon Auden's darker inclusions in the 1938 anthology, and there are other pointers to take from the volume when we consider Auden's own work. We recall that Auden's selection contains many anonymous poems from numerous traditions; Irish ("The bonny Bunch of Roses O"), American , and feudal English ("The rural Dance about the Maypole"). Earlier in his career Auden cultivates a form of light verse anonymity: an anonymity which in the modern age could only be patterned into the stance of the poem, in order to utter the binding terms of commonality, as "We made all possible preparations" suggested. At this stage in modernity those terms are oblique, but the lyric yields an immediate accessibility. A folk culture may have perished in industrial England, but "We made all possible preparations" seeks to resurrect the voice which speaks out of the culture as composite, which cannot, and need not, be traced to its author as final origin. It is light because implicitly,unsettlingly familiar; its lightness and contemporaneity lie in its ironical detachment, which aims beyond simpler satirical targets to strike at the bases of an intellectual, political and moral epoch, bases that are fast disintegrating.

The collection of socalled "Shorts", written between 1929 and 1931, are also worth remarking on in this context. Standing alone, they might not warrant any real attention; collected, they convince as exercises in the rudiments of light verse, containing snatches of black humour, farce, vulgarity, and conversations. Their throwaway quality adds to their appeal. The testing of sexual taboos becomes congenial here (more prominent in The English Auden, 552, than in the Collected Poems),

Schoolboy, making lonely maps,
Better do it with some chaps.
So too does jaded wisdom and le bon mot,
Medicines and Ethics: these
Are like mercenaries.
They join the other side when they
Have made you pay.
A proverbial use of the first person emerges also,
I am beginning to lose patience
With my personal relations.
They are not deep
And they are not cheap.

As private and as minor as these verses are, they present

us with a kind of hyper poetry language distilled into immediacy; as if Auden is toying with the viability of the proverb. Proverbs are repeatable verities, prospectively applicable across generations, across localities. Light verse and the proverb are closely related in this respect; they both look for their sustenance to the general and the common, borne of the assumption that experiences are communicable, transposable, and possibly instructive. But Auden's proverbial world offers new kinds of verities: it is one of pathologies ("The friends of the born nurse / Are always getting worse") and inversions, naming a characteristic severity towards how one should live:

Those who will not reason Perish in the act.
Those who will not act
Perish for that reason.

The "I" of "I am beginning to lose patience" is proverbial; neither explicatory or confessional, its purely semantic life is made possible by the shared experience. It is the "I" as mode and as attitude. The proverbial "I" has been given a fresh injection of life by the preponderance of other, similar "I"s in the mass media nexus, which also have both something and nothing to impart; their penny's worth of knowledge, garnered from their experience of as implicated observers, who know themselves chiefly through their being acted upon:

The bird goes up and the bat goes down:
The bird will burn and the bat will drown.

This wilfully slight verse is predicated on brevity, but its brevity is of a totally different order than, for example, the Imagism of Pound or Aldington: it offers no considered philosophy. Instead it is disposable in a similar manner to a proverb, but the conditions for such utterances are now shaped by the imaginative weather of the time. Auden's "Shorts" are composed with an intimation of the terms of social taxonomy, with its pronounced divisions of the communal body into groups determined by interests, yet they still strive toward the status of the proverbial. The terms of taxonomy have become both the instrument of the collective imagination's selfrecognition and, at the individual level, the means by which distance is preserved between subjects. It is this defining antinomy which continually informs the curiosity of Auden's light verse.

Thematically, this antinomy frequently loses its balance in Auden's early work, as we occasionally see his lyrics acquire a sourness that, ostensibly, has much in common with the orthodox modernist contempt for the age of the masses, with its demotic cultural programme. If we take a lyric such as "To Settle in this Village of the Heart", we can hear dissonance in the pitch of Auden's work, which can perhaps be explained within the framework of light verse. The poem has not attracted a great deal of critical interest, but I would argue that in the expanded context of lightness, it presents valuable insights. The voice of the lyric is, again, palpably familiar yet impersonal: the voice of affected upper class scepticism; but Auden puts it to deeper use:

To settle in this village of the heart,
My darling, can you bear it? True, the hall

With its yews and famous dovecote is still there Just as in childhood, but the grand old couple Who loved us all so equally are dead;

What the lyric presents is a mode of social thinking (or perhaps, "point of view" thinking - the thinking inspired by new social taxonomies) making incursions into the inner life, the "village of the heart". The highminded and languidly contemptuous voice describes the limits installed by the conventional relationship ("the hall /...is still there"). But the relationship itself is less important than the growing sense of entropy and claustrophobia occasioned by the bland, homogenised exteriors of bourgeois consumer living. It is the garishness of this cultural upheaval which compels the attention of the language here. Without the confidence afforded to us by the equality of love of "the grand old couple" (possibly church and state), we are left to devise the terms of our own equality: a project which, as the acidity of the speaker's tone implies, is contrary to all instincts. The speaker imagines this insidious regularity producing some extreme adverse reaction in their partner:

The identical and townee smartness,
Will you really see as home, and not depend
For comfort on the chance, the shy encounter
With the irresponsible beauty of the stranger?

The cast of thought is clearly Freudian, more specifically the Freud of Mass Psychology and Analysis of the "I" and The Future of an Illusion; if the individual's relation to culture has always been characterised by an uneasy détente between drives and compensations, then the appeal of the compensations offered by this kind of life is minimal. Culture is now both monolithic and impalpable, bearing down on the speaker; it is no longer an activity to which such voices appreciably contribute; it is instead becoming a facet of history, that is, something which is happening to them. They are now the objects in a new cultural grammar.

In a sense, however, such an attitude is not new, and here we might reflect with more circumspection on Auden's poetics. First, this kind of complaint has been voiced time and again in the early century, as far back as 1910; the perspective is affined to Forster's in Howards End.

By the thirties the growth of suburbia was a standard preoccupation among writers. (By the end of the decade, furthermore, the flagrant irony produced by suburban expansion in full recognition of the danger of foreign attack would be sharpened into a new sense of the preposterous, most notably in Orwell's Coming up for Air, in 1939). In May 1934, at Auden's time of writing "To settle in this village of the heart", such a voice is familiar enough to be parodied and theatricalised. The lyric is fairly close in colour to Auden's light verse, then, but his poetic spectrum is sufficiently wide that we ought not to mischaracterize it.

Humourless and darkly allusive, we cannot call the poem light in Amis's terms, but it is certainly of a piece with other instances of Auden's lightness, chiefly because of the voice itself, which is rendered in a strophe of quasifree verse, centring around lines of decasyllables that vary according to the stresses and emphases of spoken conversation, their looseness underscored where necessary by a subtler regularity of meter: "The sham ornamentation, the strident swimming pool". The closeness of the lyric to dramatic monologue suggests an element of ironic hyperbole: the voice is indeed satirised ("None too particular" is a little too curt, inviting mockery), but finally plaintive, capable of another order of reflection:

O can you see precisely in our gaucheness
The neighbour's strongest wish, to serve and love?

The sourness of the lyric's tone proceeds from the recognition, explained here at the coda, that there might not be a more rarefied individuality to lose in any case. The speaker sees the terms of commonality, sees his implication within the movement of history as, crucially, the aggregate of individual behaviour and propensities. The couple's "gaucheness" is the measure of their fitness for the age; their snobbery and distrust testifying to a deeper desire to simplify their inner lives and take their place within the mass, whose motto might be "to serve and love". "To settle in this village of the heart" is important, then, because it demonstrates the kind of poetic chiaroscuro which Auden could so effectively employ; the lighter shades of lyric's satire converge with a stronger element of reflection. Consequently the quiddity of the lyric expresses the challenges facing poetry under the terms of twentieth century modernity, by bestowing the general voice (that is, the light voice in this instance) with an individuated sense of anxiety.

Auden's Mature Light Verse

The continuous form in which we read "Letter to Lord Byron" in The English Auden and the Collected Poems, is perhaps contrary to the epistolary spirit exemplified by the poem in its original incarnation in Letters from Iceland. There, its sections scattered across the volume, punctuated by letters to other addressees, tourist guides and comical minihistories, "Letter to Lord Byron" seems more comfortable and more fittingly met. As Auden implies at the end of the poem ("This letter that's already far too long") light verse is most effective when its brisk pace is condensed. That said, in aping the "airy manner" of its addressee, "Letter to Lord Byron" is a professed "experiment" in resurrecting the longer narrative modes pioneered in works such as "Don Juan". Specifically, the experiment is once more one of voice: can such a manner be successfully inhabited by a voice speaking in an age where the place of the poet is found within the mass? If so, how does that voice describe its circumstances and what kind of access do we have to it, as readers? The question of autobiography, or rather, of selfpresentation, is unavoidable here. Byron's voice was inseparable from his persona: he was in a sense the first public poet, whose renown preceded him. Auden's letter depends on fruitful contrast, being an experiment in the relationship of autobiographical poetry to one's historical milieu. Where Byron was the Romantic poetashistorical actor, Auden is his modern, much less exalted progeny. Auden's capdoffing first lines make this clear:

Excuse, my lord, the liberty I take
In thus addressing you. I know that you
Will pay the price of authorship and make
The allowances an author has to do.
A poet's fanmail will be nothing new.

Auden repeatedly takes the deferential view, praising Byron's work and style ("...I have, at the age of twentynine / Just read Don Juan and I found it fine"). But behind the praise for Byron is the wish to revive the closeness of his voice in a modern setting, a closeness which the modern postal service dispatching this letter might effect, serving as metaphor:

To learn the use in culture's propagation Of modern methods of communication:

New roads, new rails, new contacts, as we know
From documentaries by the G. P. O.
Light verse is the best expedient for this propagation.

Auden's voice is digressive, urbane and never discomposed. It suggests that there is still a place within modernity for meaningful selfexposition, no matter how trivial its "airy manner" of communication might first appear: meaningful in situating the speaker in a clear relationship to the different modes of life in society, from the intimate to the historical.

"Letter to Lord Byron" is a performance of personality, then. It is choral in the sense that we follow its meanderings without complication, as Auden holds court on all things, "From natural scenery to men and women, / Myself, the arts, the European news:". But we ought to qualify this with the stipulation that the performance is too informal to be repeatable and speakable, as we have seen in earlier choral lyrics. We are not induced, as it were, to participate. It cannot be called lyric in generic terms because (like its Byronic inspirations) it carries no suggestion of song. But it presences the voice of the speaker - this time Auden himself, or a poetical selfperformance - such that it invites our company in sharing a supracultural view, out across contemporary affairs. Auden's selfeffacing lines, having produced "the flattest line in English verse" and detailing his lowly place on Parnassus, are offset by the importance of his project in preserving MacNeice's "human values":

Parnassus after all is not a mountain,
Reserved for A. 1. climbers such as you;
It's got a park, it's got a public fountain.

In the second part of the poem those values encourage an irreverent view of history: the intervening time between Byron's life and Auden's is briskly, but somehow fully recapped:

I'll clear my throat and take a Rover's breath
And skip a century of hope and sin -

For far too much has happened since your death. Crying went out and the cold bath came in, With drains, bananas, bicycles, and tin,

And Europe saw from Ireland to Albania
The Gothic revival and the Railway mania.

Auden creates in "Letter to Lord Byron" a realm of imagined civility, where one can present one's thoughts without being called to account for them in "responsible" terms. Thus his offerings on the modern infatuation with technology and progress are too funny to be elevated to the status of doctrine ("Preserve me, above all, from centralheating"): they are instead the stuff of the "point of view", here redeemed by the wideangle lens of the poem and by its engagingly conversational pace. For this reason we should guard against relegating "Letter to Lord Byron" on grounds of frivolity or triviality. Justin Replogle argues that the poem is an example of Auden's "Antipoet", who "holds life to be a blessing, and has little inclination to dissect and condemn". Be that as it may, the manner of reading experience that the poem fosters has a valence quite out of proportion with its funmaking tone. The poem exists in its own public sphere, and in the brightness and promiscuity of its voice there is the insinuation that modern experience (pace Benjamin) is perhaps manageable, according to a standpoint of openness, clarity and humour.

Although it would seem to be diametrically opposed to the definition of lyric propounded by Adorno with its troubled principle of individuation, "Letter to Lord Byron" can still be said to crystallise the motion of the self according to its history and culture; it is just that that version of selfhood we glean therein is based not upon the confinement that results from identity thinking, but upon the voice's humorous expansiveness. The force of the poem is vocal rather than formal: this voice is still capable of a historical précis that fully comprehends the fundamental shifts occasioned by mass society. England's transition into twentieth century modernity is captured, the "John Bull" of days gone by wiped out by the First World War, and replaced by the "bowler hat who straphangs in the tube/And kicks the tyrant only in his dreams,". In his dread of all extremes, the bowler hat is the cipher of behaviourism, the unwittingly generative unit of mass society ("I may not be courageous, but I save"), haunted by and subservient to "the ogre". Anthony Hecht equates the ogre with monolithic "Authority", but Auden never names it as such, being more interested in its effects: crippling stasis and cynicism towards humanity.

The bright tone of the poem is clouded in these sections as Auden describes the Ogre as a recurring force in history, and presents kowtowing to the Ogre as the recessive historical gene:

Banker or landlord, bookingclerk or Pope,
Whenever he's lost his faith in choice and thought,
When a man sees the future without hope,
Whenever he endorses Hobbes' report
"The life of man is nasty, brutish, short",
The dragon rises from his garden border
And promises to set up law and order.

The meanderings and the tangents between sections are unified at bottom; Auden's thoughts on (capitalised) Art—"To me Art's subject is the human clay" in part three serves equally as a motto for the worldview that "Letter to Lord Byron" makes available. Light verse is among the arts best suited to capturing the substance of that human clay, because of the transparency of meaning and uncompromised intelligibility that it implies. Wordsworthian natureworship is countered by the celebration of the modern quotidian and the place of people within it.

What follows in part three is a poetic account of Auden's argument in the introduction to the Oxford Book, whereby Romanticism signals the end of patronage for the artist and the birth of selfsufficiency: "He sang and painted and drew dividends/But lost responsibilities and friends". Responsibility recurs once more; the modern responsibility, as we have seen, is to respond to Romantic detachment with a corrective social awareness, as Auden himself insists, using "clay" in an ironically snobbish (perhaps aristocratic, for the benefit of his addressee) rather than a profound sense here: "The common clay and the uncommon nobs/Were far too busy making piles or starving/To look at pictures, poetry, or carving". This responsibility further entails the poet's selfaccount in part four, but the airy manner Auden has adopted lifts this out of the mundane:

My passport says I'm five feet and eleven, with hazel eyes and fair (it's towlike) hair, That I was born in York in 197, With no distinctive markings anywhere. Which isn't quite correct. Conspicuous there On my right cheek appears a large brown mole; I think I don't dislike it on the whole. This is selfexposition not mired in subjectivity: a genial, communicable personality speaking the language of the "point of view". Auden's mockery of "Das Volk" ordering "sausages and lagers", some of whom have based their notion of racial purity on an unathletic Nordic Aryan such as he, reminds us of the freedom of the spirit of light verse as it has become newly important. It finds another, broader enemy in the will to conformity and behaviourism, where "telling the truth" means divesting life of its nourishing ambiguities:

I hate the modern trick, to tell the truth, Of straightening out the kinks in the young mind, Our passion for the tender plant of youth, Our hatred for all weeds of any kind. Slogans are bad: the best that I can find Is this: "Let each child have that's in our care As much neurosis as the child can bear." In its concluding roundup of contemporary matters, "Letter to Lord Byron" perhaps strikes its only ambiguous note. Does its manner of narrating the individual's place within history make history assailable - does it instate the "tiny measure" of contribution or does it play and mock in the face of history's unbreakable influence? Auden's scepticism about "The Great Utopia" he and his generation have entertained is telling:

The Great Utopia, free of all complexes, the Withered State is, at the moment, such A dream as that of being both the sexes. The imagined civil realm conjured by "Letter to Lord Byron" is, as Auden has said, not the place for narrow sloganeering. It marks a sphere of humane civility.

This does not amount to passive acceptance of the status quo. Instead the "conversational song" of the poem convinces us of the importance of human values and the closeness and proximity of modern subjects. It encourages us to endorse its implicit willingness to return a sense of agency to one's involvement in history, a different and more valuable way of "telling the truth."

"As I Walked Out One Evening": November 1937.

After the programmatic lightness of "Letter to Lord Byron", Auden returned in "As I walked out one evening" to the lyric ballad form, apparently searching for a lightness with complementary shades of poignancy. The element of vocality is paramount in the poem. "As I walked out one evening" has what we can call a distinctively Audenic mutuality, between the employment of traditional elements of light verse poetics (the smallscale narrative structure, the clarity of address and prosodic consistency, the components of song and dialogue) and weightier themes such as transience and death. It is Auden's imagery, though, which ensures that the lyric is of its moment, capturing the quiddity of thinking without recourse to the discursive or the arcane. We are invited into the poem by another anonymous "I"; not, confessional; not, in this instance, proverbial; but purely narrative. The "I" is a clear pane through which we observe what unfolds. This is how we enter into lyric. We tessellate with the "I", we observe along with it:

As I walked out one evening,
Walking down Bristol Street,
The crowds upon the pavement
Were fields of harvest wheat.

This is an image pulling in two different directions, drawing on a wellestablished repository of the mannature metaphor, but rooted in the consciousness of its moment. The voice is casually undifferentiating - no single man or woman stands out from the crowd but there are notes of awe and of fear in the description of this concentrated human activity. We might say that this voice is also recasting the heightened visibility that characterises the social; it encounters its fellow men en masse. Lingering within this spectacle is the sense that the wheat will inevitably be harvested, a sense that ushers in the first note of transience and death which will dominate the lyric. Auden has intimated straight away through our tessellation with his speaker that death has been brought into a different kind of symbiosis with the concentration of people into masses. Collective entities eventually perish, as inexorably as does the individual body, therefore collective life might be experienced as a manner of rehearsal for death, not simply in the immolation of the self, but in our being implicated in the inevitable expiration of the collective body, in whatever form. The ballad's metrical regularity serves a distinct, almost hypnotic purpose, offering a clear inducement to the reader, drawing him or her in further, encouraging us to intuit the deeper significance of how we are positioned within this mass, at once within and without.

The poem continues in this conspiratorial vein: we eavesdrop with the speaker as the lover sings. The singing voice arrives from nowhere: in stark contrast to the undifferentiated "fields of harvest wheat", it sings the inner life. But it is the emphasis on raw sentiment, rather than personal circumstance on what might be applied generally which chimes with the preceding stanza:

"I'll love you, dear, I'll love you Till China and Africa meet
And the river jumps over the mountain
And the salmon sing in the street.

Again, though the subjectmatter of the song is weighty, and is related earnestly, we can bring it into sharper focus within the rubric of light verse. The song of Love is similarly affined to the speaker's introductory stanza in its nakedness. There is in light verse a bareness of presentation which, manifested here in the speaking "I" and the immediate way we enter into the lyric, allows for the enchantment of surroundings and actors. "As I walked out one evening" operates through this kind of correspondence between our enthralment to its voices and the fantastical events that those voices describe. So the traditional aspects of the poem defy their familiarity. The lover's ease of expression seems to redeem the stock element, the conventionality of the construction "I'll love you till". Auden's imagery leavens the sense of earnestness ("And the seven stars go squawking / Like geese about the sky"), a note that continues into the dramatic peak of the lyric. The Urvoice of Time (through its minions the clocks) responds to the quotidian warmth of Love's song portentously, with bleak abstract nouns:

Behind the quotidian lurks the inevitability of death and erasure:

"The glacier knocks in the cupboard,
The desert sighs in the bed,
And the crack in the teacup opens
A lane to the land of the dead.

Iambics have alternated with anapaests to convey the song; here the latter are more prominent as the voice of Time finds its own sense of fable. The rising rhythms hasten the voice of Time onwards to its climax. If death is perceptible everywhere, even through "the crack in the teacup", then death is a project of the imagination, in a similar vein to the fable, the story, the legend ("Where the beggars raffle the banknotes /And the giant is enchanting to Jack,"). Death is inexorable, yet indescribable. Time concludes its sermon with a return to the terms of life in light of this, with the inevitability of death as the conditioning factor ("Life remains a blessing / Although you cannot bless"). There remains the truer, more abiding version of "love", which is less a question of passion and feeling between individuals and, as we saw in "To settle in this village of the heart", more a struggle for collective existence as produced by the efforts of flawed individuals ("You shall love your crooked neighbour / With your crooked heart.") The final stanza is spoken by the narrating "I" as we are briskly ushered back into the quiet:

It was late, late in the evening,
The lovers they were gone;
The clocks had ceased their chiming,
And the deep river ran on.

What is most palpable from this coda is the pace of our imaginative investment in the respective voices of Love and Time, or, our transfixed utterance of their competing songs. The ending is simply recounted, not explicated. It is as though we are abruptly given back our own thoughts. "As I Walked Out One Evening" thus uses the speed of light verse - its simplicity of involvement, and the eagerness with which we enter into it - to vivify an ageold thematic refrain for its own time. Love is often doomed to end as abruptly; Auden's success with the lyric is to frame this truism through a historically vivid manner of perception, rooted in the mass social experience.

"It's farewell to the drawing-room's civilised cry": January 1937.

Of all Auden's most renowned early works, this

engrossing lyric is perhaps most central to the narration of "the Devil's decade": the Devil himself "has broken parole and arisen" and is running amok across bourgeois Europe.[276] How might we understand the placement of Auden's speaker, as a light verse narrator, and his description of the resurrection of this Satanic figure at his time of writing? Written in January 1937, this is evidently the poetry to complement the disaster narrative finding increasingly urgent expression. But how does the lightness of the verse configure that disaster? As I suggested earlier the element of speed and pace is crucial: the frenetic rhythms patterned into the quatrains, ratcheted by repeated anapaests, create a taut stanza, rendered stronger still by the fullrhyming couplets. The proximity and implacability of the catastrophe is domesticated in an uncomfortably literal sense, through imagery (the devil "hides in the cupboard and under the bed") and a sustained tone of levity, by turns rueful, foreboding, celebratory and abandoned.

Edward Mendelson characterises the voice as that of a "mad dictator", seeing behind its element of performance a coherent identity. John Fuller identifies the speaker as "deliberately an alter-ego of the poet", which is also valid, yet, as I will show, only to a limited degree. I would submit that, as the voice of light verse par excellence, the speaker is a protean creature, speaking out of the culture itself. Certainly its imagery, its imaginative promiscuity and its tone can be conceptualised at this level. It is by tracking the kinks in this tone that we can fully appreciate the discursive qualities of the lyric, qualities which lend it the gravitas that orientates its infectious lightness.

"It's farewell..." is evidently an attempt to shape the decade's self recognition: a declamatory intervention into the ongoing debate about what comprised the times. (For this reason I choose to examine the original version; Auden's later alterations cannot be said to improve on it.) The fitness of light verse as a response to the litany of catastrophes and failures (Franco's capture of Madrid in November of the previous year, for instance; further consolidations by the Hitler's Germany; the wider economic malaise which, but for occasional reverses, continued in earnest) is perhaps best elucidated if we take the content of the poem at face value. In other words, we should consider the sincerity of the "farewell" to all the cherished principles, all the previous complacent assumptions of security and prosperity which Enlightenment Europe had nurtured. This is a poetic instance of play, a voice uttered from within a rational culture as its premises are apparently disintegrating. Mihai I. Spariosu has given a comprehensive account of the evolution of the concept of play, and this concept can encourage us to understand the disaster narrative of the thirties and Auden's lyric in richer terms. Building on Freud's emphasis, given in "Character and Culture" and "Mass Psychology", on the progress and regress of cultures between rational and prerational modes, Spariosu offers a nuanced, agonistic alternative, contending that those opposing modes compete within a given culture at a given time, to no preestablished end. The voice of "It's farewell..." might be located in the melee of such competition, at a time when the rational - or a received version of it, the rationality of Enlightenment libertarianism - is being dismantled. Immediately, such disabuse of longstanding confidences is halfbewailed, half relished by the speaker:

It's farewell to the drawingroom's civilised cry,
The professor's sensible whereto and why,
The frockcoated diplomat's social aplomb,
Now matters are settled with gas and with bomb.

We could not call this sense of riveted anxiety ambiguous; it is perfectly consistent with a view, which we have seen elaborated in other light lyrics, at once detached and entirely implicated. Violence is the terminus of all culture the firmer reality, the latent truth of human activity. The perspective here (against "Letter to Lord Byron") is Hobbesian: fearful, yet unblinking. The accoutrements of culture such as high art ("The works for two pianos") consoling myths and legends ("reasonable giants and remarkable fairies") are as "frangible" as peace itself ("the branches of olive are stored upstairs"). Violence and chaos, embodied in the devil, are now the conditions for living. Again, the pace of the verse has a levelling effect wholly concordant with the underlying theme of rationality's decline: the stuff of art, of myth, of bourgeois luxury and of Christianity is all reduced to the level of incidental detail, material over which the voice can flit.

The speaker sees the mundane effects of modern industrial life with the pagan eyes of superstition and fear:

Like influenza he walks abroad,
He stands by the bridge, he waits by the ford,
As a goose or a gull he flies overhead,
He hides in the cupboard and under the bed.

The psychogeography is reminiscent of earlier lyrics ("Look there! The sunk road winding" particularly), but here, carried along by the momentum of the lines, it coheres more effectively: it insinuates a sense of foreboding which is more articulate and penetrative in a light lyric setting. From the first "O" of "O were he to triumph", the voice is melodramatic and overplayed. The "dear heart" being addressed is a device, a kind of ossified poeticism that the voice creates spontaneously. It is as though the voice is imbibing the excess that saturates the culture as it is burning out (the "dear heart" reappears only in the final stanza, with similar effect), and we as speaking readers revive it. Each stanza seems at this stage to divert the trajectory of the lyric, conveying a stream of thought eager to include as much as possible, only then to move on once more. When the speaker decides "I'm the axe that must cut them [the "unsound trees"] down to the ground", he is speaking as the contrived poet ashero, as the expression of one's impotence in the face of disaster, and it seems as Auden himself:

For I, after all, am the Fortunate One,
The HappyGoLucky, the spoilt Third Son;
For me it is written the Devil to chase
And to rid the earth of the human race.

These notionally autobiographical lines (Auden being the "spoilt Third son" by his own admission) could contain a coy reference to his position as the anointed one, the leader of the thirties poets, a position of inflated importance he is quick to puncture by the last line, with its delusions of omnipotence. At this point the lyric switches to a highoctane polemic that the speaker is unable to sustain for very long. Adopting the moral stance of opposition to the times (bemoaning the "sedentary Sodom and slick Gomorrah" of the modern industrial world, whose apathy and efficiency are mutually productive), the speaker soon takes on the characteristics he is harpooning ("I shall have caviare thick on my bread,"). The individual will ("I shall come, I shall punish") leads only to imitative ridiculousness and mindless selfdisplay:

I shall ride the parade in a platinum car,
My features shall shine, my name shall be Star,
Daylong and nightlong the bells I shall peal,
And down the long street I shall turn the cartwheel.

Suitably, after this momentary peak of selfglorification, the firstperson mode seems to exhaust itself. We are back to the dance of death and its pagan notion of history. Auden gives us strains of infantilism and adolescent tittering ("So Little John, Long John, Peter and Paul, / And poor little Horace with only one ball") to evoke a condensed, cyclical history. We are trapped in the repetition of bloodletting, popularly understood in the form of the paradigmatic catastrophe, the First World War ("You shall leave your breakfast, your desk and your play / On a fine summer morning the Devil to slay."). Violence is the engine of history, violence which becomes in the climactic stanzas of the lyric the last bastion of meaning. The modern world subsists in consumer indulgence and violent expiation ("And the earth shall be emptied of mortal sin"). Narratives of progress - more specifically, the "embarrassment of beliefs" of the decade - have been dislodged by the pagan oracular vision, which exists along side the Christian mythology of the lyric (the myth of the Fall, the premonitory Star), and within the clutter of consumer life:

The fishes are silent deep in the sea,
The skies are lit up like a Christmas tree,

The star in the West shoots its warning cry: "Mankind is alive, but Mankind must die."

So goodbye to the house with its wallpaper red, Goodbye to the sheets on the warm double bed, Goodbye to the beautiful birds on the wall,

It's goodbye, dear heart, goodbye to you all.

The "dear heart" and the refrain of "goodbye" remind us at the climax of the lyric of its essential mode of address: the song, the performance. By the end of "It's farewell" Auden's poetics have taken on the qualities of invocation (the stressed beats which end the line after the anapaests are especially effective at the lyric's end: "birds on the wall"; "goodbye to you all") beckoning the spectacle of destruction[282] which would, his speaker imagines, fulfil the culture of death and erasure, whose indicators simmer beneath modern industrial life. The lyric is itself a kind of wishfulfilment, then. It is voiced as a celebration of the will to destroy, for which the mechanics of light verse, paradoxically, offer the most germane poetic realisation. We are invited to recite along, to involve ourselves in the panache of the speaker's performance.

"It's farewell to the drawing room's civilised cry" stands as the most compelling example of Auden's light verse because of the way that it exhausts the choral mode. Our attention is drawn to the currents of uncontrollable collective energies that pass beneath the apparently stable terrain of mass society. In its irresistible panache and highoctane pace, the lyric induces a dizzy headedness in the reader which muddies the distinction in our minds between the moment of immersion in the poem and the moment of reflection, and this confusion defines its historicity.

Both the dangers and the seductions of the collective utterance seem to backlight the lyric: it is a warning and an inducement. "As I walked out this evening" is premised on a similar insight in its themes, but the experiential element is more pronounced here: we are appreciably aware of the high stakes of collective involvement. Auden's destructive devil is finally an embodiment of the very mutuality that grounds how we read the lyric, and by extension, how precariously we live together.

Chapter 16

Critical Essays on W.H. Auden

"Reflection on the right to will": Auden's "Canzone" and Arendt's notes on willing

Does God ever judge us by appearances? I suspect that he does. (Auden, Poems 856) WITH THIS EPIGRAPH from W.H. Auden, Hannah Arendt begins her last work, The Life of the Mind. Although it appears to be merely a witty apothegm-and its inclusion among the peculiar genre Auden called "Shorts" might lend credence to this evaluation-Auden's words go to the heart of a modernist predicament: the revaluation of appearances, which began in earnest with Nietzsche, cannot be undertaken without a gesture toward something that transcends appearances, nor can it be pursued without a perspective that immerses itself in appearances in order to break their spell-the perspective of "suspicion."

In her choice of epigraph and in her treatment of Auden's poetry throughout The Life of the Mind, Arendt indicates a strong affinity with the work of her friend; similarly, Auden, in various prose writings, especially his review of Arendt's The Human Condition, emphasizes that the two participate in a common project.1 The stakes of this project are most readily comprehensible in terms of the dangers that arise not so much from the modernist dilemma to which Auden's apothegm alludes as from two broadly defined attempts to escape this dilemma, both of which result in the occlusion of any space for the faculty of willing. On the one hand, gestures toward transcendence are converted into a steadfast conviction that salvation lies in a transcendent being or in a nostalgic return to those forms of life in which such beings were still believable; on the other hand, suspicion is raised to such a high level that it leaves no place for stable forms and gives way to a mode of isolation that can no longer even be considered a "perspective" since it does not open onto anything like a common world.

If the first danger leads to dubious calls for renewal-what Auden denounces as "a new Constantinism" the second tends to make every appearance into a novum, the ironic result of which is a doctrine of eternal recurrence. Arendt's and Auden's acute awareness of these sharply contrasting but nevertheless kindred dangers generates a particular sensitivity toward the intricate dialectic of novelty and repetition, and this sensitivity not only gives rise to certain themes that dominate both of their works— one need only think of Auden's fascination with the figure of Don Juan3-but also expresses itself in the formal experimentation that characterizes so much of their writing. Arendt invents a novel form of exposition for each of her major works, and Auden explores an astonishing variety of poetic forms, some of which come close to exhausting the resources of an uninflected language like English.4 Even the Auden poem Arendt chooses as the epigraph for her last work is evidence of this, for it is an experiment in pure syllabic form derived from the Japanese haiku-which was originally a "humorous" "opening part" (hokku) of a jointly authored composition.

Of Auden's many experiments in poetic form, none leads so quickly into the dialectic of novelty and repetition as does his largely overlooked, enormously difficult, and emphatically peculiar 1942 poem, "Canzone" (Auden, Poems 3331).5 The poem is peculiar at the very least because its form is unusual-almost unique-in the Western literary tradition and, at the time of its composition, unprecedented in the English language. Of course English poets have written canzoni, many on the model of Petrarch, but among the many poetic forms called canzoni, Auden chooses a particularly difficult one, invented and employed only once by Dante in his poem of 1296 or '97, "Amor, tu vedi ben the questa Donna."6 This poem is one of the time petrose, in which Dante celebrates his frustrated love for an unnamed lady. In this exacting poetic form there are five twelve-line stanzas, with a com niato of six lines, in which each line ends with one of only five rhyme words-donna, petra, freddo, luce, and tempo (lady, stone, cold, light, and time). The rhyme words appear in an ordered sequence whose repetition and cyclical transition from one dominant word to another corresponds to the transmutation of one element into another and to the transfiguration of something in the natural world into something divine. The poem is itself born of these transformations, as Dante indicates in the final stanza, when the coldness of the lady becomes, for the poet, the cause and condition for the invention of "the non fu mai pensata in alcun tempo [something never thought before in any time]," namely, this novel poetic form.

Dante's final apostrophe to the poem-"Canzone, io porto ne la mente donna [song, I carry in my mind a lady] "-is meant to indicate that the poet's sexual frustration can be transformed into the novelty of a hitherto unheard-of song: the poet wants the fulfillment of the will that gives rise to the poem-the will to be loved by the lady. And he implores God to bring about this, the last transmutation of a cold substance into something warm, the final satisfaction of the poet's will. In the meantime, he celebrates the novelty of the thing he can master: the poem, song or "canzone." Although he praises novelty, what he really wants remains the same; indeed, he wants nothing less than the return of the same, the reciprocal return of his warm, loving glance. Novelty here functions as compensation; it is a substitute for the eschatological or even messianic moment in which all things finally return, in Stoic-Christian terms apokatastasis canton.

Once the lady undergoes an ordered transformation, warms up, and returns his love-and this "once" occurs at, and as, the end of time-all things will have returned. Cosmic time does not run counter to eschatological time; on the contrary, the latter confirms the former, and the novelty of the song, like the stubborn uniqueness of the untransformed, still cold lady, is merely an index of the expectation of return. The satisfaction of the will depends upon the possibility that it can produce the conditions of its own fulfillment, that the will can project itself into -and thereby master-a future, bringing that which escapes the will into the ordered course of events. As Auden's "Canzone" repeats Dante's poem, it analyzes the zone of this possibility, this can-zone.

Historical as Munich

Auden at 1: Who is he now?

Who am I now?", W. H. Auden asked in a poem, written in April 1967, called "Prologue at Sixty", an age he suddenly defined as the start of his real writing life. How sadly short the ensuing "main text" would be, Auden was probably starting to guess: the physical effects of years of heavy consumption of alcohol, cigarettes and uppers and downers, of sedentary habits, and of a disrupted domestic life, were making themselves felt. His answer to his own question then – "Who am I?" – was that he was "a New Yorker, who opens his Times at the obit page" and whose "dream images date him already". Such intimations of mortality belie his insistence to friends that he was going to live to be eighty. He looked that age, though he was only sixty-six, when he died in a Vienna hotel in 1973. Auden would have been a hundred years old this month.

Who is Auden now, at 1? The older Auden did his best to set the terms of his future reception. But as well as a physical end, writers' deaths mark their final surrender of control over the meaning of their work. It was the point where Auden could "accomplish" his "corpse at last" (he is punning here on the dual meanings of both "accomplish" and "corpse"), but also the point (as he puts it elsewhere) where the poet is "stripped of excuse and nimbus" and becomes "a Past, subject to Judgement".

As early as the spring of 1931 – at which time Auden, at twenty-four, had published only one real book, Poems , though "Paid on Both Sides" had appeared in the Criterion – Ezra Pound in Rapallo was sneering about the "Auden craze" in

Britain. "Audenesque" was already an adjective by 1933. Subsequently Auden enjoyed the lifelong dignity of a controversial and highly variegated reputation. When, in June 194, a Tory MP, outraged by Auden's "refuge" from war service in the United States, demanded that the writer be stripped of British citizenship, it was the first time that a poet had been the subject of parliamentary interest since Sassoon's non serviam "Declaration" was read out in the House of Commons in July 1917. The following year, in the journal Horizon, the sociologist Tom Harrisson surveyed two years of wartime book publication and came to the extraordinary conclusion that "to judge from most war books, Britain is fighting this war to protect the world against Auden and Picasso, the Jews and any form of collectivisation".

By 1947, Auden was referring to himself as "Public Cultural Enemy No 1" in his former country. And issues of national belonging and social responsibility remained central to judgements about Auden's poetry for the rest of his career. For example, in 196 Philip Larkin complained that Auden had "abandoned his audience together with their common dialect and concerns", and he denigrated the "individual and cosmopolitan path" the poet had followed since. (As if making the same point but in reverse, Auden once told Christopher Isherwood: "Though I believe it sinful to be queer, it has at least saved me from becoming a pillar of the Establishment, and it might not even have done that if I hadn't bolted to America".) But a living author can always fight back against critics and even admirers.

Death means total powerlessness in the face of abuse or praise. For the English novelist Anthony Powell, Auden was something close to a traitor. Powell greeted the news of Auden's demise by telling Kingsley Amis, "I'm delighted that shit has gone... scuttling off to America in 1939 with his boyfriend". Yet for many younger readers, such as James Merrill, Auden had acquired almost divine status. In his long poem The Changing Light at Sandover, Merrill refers to the memory of Auden, guest of honour at a party in Athens, with an epithet, "Father of forms", which was often used of Zeus.

Auden himself foretold how "the words of a dead man", like a Dionysian sacrificial offering, "are modified in the guts of the living". Robert Lowell wrote shortly after Auden's death of seeing a girl reading Auden's last book.

She must be very modern,
she dissects him in the past tense.

Lowell concluded, with a rival's relief, that Auden was "historical now as Munich".

The prospect of becoming "historical" brought from the 196s' Auden a fusillade of late self-characterizations. He seems to have begun pondering the total arc of his career around 1963, the year in which the first full critical study of his work, Monroe K. Spears's The Poetry of W. H. Auden: The disenchanted island, was published, with his input. This was the year in which Robert Frost, William Carlos Williams, Louis MacNeice and Sylvia Plath all died, and Auden's partner Chester Kallman left New York for good. The "dead we miss are easier / to talk to" than the living, Auden wrote, as if with one foot already planted in the Elysian fields. "Thoughts of his own death" began to preoccupy him, "like the distant roll / of thunder at a picnic". By the summer of the following year, he was writing what he cannily but morosely called "Posthumous" poetry, "not all of it printable" as he told a friend – poems, that is, which he could not or would not publish during his lifetime. Three of those proleptically "Posthumous" poems made their way into the Collected Poems of 1976.

A number of other such poems, however – mostly in the tanka and haiku forms with which he became fascinated in the 196s – will eventually be included in Edward Mendelson's ongoing edition of Auden's Complete Works. One of these is "My Epitaph", scribbled on the menu in a New York Chinese restaurant in 1965: "posthumous" both in its graveyard conceit and in its unprintable nature:

A cocksucker? Yes.
A poet? I believe.
Good. And a Christian?

Some things could only be confessed publicly once one

was dead. After all, in 1963 Time magazine had at a late stage cancelled a cover story on Auden after the periodical's editors discovered that he was a homosexual. And Auden had been frantically annoyed in 1965, the year in which he wrote "My Epitaph", when Fuck You, a Lower East-Side samizdat "magazine of the arts", pirated the text of "The Platonic Blow", a poem about fellatio which Auden had written in 1948 but, for obvious reasons, had never published.

On the face of it, "My Epitaph" suggests that whether one is a poet or not is a more significant fact than whether or not one is a cocksucker and a less significant matter than whether or not one is religious. But Auden's poems, and his career as a whole, demand that we watch for gaps and to listen for lacunae. For example, the "missing" syllable in the second line here between "poet?" and "I believe" is a morally meaningful, self-doubting silence. Poetry is this poem's bridge and pivot: it is only in poetry that Auden can articulate his human shortcomings, and religious clarity is therefore inseparable from poetic magic. This little poem makes a memorable claim for the centrality of poetry to the meaning of Auden's life. But it is also a bid for posthumous interpretive power. "This, finally, is who I was", Auden's poem says. By 1965, then, the stock-taking had already begun. Now, on the occasion of his 1th birthday, if we ask who Auden is, we are not posing a new question, but are stationed further along the curve of examination which the poet himself inaugurated in his mid-fifties. And there is more to be said (and to be discovered) about him than those three things that his "Epitaph" puts in the foreground.

One difficulty about producing an accurate overview of Auden's career is that his oeuvre is so sprawling and various. He had an anxious, Victorian prodigality, telling a friend, "unless I write something, anything, good, indifferent, or trashy, every day, I feel ill". The problem is not with the poetry. The expanded edition of Katherine Bucknell's collection of Auden's juvenilia, published in 23, has raised a large number of early poems to the surface, and now only a few later pieces remain to be collected: as well as the once-unpublishable poems such as "My Epitaph" and "The Platonic Blow", there is the mesmerizing but unfinished dream vision beginning "In the year of my youth when yoyos came in" (written around 1931), a very few rejected drafts, and various occasional squibs, birthday poems or verse compliments. The general contours of Auden's poetry are by now relatively clear, if dauntingly vast in scope; as are those of his work in the theatre, in opera and in films.

But much of Auden's output of prose remains, for most readers, terra incognita. Aside from the inner drive to create something "every day", Auden wrote copiously because he needed the money. After an early stint as a schoolteacher, he never held a steady, long-term job, not even in a university, and never taught so much as a semester of creative writing. The price of such independence for Auden, especially once the spendthrift Chester Kallman came on board, was a very close relationship with his typewriter: he once wrote about his study: "from the Olivetti portable, / the dictionaries (the very / best money can buy), the heaps of paper, it is evident / what must go on". Yet very little of what Auden wrote can be discounted as hack-work. The prose as a whole is remarkable, full of fresh ideas and commanding yet eccentric speculations and intuitions. When it becomes readily accessible in its full extent, it will surely alter preconceptions about Auden. s.

A second factor inhibiting an overall assessment of Auden is his strong evolutionary urge as an artist. When his father wrote to him, in 1939, that he preferred Wystan's old poems to the new, he wrote in reply: "The writer's problem is that of everyone: how to go on growing the whole of his life, because to stop growing is to die". And in 1946 he insisted to an audience in New York that a "major poet is always willing to risk failure, to look for a new rhetoric". His subject on that occasion was Shakespeare, but Auden was also thinking about his own career. The will to change, to find "a new rhetoric", was so strong in him that there is in fact something almost eerily provisional about his poetic self. Auden was, in effect, several different poets working under a single name. To make a general point about his work as a whole is almost inevitably to mischaracterize at least some of those "Audens". The poet who brought the television set, the sick joke and the word "sexy" into poetry for the first time, Auden was the master of the diagnostic, Arnoldian, authoritatively vatic voice. But he was also the major dismantler of "His Majesty King Ego" and that poetic voice's pretensions to power over its audience.

This anti-authoritarian thrust, which included attacks on his own authority as a poet, is clear in his elegy for the "silly" Yeats, who in Auden's poem lies semi-delirious, not surrounded like Cuchulain by the onrushing sea and the whirrings of his heroic sword, but instead – a rich, half-conscious bourgeois – confusingly impinged on by "nurses and rumours" as he dies in his bed. Auden was a public poet, capable of writing an ode which could link our private "fears" with the continental crisis of a civil war; but he was also the poet who opened up for male writers, in "Thanksgiving for a Habitat", the domestic and homely sphere in poetry. In this sequence, written in the early 196s, there is a poem for almost every room in his Austrian farmhouse: though here, as often with Auden, a silence is filled with meaning – there is no mention of Chester Kallman's bedroom.

Added to Auden's enormous output and his protean qualities as a poet is the fact that his interests range so widely. (His work is far more diverse intellectually than – for example – that of Ezra Pound; The Cantos present themselves as encyclopedic, but make virtually no reference to the most prestigious culture of the modern world – science.) Even after the publication of John Fuller's indispensable W. H. Auden: A Commentary , with its tracking of allusions to subjects as disparate as the Abdication crisis of 1936 and the Zulu Empire, there is still much basic information which is unknown about Auden's life, his studies and writing.

Fuller says drily at the start of his book, "there are limits to one man's understanding of such a polymath as Auden". What is more, Auden's life, both in mental and physical terms, was an extraordinarily mobile one. It is often still not easy to determine where he was when, whom he met where, what he was reading, and so on. With two passports, at various points he had long-term homes in five countries: England, Germany, the USA, Italy and Austria. He made twenty-nine separate journeys that lasted more than two months; twenty-six of those lasted more than five months, blurring the meaning, especially in his later years, of home and abroad, domestic and foreign, here and there.

In addition, Auden's homosexuality helped to enforce the social mobility and unpredictability which he thought essential to his freedom as a writer. Thus, in the United States, Auden was able to move back and forth between vastly disparate worlds, from the ultra-stolid milieu of the British Embassy in Washington, to the golden craziness of the international operatic and ballet elites, to the seedy fertility of the East Village underground scene, rubbing shoulders with Christians, poets and cocksuckers alike.

Auden's social reach in the 196s could take in Dag Hammarskjöld and Hannah Arendt at one end, and – crossing by way of people such as Larry Rivers and Frank O'Hara – murky figures like the convicted Canadian thief named Coney Burns at the other. Burns had come across an Auden poem in an anthology in the prison library and wrote to the poet. Their friendly exchange of letters about literary and ethical matters continued even after Burns had escaped (temporarily) from prison and was on the lam.

Social ambiguity has been compounded by an only slow-fading reticence about Auden's love-life. This means that it has only recently become possible to discuss directly in print, or even to name, Michael Yates , who was a schoolboy of thirteen when the twenty-six-year-old Auden fell in love with him in the summer of 1933, and whom scholars have had to refer to by such periphrases as "the person who is the subject of the poem 'Lay your sleeping head, my love'". Nothing substantial about Auden's and Yates's relationship, or on its bearing for Auden's poems has yet appeared.

"Lay your sleeping head, my love", written in January 1937, is one of the century's most famous lyrics. Many of its key phrases come directly from W. B. Yeats: the "living creature" from "The Poet Pleads with the Elemental Powers";

"the entirely beautiful" from "A Prayer for My Daughter"; and the "stroke of midnight" from "Broken Dreams". The poem's final cadence comes from Yeats's "A Prayer for My Son". The latter poem ends with thoughts about "A woman and a man" protecting Yeats's sleeping son "till the danger past, / With human love"; Auden's poem, also about a sleeping boy, ends: "Nights of insult let you pass / Watched by every human love". "A Prayer for My Son" also provides the note of anxiety about the beloved's future.

Auden writes more delicately, but still in strikingly threatened terms, about the loss of "Certainty, fidelity", about "fashionable madmen" and those "Nights of insult". (No doubt the sense of havoc and uncertainty in Europe in the mid-193s – with, in H. A. L. Fisher's words, "one emergency following upon another, as wave follows upon wave" – accounts for the note of trepidation in Auden's poem.) The poem addressed by an adult to a sleeping child is a traditional scenario, of course, and Coleridge's "Frost at Midnight" is another example to which Auden's lyric seems to allude.

But Yeats's rhetoric in Auden's poem seems to crowd out more distant references. Poets often make cryptic play with the names of their lovers – Yeats did it, for example, in "Fallen Majesty", where he imagines himself the sole surviving witness to the glory of what was Maud Gonne: "this hand alone... records what's gon[n]e". Here Auden matches, with identical last words, Yeats's poem about "my Michael", Michael Yeats (who died in Ireland recently), with a poem about his own homophonically identical Michael Yates. The identity of the sleeper in Auden's poem had to remain veiled; but the love that dared not speak its beloved's name in 1937 could at least whisper it through the language of parallelism and allusion.

As well as using Yeats's "A Prayer for My Son" to cipher Michael Yates's name into his own poem, Auden invokes it to explore the similarities and differences of his own case to that of a father and son. When "Lay your sleeping head, my love" was written, Auden was nearly thirty, Yates sixteen. Auden's feelings for his lover surely included a sense of protectiveness which we conventionally but limitingly associate with the feeling of parents for their children. And, indeed, in the only public statement that Yates ever made about his relationship with Auden, evidently embarrassed, he chose the parent-child analogy, while acknowledging its obvious lack of a perfect fit:

There was this considerable affection, you know, which I had for him too in a way. I suppose you could use the word "son", but that wasn't quite his feeling.

This is the point of Auden's inserted "every" in the final line of his poem: "Watched by every human love", including, that is, not just the love of parents for their children but the socially unsanctioned love of a man for a boy half his age. Many of the important and more "subversive" meanings of Auden's lyric come from its juxtaposed relation to Yeats's poem. But because Michael Yates's relation to Auden was only recently made public, no one has previously linked "A Prayer for My Son" and "Lay your sleeping head, my love".

Among other crucial episodes in Auden's life, almost nothing has yet been published about his meetings with anarchists in Spain in 1937, or his visit to Nazi Berlin in January 1939. Such events matter, not because the life somehow authenticates the poetry, but because knowledge of them often clarifies some of the deeper structures of his poems. Thus, Auden's poem Spain is, as critics have frequently remarked, at war with itself, pulling in two directions at once.

But why? Because the international Left was at war with itself about how to respond to Franco's uprising in Spain. Auden's poem dramatizes that being in two minds: the communist centralizing drive towards a single poetic message, a "mando único" of "to-day", conflicts with an anarchistic, centrifugal, image-based enactment of poetic libertad "to-morrow". Auden's, and the Left's, experiences of Spain are formalized as two contending modes of organizing the poem. But without knowledge of his actual meetings both with orthodox Party members and with dissident anarchists on the Aragon Front, this far-reaching but stylized account of the "struggle" on the Republican side is hard to explain.

Another difficulty we face is that "Auden" now means so many different things to different people. In The Changing

Light at Sandover, again, James Merrill captures Auden's characteristic shape-shifting by having him surface in the afterlife sporting a "NEW PROLE BODY". And in terms of literary influence all sorts of writers have found something in him to follow. For example, the young Derek Walcott was introduced to Auden's work on the little island of St Lucia by the poet and educator James Rodway, who owned a collection of Faber books of poetry.

"I remember, during that period, reading Auden with a tremendous amount of elation, a lot of excitement, and discovery", Walcott has recollected. "I think Auden actually dared a lot more than either Pound or Eliot. I think his intellect was far more adventurous, far braver, far stronger, and far more reckless than either of them – plus, of course, there was also that tremendous intelligence behind the poetry." Echoes of Auden are everywhere in Walcott's own early poems. And when Walcott compiled and published his first book of poetry, 25 Poems, in 1949, he indicated how much those Faber volumes meant to him. His biographer explains that he "used a Faber volume of Auden as the typographical model.... He wanted a typeface that looked like one of the Faber volumes".

Auden's impact on poetry extended outside the English language. Auden became, in the 194s and after, the poet of a deliberately willed uprootedness; he turned himself into the first great poet of that most symptomatic of all social groups in the modern world: those who will not or cannot go home. Correspondingly, his works have slipped back and forth across cultural and linguistic borders. The young Yehuda Amichai served in the all-volunteer "Palestinian Brigade" in the British Army during the Second World War, and was stationed in Egypt. There he somehow picked up a Faber anthology of modern poetry, and was deeply affected by what he saw as the wryness and unpoetical flatness of Auden's work. It encouraged him to explore the use of a Hebrew deprived of traditional rhetorical flourishes and melitzah (melody or sweetness).

Although he had grown up speaking German and wrote his poems in Hebrew, Amichai told an interviewer around 198 that "he was most influenced not by the German poets, as one would expect, but by English poet W. H. Auden".

But to think of Auden's influence in merely literary terms is to place an unnatural limit on the ways in which his works have travelled through culture. Like Elizabeth Bishop or Sylvia Plath, Auden is a poet with "reach" – a figure of international stature within the realm of literature, but at the same time read by people who do not normally read much, or any, poetry. Even during his lifetime he was "scattered among a hundred cities", where readers often made sense of their lives, and on occasion their likely deaths, through his words. A young mathematician named David Haden Guest, serving in the International Brigades in Spain, wrote to his old tutor in England in July 1938, and cited the most famous phrase from Auden's poem about the civil war to justify his own involvement in it:

I have myself a lively and intense desire to explore whole fields of theoretical work, mathematical, physical, logical, and far beyond these when the conditions for this will become again possible. But, of course, this is not possible now. "Today the struggle". There were only a few more "todays" for Haden Guest: he was killed by a sniper at the Battle of the Ebro later that month. Faced with his work's implication in stories such as this, it is no wonder that Auden was desperate to believe, probably against all his deeper instincts, that "poetry makes nothing happen".

Ian McEwan was thus spot on when he made Robbie Turner, one of the central figures in Atonement, keep on his bookshelves a talismanic copy of Auden's Poems and an autographed copy of The Dance of Death . During the disaster of Dunkirk, the text which Robbie carries into "the storm of approaching German armour" is a London Mercury clipping of Auden's poem "In Memory of W. B. Yeats", folded together with a letter from his lover in the top pocket of his uniform, near his heart. Auden's poem becomes the explanatory voice of the fictional character's experience. While Robbie watches the detonations lighting up the sky, he remembers lines from the poem (he has them literally by heart): "In the nightmare of the dark / All the dogs of Europe bark". More positively, Auden once claimed that the "nicest poetic compliment" he ever received came in 1957 when his friend the Catholic activist Dorothy Day was arrested and held at what was then called the "House of Detention for Women" at the corner of 6th Avenue and West 1th Street in Manhattan.

She told him that as the women prisoners were marched down for their weekly shower, a prostitute recited the last line of Auden's poem "First Things First" (which had recently appeared in the New Yorker): "Thousands have lived without love, not one without water". "When I heard this", Auden commented, not wholly ironically, "I knew I hadn't written in vain!" Such moments testify to the ways in which a readership actually uses (rather than just reads) a writer's work.

Auden's language can seem as if it has worked its way like a gas into every cranny of modern culture. His libretti, with Kallman, for Britten, Stravinsky, Henze aside, there are innumerable "classical" settings of Auden's poetry all the way from Benjamin Britten's and Lennox Berkeley's early works in the 193s, and Elizabeth Lutyens's and Leonard Bernstein's in the 194s onwards to the present.

Although Auden came to be associated with the "high" world of opera, he drew on popular song lyrics, such as those of Cole Porter, in his own poetry. Now his writing has cycled back into the world of pop. For instance, Michael Bracewell, calling on Auden's "sexual difference, residence in pre-War Europe and a fascination with the glamour of science and technology", has even identified him as the "grandfather of the robot dandys" of early 198s synthpop such as Gary Numan, Kraftwerk and The Human League.

More recently, the former fashion diva Carla Bruni released an album, No Promises, which features an Auden-scripted song "Lady Weeping at the Crossroads"; and the singer Lois has a number called "A Summer Long", which includes the lines: "'Nights of insult let you pass / Watched by every human love' / That's the page that I tore out / And pasted to the wall above". (The quoted lines are "torn" from "Lay your sleeping head, my love".) These stray examples suggest how pervasively Auden's work is now a part of the cultural weather of our time. Two recent events added peculiar impetus and width to the "scattering" of Auden. When the Princess of Wales was killed in a car crash in Paris on August 31, 1997, many British people gave themselves over to unprecedented expressions of communal grief. Great mounds of cut flowers appeared all over London, especially outside Buckingham Palace and Kensington Palace; and according to one report, there were cards from "every corner of the globe", including, "inevitably, lines from W. H. Auden, immortalized in Four Weddings and a Funeral" (the 1994 film in which the John Hannah character recited Auden's "Funeral Blues" – "Stop all the clocks", etc. – over his lover's coffin). In the following days, that poem seemed to be everywhere.

Discussing arrangements for the funeral, a leader in The Times recalled a great poem written for a state funeral, Tennyson's "Ode on the Death of the Duke of Wellington", but concluded that a different tone was wanted now: "Not Tennyson's pomp and circumstance but Auden's sad lines... strike the right note". Since then, the poem has been recited at tens of thousands of private funeral services across Britain. In this case, too, Auden would surely have felt that he had not "written in vain".

The public response to Auden's "Funeral Blues" was remarkable. But the mass recourse to his "September 1, 1939" four years later was even more striking. Though Auden more than once disowned it as "trash" or a "damned lie" or "infected with an incurable dishonesty", this intensely dramatic poem had already enjoyed a long public life. It is one of those very rare poems, like Yeats's "Easter, 1916" or Allen Ginsberg's "Howl", which re-enters history to become itself an event.

Auden published the poem in a periodical in 1939 and in his book Another Time in 194. Almost immediately it was circulating in the Anglo-American cultural bloodstream. The April 6, 194 issue of a Communist newsletter called Report to Our Colleagues, probably written by J. Robert Oppenheimer (later to become the "father" of the Atomic Bomb), attacked Roosevelt, argued against American participation in the

European war, and had a quotation from Auden's poem as its epigraph. A year later, the popular British novelist Robert Westerby published Hunger Allows No Choice, a title culled from the eighth stanza of "September 1, 1939". Indeed, the poem has been a fruitful source of titles for many other authors: for W. Michael Reisman's Folded Lies , an exploration of corruption and bribery, as well as Larry Kramer's play The Normal Heart ; for Madelon Powers's Faces Along the Bar , a cheery history of saloons, as well as Allen Weinstein's The Haunted Wood , a fevered history of Soviet espionage, and, inevitably, Robert G. L. Waite's The Psychopathic God: Adolf Hitler . Some phrases from the poem have done double service: David Patterson has published The Affirming Flame: Religion, language, literature , and Maurice S. Friedman The Affirming Flame: A poetics of meaning . From Lyndon Johnson to Dan Quayle, presidents and presidential candidates, or their speechwriters, have similarily ransacked the poem for nuggets of rhetoric. (With the uses of his earlier poem in mind, Auden condemned, in "Ode to a Terminus", 1968, "all / self-proclaimed poets who, to wow an / audience, utter some resonant lie".)

On or around September 11, 21, however, "September 1, 1939" began a quite new chapter in its existence. As people sought to come to terms with the events of that day, the usually marginal genre of poetry became very popular; and this watershed poem of Auden's in particular felt uncannily fresh, as if somehow it had been written after, and about, the event which it preceded by more than sixty years. What might be called the first poem of the Second World War was taken up on what seems like the threshhold of another period of global conflict. The more formal manifestations of the poem's revival might have been predictable: it was read at impromptu memorials by Adrienne Rich and Paul Muldoon and others. But the poem was suddenly meaningful not just to literary readers, to politically engaged citizens of the Right and Left, or to newscasters and pundits, but also to "ordinary" people. It worked temporarily as Dr Johnson said Gray's "Elegy" did, as a poem which "abounds with images which find a mirror in every mind, and with sentiments to which every bosom returns an echo". On September 18, 21, Eric McHenry posted an article about Auden's poem on Slate's "Culturebox" section. McHenry's piece was titled by the Slate editors "Auden on Bin Laden". It began:

Last Wednesday I e-mailed W. H. Auden's poem "September 1, 1939" to members of my family. Two days later a friend e-mailed it to me, having received it from another friend who was circulating it. On Saturday my mother told me that Scott Simon had read portions of it on NPR. And Monday my wife, a prep school teacher, saw it lying on the faculty photocopy machine. The poem also began to emerge in the discursive hinterland of the Web, the newsgroups. In one typical instance, after another person had posted some of Auden's lines to express her feelings about what happened on September 11, "Ilene B", a correspondent to a newsgroup for people without children, commented on September 13:

I'm reminded of the beginning of the Gulf War. I was working nights at an AIDS hospice, and had just joined the Army Medical Reserves. I was hanging around the hospice kitchen, taking a break from CNN. Someone had handwritten, framed and posted the Auden poem, "September 1, 1939". I just kept reading the line, "We must love each other or die". It was very poignant. On September17,21, "G*rd*n", posting to alt.society.anarchy, wrote:I went into the city today to see what the 21st century looks likc. There were cops, firemen, construction types, generator trailers, dust and ashes everywhere – not very pretty. I learned that "the unmentionable odour of death" is not always a metaphor.

"September 1, 1939" seemed, as one post on another site put it, "Better words than I can summon... to describe the sense of dread most people feel right now". And the poem has since become redefined, at least for now, as a "peace text". At a march in Adelaide, South Australia, in February 23, to protest against the imminent invasion of Iraq, a placard read: "I and the public know / What all schoolchildren learn, / Those to whom evil is done / Do evil in return. / W. H. AUDEN".

Auden as prophet; Auden as thinker; Auden as activist;

Auden as comforter – all these figures were alive in people's minds in recent years. The words of "September 1, 1939" have been appropriated by speechwriters; xeroxed and distributed by political dissidents; hung up in an AIDS hospice kitchen; intoned on the radio; photo copied in prep schools; displayed at the close of a TV news show; posted on a thousand websites. All these scenes and moments evoke the ways and contexts in which poems gain and lose meaning, get re-read, re-thought and re-deployed. They are instances of the infinitely diverse and circumstantial routes by which a piece of writing moves through a culture.

But what if you want, not to pore over the sum of different readings of Auden, but instead to get back to the source, to Auden's poetry in its own historical moment? How easy is that? Auden's own late, neurotic obsession with revising his poetry is well-known. Edward Mendelson has steadfastly maintained that the elder Auden knew what he was doing when he reworked earlier poems. But most readers think the opposite: that precisely because Auden was such a metamorphic poet, he found it almost impossible to work himself back into the inspirational mood or to re-experience the historical pressures bearing on a poem's composition.

The general verdict has been that almost everything of the young poet's which the old poet touched with his blue biro turned to ash. But in returning to the "original" versions of poems such as "Spain" or "In Memory of W. B. Yeats", perhaps we of the majority persuasion have congratulated ourselves on our own good judgement too soon. Auden seems to lose every skirmish over earlier and later versions of the same poem. But to an unacknowledged degree, he has consistently been winning the larger interpretive war. As Auden turns 1, it is thus striking to see how lastingly successful the later Auden, and a few literary friends, have been in establishing the basic outlines of his career and work.

There is thus the metaphorical issue of his "eyesight". Later in life Auden came to define himself as a non-visual writer and to make much symbolic play on his personal short-sightedness. Readers have responded by playing down the "visual" qualities of his writing – even though we know him to have been an enthusiastic photographer through the 193s. The idea of Auden's unvisual imagination begins with the first and most potent of all the Auden mythographers, Christopher Isherwood. In Lions and Shadows , the first description offered of the very young "Weston" is that his "normal expression was the misleadingly ferocious frown common to people with very short sight"; and many years later when Isherwood re-encounters Weston he finds "his small pale yellow eyes... screwed painfully together in the same short-sighted scowl".

Until Lions and Shadows appeared, Auden's poetry had been characterized by the critics as marked by clarity, "hardness", stark imagery, striking details. The reviews of Look, Stranger! refer repeatedly to Auden's visual power. Dilys Powell saluted his poetry's "ability to surprise and excite by its images and metaphors", praising one poem as "a piece of precise description". F. R. Leavis, in the course of an extremely hostile review, acknowledged "those striking and so characteristic phrases and images". And Janet Adam Smith highlighted the way in which Auden's "hoard" of "phrases, gestures, actions" are always enough to provide "him with the effective word and image".

As far as I have been able to establish, Auden made only two references to his being short-sighted in all the time between March 1922, when he took up poetry at the age of fifteen, and March 1941. It seems as if the myth about the literary significance of Auden's short sight was created by Isherwood (eager, of course, to monopolize the "camera aesthetic" for his own writing) in Lions and Shadows, and then taken up by Auden and others. In March 1938, Geoffrey Grigson, one of Auden's great supporters, reviewed Isherwood's book enthusiastically, calling it "a reference and key book of the Auden Age and the Auden Circle". Less than a year later, when Grigson picked a public quarrel with Auden over the latter's advocacy of the paintings of William Coldstream, he used ammunition that Isherwood had put in his hands. Aside from rubbishing Coldstream, Grigson attacked "short-sighted" Auden for daring to have such an opinion about art when "he has many of the most sensitive and visually expert persons in England against him in this business".

In a way that is not untypical of the masochistic streak in his persona, Auden began to think creatively about the implications of his "deficiency" of short-sightedness only after it had been highlighted for him, thrust in his face if you like, by Isherwood and Grigson. From the early 194s on, it was something that he started to emphasize. At a banquet at Yale in 1941, Auden criticized "our distrust of language and mathematics, those two great instruments by which we relate the particular to the universal, fact to pattern, our fear of making children learn by heart, our indulgence of the visual sense, as exemplified by Life Magazine". A week or so later he was telling Stephen Spender that "I unfortunately lack your great gifts of sensual perception but they are not in my nature and I shall never have them".

Spender subsequently described his first meeting with Auden in World Within World (the meeting occurred in 1928; the book was written in the late 194s) in something like Isherwood's terms: "Auden, after having cast a myopic, clinically appraising glance in my direction, did not address a word to me". Recounting his first visit to Auden's rooms in Christ Church, Spender again focused on the eyes: "He had almost albino hair and weakly pigmented eyes set closely together, so that they gave the impression of watchfully squinting". Spender prided himself, not unjustly, on the sensory immediacy of his poetry. And consciously or not, this description of his friend makes Auden deficient in the area in which he himself was strongest. In this way, his own poetry's character was differentiated and protected from the encroachments of Auden's altogether more potent literary persona. From these promptings, critics have come almost programmatically to play down the often remarkable "visual" aspect of Auden's early writing. In this they have taken the hint too readily from Isherwood, and from the middle and late Auden, a figure always active, occasionally forgetful and exceptionally adroit at stage-managing critical understandings of his early career. These sly hints and signals by Auden, joined with the images of myopia drawn by Isherwood and Spender, soon became a misleading critical platitude. In the year following Auden's death, for instance, the critic Geoffrey Thurley spoke (not unapprovingly) of "Auden's deficiency in local actualization", commenting that "I seem to remember a famous critic dismissing Auden with the remark that he 'couldn't pass an optician's test'; yet in fact Auden's notorious short-sightedness made a positive contribution to his art". In his biography of Auden, Humphrey Carpenter writes completely wrongly of the teenage poet that he had not written many poems like this before he realised he had no real aptitude for noticing the details of nature. He put this down largely to defective sight.... In fact, none of his senses seemed to be highly developed; everything had to be scanned by his intellect before he could really become aware of it.... He eventually made his lack of sense-perception into a virtue.

Short sight thus became part of the distorting iconography which still defines Auden as a poet indifferent to the outer world, deaf and blind to sensory life, unfeeling, unimaginative – in short, that unappealing freak, an intellectual poet. This is a travesty of his poetry.

One task for readers of Auden's poetry, then, is to detach his work from the fables and half-truths, many of them originating with Auden, which currently enshroud it. That Auden felt wholly unaffected by the First World War; that he took no interest in politics before he went to Berlin, and had no idea what the 1926 General Strike, in which he briefly drove a car for the TUC, was about; that he read Freud while at school; that he was a supremely self-confident individual; that he never had dreams; and that he identified strongly with his mother, and not with his father; all these shibboleths can be traced back to the writings of the later Auden and such carefully indiscreet friends and allies as Spender and Isherwood, both of whom had a stake in creating a particular myth of him. None of them is actually true.

In the same way, we have more generally to re-address the question of his early politics. Doubtless in the 193s Auden believed himself to be a well-meaning "bourgeois" and a "selfish pink old Liberal", leaning further left than right. But whatever Auden does not speak of, we cannot pass over in silence. Again and again, Auden's poetry in the 193s swings towards writing about England or Britain as a blessed enclave momentarily exempt from the terrifying pressures of history, both literally and figuratively an island. And within England, Auden's imagination often sought out further nests or retreats, places protected, for example, by the "creepered wall" of "this English house" which shuts out threatening "multitudes"; immured in "gardens where we feel secure" and, "gentle, do not care to know, / Where Poland draws her eastern bow".

Up to the year 1936, the young Auden generated poems of intense feeling by putting a small, tightly-knit group of friends in such sheltered spaces. Here Auden and others hoped that a new, more modest, modern and humane national character – uncontaminated by the nation's escapades during the delirium induced by capitalism, militarism, industrialism and imperialism – might emerge. If there was less of a certain kind of left-leaning politics in Auden's poetry in the early 193s, that does not mean that there was no politics at all. A good clue to the political solutions he envisaged is given by the frequency of the words "England" or "English" in these poems: as when he writes about "our English land" (in "Get there if you can..."), or the "English earth" (in The Orators, an "English study"), "the English heart" (in "In the year of my youth..."), or "the English cell" (in Part Two of "A Happy New Year").

Auden's voice coalesced in the early 193s, a period which witnessed what one commentator describes as a moment in which the "anglicization of Continental styles and values was being openly contested by a militant cultural nationalism". In this context, some readers saw Auden not as an anglicized version of Bertolt Brecht or Ernst Toller but as – deep down – a dangerously right-wing writer. This view was not limited to those committed socialists who bemoaned Auden's bourgeois eccentricity and artistic individualism. The liberal Isaiah Berlin, for example, wrote to a friend in 1935 that "it is as though Auden, fundamentally a patriotic poet, writes most eloquently when vaguely fascist, & conscientiously has to transfer this to the enemy because people he respects are all left-wing". Berlin's statement seems extreme, but it is true to say that the young Auden in his verse was "fundamentally a patriotic poet" in the early 193s, albeit one who did not lapse into a crude or explicit chauvinism.

In Theory of the Avant-Garde , Peter Bürger located the rise of the avant-garde in Europe, with its mandate to re-integrate the arts and society, in the late 191s, with the advent of Dadaism and the art of montage. His field of reference is insistently, and perhaps parochially, Germanic. In an Anglo-American context, the moment came later and from the right, in the 193s, when writers such as Yeats, Eliot, Pound and Auden sought to close the gap between art and everyday life. With that attempt came hopes that poets would regain some of the prophetic authority they had lost since the Enlightenment. In a country traumatized by her war losses, by class strife, economic malaise, and cultural pessimism, Auden imagined that his poetry would play a regenerative role; he aspired, without turning poetry into "agit-prop", to make it instrumental, diagnostic and curative again.

And Auden's poetry did play that role, for some people, if only imaginatively. We have already seen how Anthony Haden Guest used Auden's poetry to justify his own involvement in the Spanish Civil War. Another instance of Auden's charismatic relation to his audience is that of Charles Madge (later to become an important British sociologist), who had been suffering from a debilitating spinal disease which forced him to lie flat on his back for long periods. He describes in his poem "Letter to the Intelligentsia" the symbolically uplifting effect of this new poetry:

But there waited for me in the summer
morning,
Auden, fiercely. I read, shuddered and knew
And all the world's stationary things
In silence moved to take up new positions.

Madge casts himself as a cerebral Lazarus, raised from the dead by the curing power of Auden's work.

Like the later T. S. Eliot, Auden in the early years of his career attempted to write the poetry of revived and redefined Englishness, of life in small, rural and often same-sex collectives in the southern half of the country, where he hoped a revitalization of the national spirit might take place. (One such site was The Downs School, at the foot of Elgars's Malverns, where Auden met Michael Yates.) This was the world of poems such as "Out on the lawn I lie in bed" and "Look, stranger, on this island now", the time when Auden referred to himself as a "Little Englander" and began to conceive of his own mind as a map of the national psyche, believing that the symbols he instinctively gravitated towards in his poems were "national emblems".

Auden, then, was a "patriotic poet", a celebrant of a closed, predominantly male, English Gemeinschaft, and one who believed that contact with England was an essential precondition of his inspiration. Wyndham Lewis, one of the younger Auden's favourite authors, wrote in 1927:

To be "young" is to be in impulsive "revolt": so a youth-movement must be a "radical" movement, it is felt. But the most characteristic, and the most admirable, "youth-movements" in Europe to-day are not at all "radical", but quite the reverse... Europe has had the lessons of War and Revolution burnt into it.

This was, to a marked degree, true of Auden and the writers gathered round him. But far from being a socialist or left-leaning liberal as is usually assumed, Auden, as a few of his readers noticed, was something much more like an idealistic, lyric nationalist. In the early 193s Auden privately went so far as to acknowledge a "tendency to National Socialism" in an English context, and he longed for what he called in one poem "an eternal tie" with his nation, with the "island". Modernity's three great ideological inventions have been communism, fascism and nationalism. Fascism collapsed in 1945. Communism crumbled across most of the world in the late 198s and early 199s. But in a multiplicity of different forms, nationalism, the oldest of the three, has proved the most durable. In the words of one scholar, it is the "single red line" that "traverses the history of the modern world from the fall of the Bastille to the fall of the Berlin Wall". As such, the phenomenon of "nation-ness", reaching as deeply into our lives as a sexual or religious identity, cannot be judged by moral criteria alone: the nation-state and the collective solidarity promoted by nationalism in the 192s and 193s are historical facts. And so it is with Auden's lyric nationalism. By reorienting discussion of his politics away from the left-right axis on to the ground of nationalism and its opposites, it becomes clear that, early and late, one of the fundamental features of Auden's poetry is its engagement with, first, national belonging, and then with the consequences of disaffiliation from national ties. It was because Auden began his career as a poetic nationalist that he could later reach for a "new rhetoric" and evolve into the most important cosmopolitan poet of the century.

Schlegel called the historian "a prophet looking backwards". If we want to know who Auden will be in his second century, the best thing we can do is return to his cultural origins, to the world in which, a hundred years ago, he began. It was a world of virulent nationalisms, of strong collective bonds to class and country, and one in which the precondition of gaining a reputation as a "great" poet was to be recognized as a "national voice". The next hundred years of Auden's work should start, then, not with a candid appraisal of his virtues or vices, as Auden himself attempted in "My Epitaph", nor of his "ideas", but with a fresh account, free from the thrall of the older man's self-conceptions and impositions, of why Auden's poetry took the forms and themes it did – then on that island.

Communist Poetry of the 193s and Modernism

Virginia Woolf's critique of 193s poetry as being too often an exercise in didacticism is perhaps warranted from an overall perspective. The overwhelming import of the fascist threat that rose in Franco's Spain, however, holds a unique place in the literary history of this time. The Spanish Civil War served as a call to arms that legitimised for many the embrace of a far-left alternative to awaken the closed eyes of many in Britain and throughout Europe. As the subject for the adoption of a loudspeaker mentality, very few moments in modern history are more deserving. What may be lost amid the generalised opinion of Virginia Woolf is that so many of those poets had but one issue to drive them. Far more instructive in analysing her assertion is how writers of talent who chose to tackle the issue of radical liberalism succeeded or failed. The real question that must be addressed is whether active engagement with beliefs is better suited to turning propaganda into art, or whether the key lies in detached, observational analysis. In other words, is propaganda more likely to reach the level of art if one is fully or only partly committed to the cause?

W. H. Auden was never a card-carrying member of the Communist Party, but like so many artists and intellectuals of the time his response to the widespread advancement of fascism manifested itself in the embrace of certain leftist ideals commonly associated with the Party. Although the iconic symbol of the dangers of right wing extremism today is Hitler, Germany and the Nazis, for most of the 193s the poster boy for all that progressive liberalism hated was located in Spain and that face was Francisco Franco. The Spanish Civil War provide fodder for many archetypal modernist works of art, from Ernest Hemingway's novel For Whom the Bell Tolls to Pablo Picasso's massive mural Guernica, neither of which can escape the critique of being at least partly didactic. In those days before the rise of the Soviet Union and threat of nuclear annihilation, it was still not yet dangerous to be a fellow Traveller, Communist sympathiser or just plain Red. Seen from that perspective, then, Auden's poem "A Communist to Others" need not necessarily by its very title and subject be designated mere propaganda.

It might be considered more highly if it was; as it is "A Communist to Others" suffers the fate of much proletarian literature in that it is crafted with unfortunate tones of an intellectual speaking down to the common worker while positioning himself as one of them. The consciousness that infuses this poem is one that is, fortunately, entirely aware of that particular paradox: "We cannot put on airs with you / The fears that hurt you hurt us too." The speaker is recognising the distance that exists while promising not to become merely a dialectician conducting a seminar in class consciousness. That sentiment is undermined, however, by the lines that come directly after: "Only we say / That like all nightmares these are fake / If you would help us we could make / Our eyes to open, and awake / Shall find night day."

On the surface, these lines appear to indicate that the elitist is placing himself in a somewhat submissive position, as if asking for help suggests that his capacity is not enough without assistance of the comrades being addressed. It is that "Only we say" that is troubling, however, in regard to Woolf's observation that the poetry of this era often gives in to the danger of becoming a didactic, secular sermon sanctifying not the opium of the masses, but Marxian theory. Like a religious sermon urging potential converts to the word of Jesus Christ, a secular sermon is probably not best served with a generous helping of subtlety.

Of course, the interpretation that Auden's poem is a workers rights polemic becomes more complex if, as Stephen Spender asserts, the poem is for Auden "`an exercise in entering a point of view not his own'." In addition, Spender makes the claim that it was precisely because Auden was not a Communist who could write, but a writer who was sympathetic to some aspects of the ideology who was also conscious of its limitations that he could better write artistically on the subject matter. When viewed from that perspective, however, the poem is all the more a failure. If even a somewhat detached engagement with political propaganda can seem so heavy-handed at times, then Woolf's assessment about the preachy quality of 3's poetry rings true.

Unfortunately, Spender may have been mistaken in his assertion that a true believer was not better equipped to write about leftist ideology. John Cornford certainly does not allow for interpreting his poetry as an exercise; he was a committed Communist. Under Spender's terms, then, his poetry should be less successful than Auden at artistic propaganda. At least in terms of "Full Moon at Tierz" this is debatable. While the final exhortation of the poem urging readers to "Raise the red flag triumphantly / For Communism and for liberty" certainly sounds like something that may have been lifted straight out of Karl Marx's The Communist Manifesto, or a fiery 1917 speech by Lenin, the elegant nuance of what comes before makes Auden's detachment all the more didactic in comparison. "Here, too, our freedom's swaying on the scales. / O understand before it's too late / Freedom was never held without a fight. / Freedom is an easily spoken word" is poetry that, separated from its subject matter, could be applied to any political literature. In fact, its lyrical quality is closer to an anthem. Or, possibly, a love poem.

That is the missing ingredient from Auden's "Communist" poem and Cornford and presents the crux of the problem of Spender's assertion. While doubtlessly a committed Communist could place ideology over art, the same can be said of any poet and any firmly held conviction. What Woolf's criticism is really driving at is that Modernist poets had to turn their backs on Romanticism as part of the effort to define themselves by what they weren't. The poets of this era had witnessed amazing technological achievements as well as unbelievable horrors. As a result, the literature of this period was typically pessimistic and at times deeply cynical. It was a clarion call to the masses who had been hypnotised by the technological progress, but who were too quick to suppress the unspeakable evil that could be waged with that technology. In the midst of sounding a wake-up call there was little time for such flights of fancy as love poems.

Instead, the romantic feelings of many 193s writers were sublimated into a passion toward stemming the tide of fascism creeping across Europe. In a very real way, "Full Moon at Tierza" is a romantic poem as much as it is propaganda. The tone is certainly not one of Woolf's loudspeaker, although its allusions to specific Communist events and figures like the Seventh Congress and Dimitrov disallows the idea that it is not in any way didactic. What Cornford does that Auden does not, however, is balance the message with vibrant imagery and a personal conviction. What is certainly clear is Cornford believes more than Auden; what else is clear is Cornford sincerely views the Communist cause as a means toward establishing equality. His embrace of the ideology is on full display in "Full Moon at Tierza" and that embrace carries with it another supremely importance difference between Cornford and Auden; one that undermines completely Spender's argument.

The language and imagery in "Full Moon at Tierza" is the work of someone who doesn't merely write about his beliefs, but cherishes them the way another person might cherish a lover. More than that, Cornford lives them. Cornford's Communist beliefs are grounded in the fact that he was also an activist, and that he saw firsthand the horror of the opponent. If Auden's poem feels like an elitist speaking down to the working class, Cornford's poem feels like one worker talking lovingly about the possibility of achieving equality to another worker. Like any good propagandist, or preacher, in this poem Cornford, proving Spender wrong, combines the larger ideological message complete with its expected didactic qualities with a far more subtle personal message of conviction. With "Full Moon at Tierza" John Cornford gives ample enough evidence to tarnish the clear ring of truth in Woolf's assertion.

Even more unfortunate from the perspective of both Woolf and Spender is that Cornford is able to achieve the same effect even when his language is stripped of its romantic qualities and he is acting as a reporter. When "A Letter from Aragon" is analysed alongside "Full Moon at Tierza" it becomes apparent that in the hands of a true believer function eclipses form. In style, Aragon appears to have far more in common with Auden's poem than Tierza. Both are clearly propagandistic and polemical, and both affirm the causes of liberalism.

But while Auden's rhetoric lacks a fiery centre and betrays his alienation from the words he is writing, Cornford's admittedly preachy content builds to an undeniably blistering call to arms that positions the workers in Auden's poem as the potential victims of fascism. Here there is precious little evidence of the romantic imagery that fills the Tierza poem; Cornford proves that even a true believer can look at the situation in unsentimental terms and write passionately about it. That is to say, with passionate language. Even though the word choice in this poem is less elegant than, say, the "freedom" passage from Tiera quoted above, and even though it often comes across as bare, stripped-down, reportage it nonetheless manages to display the very same passionate conviction that Tierza contains.

If "Cornford is using poetry as a vehicle for politics" (Brown 25, 1960) then these poems both serve to illuminate the point that while perhaps not all 1930s poetry could avoid engaging in pedagogy to the detriment of artistry, it could be done. Because both of Cornford's poems are so vastly different in tone, language and syntax, they represent a strong case against Woolf's assertion. Even more so is the fact that in the more "romantic" poem Cornford introduces more stringently propagandistic language at times, including the far less elegant conclusion, and yet still manages to turn it into a love song of Communism. Eschewing the loving indoctrination of a fellow worker with luscious imagery in "A Letter from Aragon", he still manages to convey the same feeling.

What is strikingly pronounced in this poem is that despite seeming to be more didactic and propagandistic than "Full Moon at Tierza", it actually contains far less overtly pedagogical instruction on the subject of communism and ideology. It is practically impossible to imagine a writer such as Auden—one who was not fully committed to the communist cause—being capable of writing both these poems. Indeed, in the hands of many lesser artists or less committed Communists, the result in both cases would seem almost predetermined to end up categorically confirming Woolf's contention, while at the same also categorically refuting Spender's.

Doubtlessly, Virginia Woolf is at least partially correct in her assessment of 193s poetry as very often being little more than a vehicle to instruct on the political and social causes of the day. Yet, as the subject for loudspeaker poetry, the hope for a society based on equality seems particularly fitting. While many poets celebrated by the leftist movement specifically for their ideological certainty are now forgotten in part due to lack of artistry in promoting an agenda, the cases of Auden and Cornford are unique. Both were excellent poets in their own right. The fact that Auden fails to counteract Woolf's thesis while Cornford succeeds in the presentation of two distinctly different stylistic imperatives to action requires a reassessment of the very idea that propaganda and art cannot co-exist.

Giving Things Their Proper Names: Carl Linnaeus and W. H. Auden

This year we celebrate the 3th anniversary of Carl Linnaeus whose binomial system has made it unlikely that the names of living things will perish. We also celebrate the 1th anniversary of Wystan Hugh Auden who gave his time the proper name: The Age of Anxiety.

An avatar of the 18th century Enlightenment, Linnaeus set the stage for Darwin by recognizing similarities between man and ape: he named our species Homo sapiens. In an age when the word was unspoken, Linnaeus recognized that even plants had sex. He put Sweden on the map of natural science and changed forever the way we label living things.

An avatar of the Enlightened Left in the 20th century, Auden brought English poetry into the modern world: he set planes and trains and automobiles to verse. At a time when "In the nightmare of the dark /All the dogs of Europe bark," while Yeats was chasing the Celtic occult, and T. S. Eliot worried over "Murder in the Cathedral," Auden addressed Murder in Madrid. And after Guernica and the Hitler war, he retained high hope for a new world of reason, paying our profession a compliment we barely deserve:

The true men of action in our time, those who transform the world, are not the politicians and the statesmen, but the scientists. When I find myself in the company of scientists, I feel like a shabby curate who has strayed by mistake into a drawing room full of dukes.

Linnaeus, King of Flowers: The images of Linnaeus and

Auden show them in the process of forging the temper of their time. Both were prodigies: Linnaeus proclaimed not immodestly "Before the age of 23, I had thought out everything." He may have been right. By 174, "Carolus Linnaeus, Med. Doc." had become the founder and first president of the Royal Swedish Academy of Science and was also practicing medicine in Stockholm. After seven years of medical study and botanical research in Lund and Uppsala, Linnaeus earned his M.D. from the University of Harderwijk, a Dutch diploma mill that exists no longer.

In the same year he gained international attention for his Systema Natura . Linnaeus' first effort at botanical nomenclature at age 22 had been "Præludia sponsaliorum plantarum" [A Prelude to the Wedding of Plants], based in good part on his 23 mile collecting trip through Lapland to the Arctic Ocean. The Systema Natura went further into the maze of gender. He divided plants into classes by the number of "male genitals," the stamens, and then into orders by their pistils, the female "genitals." The supporting structure, the calyx, became the "nuptial bed." His sexual taxonomy may have gone a tad overboard, with some structures compared to labia minora and majora, and an entire class of flowers named Clitoria .

Whatever the sexual overtones, Linnaean botany was not only proved correct but heuristic, based as it was on specimens collected worldwide. In Sweden, Linnaeus had gathered plants from Lapland to the Baltic; in Leiden he consulted Boerhaave and gained access to Clifford's collections of the Dutch East India Company; in Amsterdam he drew Seba's marine flora; at Oxford he scoured Sherard's global Botanical Garden; in Paris, he picked through the Jardin des Plantes with Jussieu. His botanical skills earned him a corresponding membership in the French Academy.

A year after Ehrensvärd engraved his portrait, Linnaeus was appointed Professor of Medicine in Uppsala , and for the next three decades he and his students worked out the problem of assigning finite names to the infinite objects of nature. Key to the enterprise was a system of names. In Philosophia

Botanica Linnaeus announced binomial taxonomy, "A plant is completely named, if it is provided with a generic name and a specific one," adding that the characteristics of a species are dictated by its genus. Additions and corrections to the Linnaean Systema Natura followed apace: the first edition of 1735 was only 12 pages long, but by the twelfth edition of 1768 it had grown to 23 pages and encompassed some 15, species. Nor was medicine given short shrift: Linnaeus first classified fevers (and hinted at contagion) in "Exanthemata viva" . Later, he extended his system to all of human disease in the Genera Morborum . But botanical science and its application remained his first love. Dubbed the "King of Flowers" in Sweden, Linnaeus made certain that if the treatment of a disease was herbal, the name of the herb was binomial.

Linnaeus and the Darwins: Linnaeus and binomial botany spread rapidly across Europe. In England, his first translator was Erasmus Darwin, F.R.S., Charles Darwin's grandfather. A beacon of the English Enlightenment, Erasmus Darwin was a prodigious physician, naturalist, and anti-slavery advocate. He was also a man of mirth and spirit who appreciated Linnaeus' erotic description of plants. Linnaeus had compared flowers with nine stamens and one pistil to "nine men in the same bride's chamber, with one woman." Following suit, Erasmus used Linnaeus's polygamous imagery for his own purposes in The Botanic Garden :

Sweet blooms GENISTA in the myrtle shade
And ten fond brothers wood the haughty maid
Two knights before the fragrant altar bend
Adored MELISSA...

Charles Darwin was familiar with Linnaeus not only from his grandfather's couplets, but also from his own botanical studies. Half a century after The Botanic Garden, Charles Darwin paid homage to the King of Flowers in On the Origin of Species :

Expressions such as the famous one by Linnaeus...that the characters do not make the genus but that the genus gives the characters, seem to imply that some deeper bond is included in our classification than mere resemblance. I believe that this is the case and that community of descent is the bond. Community of human descent followed directly from Linnaean nomenclature. Linnaeus decreed that man is an Animal , a Mammal (class), a Primate (order), and it follows, therefore, that Homo sapiens (genus and species) is subtended by the order of Primates. A bond, deeper than mere resemblance, would dictate that Homo sapiens shares Darwinian "community of descent" with apes.

Recent scholarship has shown that the decision to classify man with apes was taken jointly by Linnaeus and a fellow Uppsalian naturalist, Peter Artedi, when both worked in Amsterdam in 1735. Ironically, Artedi (now known as the King of Ichthyology) was drowned in an Amsterdam canal in the early hours of September 28th, 1735, after an evening's bout of drinking with his patron, Albertus Seba. Linnaeus published Artedi's works, manuscripts, and biography, fulfilling a pact that if one should die, then "the other would regard it as a sacred duty to give to the world what observations might be left... " Erasmus Darwin picked up on the Artedi/Linnaeus notion of human origins in his "Zoonomia" and "The Temple of Nature" only to be mocked by Coleridge for suggesting that man had "descended from some lucky species of Ape or Baboon."

It seems fitting, therefore, that Dr. Darwin's grandson put evolution into play once and for all. The Darwin-Wallace paper that first proposed the theory of evolution through natural selection was first read in London before members of the Linnean Society.

Proper Names: Auden and Mann

The photograph of W. H. Auden shows the poet with Erika Mann on the 15th of June 1935, shortly after their marriage in the registry office of Ledbury, a rural town by the Malvern hills. It was the office nearest the Downs School, a prep school where Auden was teaching his last term. The snapshot was taken by Alec Bangham (better known for liposomes) and documents a change of proper name, as does an entry in the Ledbury register:

The photo and registry not only illustrate Auden's belief that proper names are poetry in the raw, they are also a document of the terrible thirties when the night was full of wrong:

Earthquakes and executions: soon he would be dead,
And still all over Europe stood the horrible nurses
Itching to boil their children. Only his verses
Perhaps could stop them...

Each of the names on the register reminds us of nights full of wrong, of political earthquakes, and executions. We read that Erika Julia Hedwig Grundgens, formerly Mann, (occupation not stated) was married to Wystan Hugh Auden (School Master) on June 15th, 1935. The registry also lists the occupation of their fathers: George Augustus Auden (Medical Practitioner) and Thomas Mann (Professional Writer), proper names indeed! Auden's father, a pioneer of public health, was an amateur of Norse myth and had named his son Wystan accordingly.

The bride's father, author of The Magic Mountain and Buddenbrooks, had won the Nobel Prize for literature in 1929. Marriage to Auden, a British subject, conferred a new nationality and proper name on Erika Mann, a stateless refugee from Hitler's Germany.

She had arrived at the Malvern Hotel just a day before the wedding from Switzerland, where she was living in exile with her father. In Germany, she had been a film actress (Maedchen in Uniform), an international motorcar rally driver (Ford Motor Co.), and the MC of a satirical anti-Nazi, gay/lesbian cabaret, the Pfeffermühle (à la Joel Grey in the musical Cabaret). Mann and her cabaret were forced to flee Germany in consequence both of her politics and sexual orientation. In April of 1935, she proposed a pro forma marriage to Christopher Isherwood in Amsterdam as a means of gaining British citizenship. Isherwood was author of Goodbye to Berlin on which the musical Cabaret was later based, and bits of Erika Mann's career float through those Berlin stories.

Isherwood declined Mann's request, pleading prior domestic arrangements. He nonetheless put Mann in touch with Auden, his school-chum, co-author (The Dog Beneath the Skin; et al.) and sometime lover. Auden cabled back a one word response to Erika's appeal: DELIGHTED !

Arrangements were made for a registry office marriage near the Downs School at the end of summer term. The photo and registry entries confirm the event. Directly after the wedding lunch at a local pub, Auden went back to teach classes and on the next day Erika Mann returned to Switzerland with a British passport. She telegraphed Auden almost immediately: MEINE LIEBE, DEINE LIEBE, ALLE MENSCHEN SIND GLEICH [my love, your love, all men are equal]. It's a banner worth raising against homophobes today.

Term over, Auden left the Down School forever and embarked on a soon to be well-documented voyage to and around Iceland with Louis MacNeice). That trip to the mythic North of his father's dreams confirmed Auden's notion that, somewhere in this world, on some island, Alle Menschen Sind Gleich:

Fortunate Island
Where all men are equal
But not vulgar—not yet.

The marriage of W. H. Auden, arguably the best poet in English of the twentieth century, to Erika Mann daughter of Thomas Mann, clearly the best German novelist of the century, is the stuff of history, raw. But a darker tone is struck by another name on the register, Gustav Grundgens, Erika Mann's first husband. Grundgens, an actor and director, was a willing player in the Nazi game of rank and honour. Greatly favored by both Göbbels and Göring, he became celebrated for his portrayal of Faust, or Mephisto, a role he repeated with plaudits to Nazi-packed houses in Munich and Berlin. He rose to direct Berlin's official Staatstheater during the war and produced popular fare for the Nazi state: one imagines a chorus of brown-shirts yodeling "The Hills are alive with the sound of Hitler..." Always the survivor, Grundgens emerged from the fall of the Reich in a Faustian transformation, a rehabilitated, honored German hero of "Kunst."

Erika took another path. She became a journalist, wrote

several books with brother Klaus exposing pre-war fascism, reported on the Spanish Civil War, and then wrote courtroom dispatches from the Nuremberg trials, while Grundgens was vamping the Munich stage, others had been busy in the Munich suburb of Dachau. Professors Pfannensteil of Marburg, Jarisch of Innsbruck, and Linger of Munich froze scores of inmates to death and reported detailed autopsies to "proper" scientific congresses. In Dachau also, Professor Beiglbock of Berlin forced Poles and Jews to drink gallons of seawater: descriptions of the victims' hallucinations and heart failures were neatly recorded in what passed for scientific manuscripts. At the Natzweiler camp, Professor Dr. Eugen Haagen—formerly of the Rockefeller Institute—worked to transmit viral hepatitis from prisoner to prisoner and managed successfully to kill several hundreds with experimental typhus. Pfannensteil, Jarisch, Linger, Beiglbock and Haagen— the proper names recorded by the Nuremberg tribunals are raw poetry, indeed: fleurs du mal.

Auden And The Limits Of Science

The Mann-Auden marriage was a noble gesture on behalf of an exile in an era when:

Exiled Thucydides knew
All that a speech can say
About Democracy,
And what dictators do,
The elderly rubbish they talk
To an apathetic grave;
Analysed all in his book
The enlightenment driven away.

Auden and his fellow anti-Fascists of the thirties were convinced that the journals of science contained clues to the equality of man. Auden believed that the laws of physics govern servant and master alike, and that it was the job of the poet to instruct both in the language of their common history, "Without science, we should have no notion of equality: without art no notion of liberty."

Auden himself was persuaded that science, like poetry, is a "gratuitous, not a utile, act, something one does not because one must, but because it is fun." Oliver Sacks who was a friend explained that "He had the analytic brilliance and vigour of a physical scientist; he had an intuitive penetrating, almost clairvoyant sense of what was going on in people, physically and spiritually, what was amiss and what was aright." His oldest friends, Isherwood and Cyril Connolly, have called him a schoolboy scientist at heart; Stephen Spender acclaimed him as the diagnostician of our fears. Auden was ashamed by the extent to which the children of art and science enlisted in the service of injustice and moral squalor. Commissioned as a Major at the close of the Second World War, he visited Dachau and Natzweiler where the methods of science were mocked on behalf of

The grand apocalyptic dream
In which the persecutors scream
As on the evil Aryan lives
Descends the night of the long knives

Examples of scientific disgrace were paralleled in the realm of the arts not only by the Grundgrens of the stage, but also the complicities of Heidegger, the Wagnerians of Bayreuth and Oberammergau, and the films of Leni Riefenstahl. Auden was persuaded that our best chance lay in establishing limits to the collaboration between intellect and tyranny. He spelled out his hopes in his "Ode to Terminus," the Roman God of Limits:

In this world our colossal immodesty
has plundered and poisoned it is possible
You still might save us, who by now have
learned this: that scientists, to be lucky,
must remind us to take all they say as a
tall story...

There's another strain here: a restatement of "Without science, no equality." Auden is speaking to us from the experience of a generation which had relied on experimental science and its diversities as a shield against the biological hierarchies of fascism. How could the brightest of Europe have been deluded into surrendering equality for the grand apocalyptic dreams of one ideology or another? In "Ode to

Terminus" he appealed to us to give things their proper names: This, whatever microbiology may think, is the world we really live in and that saves our sanity, who know all too well how the most erudite mind behaves in the dark without a surround it is called on to interpret, how, discarding rhythm, punctuation, metaphor, it sinks into a driveling monologue, too literal to see a joke or distinguish a penis from a pencil.

One is sure that Linnaeus would have appreciated Auden's taxonomy: the last two objects are members, literally, of two different kingdoms.

A Poetry of Atonement by Rowan Williams

Two things often said about great poets are that they create the taste by which they are appreciated, and that they have the capacity to constantly reinvent themselves. Auden illustrates these features perhaps more dramatically than any other of the great names of the 20th century.

From his very earliest work (represented here by The Letter of 1927), he created a distinctive verbal landscape, tone and, especially in the early poems, a distinctive visual landscape as well. But, while some aspects of tone or register remain absolutely consistent, the landscape steadily expands with disciplined energy and, increasingly, with a particular skill in producing a sense of aphoristic solidity, a certain timelessness of perspec-tive, unyielding, compassionate, distressingly honest at times.

Born in 197, the third child of a doctor and his intensely intelligent and artistic wife, he was already writing and publishing serious, complex, authoritative poetry when an undergraduate at Christ Church, Oxford. To his contempo-raries, he had something of a mystique, and was widely seen as a guru in matters of poetic taste; that mystique survived through the 3s, when he and some of those most marked by his influence and friendship became an extraordinarily "iconic" presence in British cultural life. The fact that all of the group were in varying degrees involved in the tangled politics of the time, with strong affiliations to the communist cause, gave special force to this presence. Some of the poems of the 3s were instantly recognised as having a lasting and classical quality, like the unforgettable Lullaby.

So it was all the more startling, even shocking, when Auden left the UK not long before the outbreak of the second world war, and made his home in New York. The new context, and the impact of his deepest and longest-lasting sexual relationship, combined with a return to the High Church Anglican Christianity of his childhood to effect a marked change in both the style and scope of his work. Several very long and ambitious pieces deal with issues of art and politics and theology, guilt, love, creation and violence. He is more than ever in his later work a "learned" poet, yet the combination of an intimidatingly erudite background with colloquial language, irony and unfailing emotional directness makes him very different from other poets who paint from a dense palette of historical and literary allusion. Somehow you don't simply respond by thinking, "inaccessible".

In his last years, personally none too happy, he moved around more between the USA and Europe, especially Austria, where he and his partner owned a house; and the poetry becomes just a little drier, with rather more pastiche and resort to condensed, formal or epigrammatic vehicles. But the intelligence is still unceasingly at work, more elegiac, sometimes more self-indulgent, often self-deflating. He died of a heart attack in his Austrian home in 1973.

The early poetry is full of what was to him the uniquely "authoritative" landscape of Pennine limestone, isolated communities, cold skies and deep-rooted, revengeful violence. This serves not as a backcloth for regional mythmaking, but as a set of framing metaphors for the social and political tragedy of the era. And, perhaps more importantly, for the sense of doubleness and loneliness, being suspicious and creating suspicion, that was bound up at this point in his life with Auden's homosexuality. The convoluted political context, with its rhetoric of covert operations, espionage and treachery, is inextricably connected with a muted but intensely felt sexual politics - of a very different kind from what we associate with the phrase in more recent decades. The poetic voice is often that of someone working as a kind of double agent or negotiating difficult border country. In what for some might seem a paradoxical development, the recovery of Christian belief and imagery allows for the poetry of hard but accepting self-awareness and a sense of absolution mysteriously granted in advance, and of an elusive but overwhelming order of joy to which the poem compulsively moves (Whitsunday in Kirchstetten).

The technical skill is always exceptional. You'd call it dazzling if it were not so all-pervading (if not unobtrusive, at least) apparently intrinsic to the poetic argument and energy. If I had to find one word for Auden's poetry, it might be "satisfying" not remotely in the sense of comfortable, but full of that sense of creative necessity that poetry conveys when it is most itself: this is how it must be said, this is (borrowing Geoffrey Hill's language) a poetry of "atonement" where something is at the same time finished and set free in the fabric of the words.

Indiscretions at the High Table of Verse

'The great paradox about Auden is this: how can the writer of the sanest, most liberal and chaste poetry in English of the 20th century also be the crotchty, opinionated old fossicker of the Table Talk?'

A neglected literary parallel, thrust beneath our noses by this quirky edition of table talk, is that between Auden and Wilde. Auden too is much given to outrageous camp epigram, and both manage the difficult feat of making camp a basis of morality and art. 'Brunnhilde is not a young woman. She is as old as God and much heavier' is Auden but the model is Wilde's favourite Paterism: She (the Mona Lisa) is older than the rocks among which she sits....' Auden thought Wilde 'important not as a writer he couldn't write at all but as a behaver. Still he did say some acute things.'

The great paradox about Auden is this: how can the writer of the sanest, most liberal and chaste poetry in English of the 20th century also be the crotchety opinionated old fossicker of The Table Talk? Much of this book flatly contradicts, without any acknowledgement of doing so, the Collected Poems which is simultaneously reissued. You admire the poems on Yeats, Voltaire, Montaigne? Well: 'I don't like Montaigne at all'; 'I can't stand the French.... I suppose Voltaire and the others performed a historically useful service but they're such vulgarians'; Yeats? 'He was a horrible old man.' Or perhaps you've always savoured the bit in Letter To Lord Byron about Wordsworth ('a most bleak old bore'). Here we have: 'I don't dislike Wordsworth at all.'

A clue to all this may be supplied by an essay in last year's first volume of Auden Studies (The Map Of All My Youth, OUP, £27.5). Katherine Bucknell points out the importance to Auden of I. A. Richards' distinction in Science And Poetry between 'statement' and 'pseudo statement'; Richards' position made explicit the possibility of poetically justified lies.

Auden's recognition of the problem that he was sometimes seduced by irresponsible rhetoric such as 'History to the defeated/ May say Alas but cannot help or pardon' led him to revise and edit out these elements from the canon. But, happily for us, it seems that he left in many poems which sound true for us but which for him might have been merely plausible.

Alan Ansen befriended him during a course of lectures Auden was giving on Shakespeare in New York in 1946. He decided to play Boswell to him, without that 20th-century Boswellian aid, the tape-recorder. The result, after some editing by the Auden scholar Nicholas Jenkins, is a lurching cascade of opinion and declarations with no necessary connection between them. Auden was by now a practising Christian, and thoroughly at odds with his extravagent young self. He matches Eliot's notorious Anglo-Catholic, Conservative, Monarchist credo almost exactly: 'I am a convinced monarchist'; 'I was down in Washington last week with the Guild of Episcopal Scholars. I'm a member'; 'I'm a capitalist now.' But of course table talk is highly dependent on mood, alcohol consumption, the occasion, and the person addressed. Considered, weighted, and cadenced prose it is not, but there are flashes of the insight and wisdom we expect, colloquially expressed. And he impresses as usual as a stern and unflinchingly orginal moralist: 'I think poetry is fundamentally frivolity.... The only serious thing is loving God and your neighbour.... You can't say about loving your neighbour that you have no talent for it. It's required of everyone.'

Richard Howard, is a judicious introduction to the Table Talk, concludes: 'We must not hold it against the poems.' The new Collected is a delight. There are a few textual changes, but the greatest joy is to have the official canon at least set in a decent typeface (the last edition was eccentric). This is the greatest oeuvre in English 2th-century poetry. No one else comes remotely near his range of form and content, his memorability, his intelligence, his power of evocation.

Julian Symons, in Auden Studies, claims to be a reader 'who still rather unfashionably regards Auden as the greatest 20th-century poet writing in English.' 'Rather unfashionably?' In a scenario worthy of his early spy poems, the Audenites have captured the commanding heights of the literary economy: they've got the key foreign outposts (Joseph Brodsky and Derek Walcott), Magdalen College, Oxford (seat of Auden Studies), the TLS, Faber, the poetry editor of Chatto & Windus, Poetry Review. Auden himself pulls off a coup in the Table Talk: planting the idea of Craig Raine's Martian poetry which swept the poetry world in the eighties and brought Raine to the poetry editorship of Fabers for 1 years: 'If you would present highbrow poetry as a type of riddle with a definite answer, it might catch on with a good many people.' That thirties business the Apostles, Burgess, Maclean, Philby, etc now looks like a brilliant front for the real campaign: the installation of Auden at the heart of our literary life, which is where he belongs, indiscretions at table notwithstanding.

Mapping the Mind and the Body: on W.H. Auden's Personifications

Despite our traditional view of the body and mind as divided, one figurative way for representing the two in our thought and in our language is the unified method of metaphor. For example, because we have easier access to bodies than to minds, our everyday notion of body language means we "map" from the body to the mind to interpret the behaviour of others. As Simon Baron-Cohen has argued, this normal psychological mapping provides us with a "theory of mind" that some autistic children appear to lack for successful social cognition. We may not be fully aware of such mappings, but they conceptually link the body to the mind, making the body indexical of the mind in a way that closely integrates them and nearly negates dualism.

Apart from these non-verbal mappings, mappings from the body to the mind in language, according to Eve Sweetser, motivate how physical verbs like grasp take on mental meanings like "know" during a language's evolution. As we would imagine, these connections between mind and body, between the mental and physical, also appear in literature, particularly in bodily descriptions, the language of emotions, and the use of mind or body metaphors. W. H. Auden is one case in point since he was forever writing about the mind and the body in his poems. Usually, Auden depicts body and mind in general via metaphor and personification in particular. What makes Auden's mind and body personifications strange, however, is that they are unlike the imaginary abstractions we often associate with personification.

Personification was vital to Auden. According to Bernard Bergonzi, the four main features of Auden's poetic style were the "copious use of the definite article; unusual adjectives and adjectival phrases; surprising similes, which have a reductive or trivializing effect; and personified abstractions". Indeed, Auden's personified abstractions bothered readers like Karl Shapiro, who wrote in his 1947 Essay on Rime, "An all-purpose abstraction is a form / Dear to the tired mind that must malinger / And precious to the talentless History is but one / Of Auden's ill-starred words. Luck is another" (qtd. in Bergonzi 68). Irvin Ehrenpreis also found that "Auden at his best did not stop at personification; he embodied the abstractions in curious or supreme examples" such as southern Italy's limestone landscapes in the poem "In Praise of Limestone" . Shapiro, Bergonzi, and Ehrenpreis have all recognized Auden's tendency to personify and embody abstractions. However, Auden also tended to personify the mind and the body, entities which are perhaps less abstract than we recognize.

We personify when we metaphorically ascribe agency to normally inanimate objects, turning non-existent or imaginary entities into realistic actors or agents. As the cognitive linguist would describe it, to personify is to "map" information from a "source domain" onto a "target domain" (what I. A. Richards once called vehicles and tenors). Mapping occurs simultaneously at conceptual and linguistic levels. Novel metaphors in language often reflect conventional metaphors in thought. In eroding classical boundaries between figures of thought and figures of speech, personification is apt for study from the cognitive viewpoint because a metaphor in language normally reveals a related conceptual metaphor in thought. Simply put, one metaphor can hide another. Therefore, it is fruitful to consider personification as both a product of thought and a product of speech. Personification is one of our most basic and frequently utilized metaphors. Its high frequency in children's literature suggests that we can understand it very early in life and that it is our "prototypical metaphor" built from "nonhuman topic—human vehicle" mappings. Not surprisingly, the same holds for Auden, who presumably knew that the personification of abstractions in literature reached its apex in eighteenth-century English poetry. The figure seemed to fall into disuse after Wordsworth's radical break with the trend in "Yew Trees".

Personified abstractions that allegedly functioned allegorically, popular in the seventeenth and eighteenth centuries, were therefore more or less abandoned by the Romantics. As Steven Knapp has suggested, personifications such as Sin or Death in Milton's Paradise Lost, for example, became problematic in the eyes of eighteenth century writers. The view that personification as a poetic device could no longer be easily defended followed from the divisi on between "arbitrary magic" and "rational Aristotelian mimesis" for critics like Addison and from Lord Kames's separation of the "natural" personification of "insensible objects" from the "unnatural" personification of "deities, angels, devils, or other supernatural powers". Since no Romantic would have wanted willingly to write seemingly "unnatural" poems, "natural" "mimesis" was apparently preferred. The issue, as Knapp puts it, was no minor one: Auden. - book reviews

Commonweal, Oct 11, 1996 by Celia Wren

The poetry of Wystan Hugh Auden impresses itself on the mind before it does so on the ear. Weighty ideas about history and human nature, bearing down on the words, seem to have worn off the usual verbal varnish: syntax can seem unwieldy, or imagery oddly juxtaposed, or rhymes too easy, as though they were meant sarcastically (take for example the lines from his sonnet sequence "In Time of War:" And strangers were as brothers to his clocks,/And with his spires he made a human sky;/Museums stored his learning like a box,/And paper watched his money like a spy.") Subjects seem unrooted, drifting among vague mysterious energies. Lines draw their power from the ideas beneath them.

Replying in the late '6s to criticism that a poem of his was prosaic, Auden wrote: "In so much 'serious' poetry I find an element of 'theatre,' of exaggerated gesture and fuss....I want [the reader's] reaction to be: 'That's true,' or better still, 'That's true: now, why didn't I think of it for myself?' To secure this effect I am prepared to sacrifice a great many poetic pleasures and excitements." Thrifty with clarity as well as poetic excitements, Auden's poems can seem at least abstract, if not, as Anthony Hecht once put it, "Orphic and obscure." But to Auden they were true, and when his ideas of truth changed, he sometimes revised early poems, heedless of protests from devotees By concentrating on the ideas Auden moved between and through, rather than on minute biographical details, Richard Davenport-Hines gives his book a hint of Audenesque mystery. As he acknowledges in an afterword, he has not tried to write a definitive biography: Humphrey Carpenter's 1981 W. H. Auden left Davenport-Hines "free to write a biography that is more thematic, or selectively emphatic."

His choice has been to do an interpretive reading of Auden,s life and work, dwelling on the ideas that preoccupied the poet at various times: his stoicism about suffering and his conviction that the glory of human love lay in its imperfections, his interest in Freudianism, his cynicism about civilization, his fleeting visions of utopias, and his re-discovery of Christianity when he was in his thirties. Davenport-Hines weaves this intellectual chronicle into the account of the poet's life, quoting amply from Auden's prose as well as from his poetry.

The portrait he draws is of a brilliant intellectual with a gift for philosophizing, a keen sensitivity to history, and a commitment to his craft that made him exasperatingly self-centered. Throughout his life Auden demonstrated a contrarian and even curmudgeonly streak that led him to state, in the 195s, that "Alienation from the collective is always a duty." Born in York, England, in 197, he discovered his homosexuality at a young age and began to rebel against the inhibited mood of the times at just about the same time as he was dazzling his contemporaries at Oxford.

When his father volunteered to finance a year in Europe, Auden chose Berlin because the risque delights of Paris were already a cliche. He did try to be useful in Spain during the Civil War ("As I have no dependents, I feel I ought to go;" he wrote, "but O I do hope there are not too many Surrealists there") but he soon regretted his poem "Spain" with its militant refrain "But today the struggle." In 1938, after a trip to China with Christopher Isherwood, he renounced overt political activity, a move that alienated many idealistic contemporaries. From henceforth he was to believe that art could not change the world; as he put it in his elegy "In Memory of W. B. Yeats": "poetry makes nothing happen." In 1939 he emigrated to the United States, and later became an American citizen, apparently because he found British literary society too claustrophobic. Shortly after the move he met the love of his life, Chester Kallman, with whom he was to share credit for a number of opera librettos (including Stravinsky's The Rake's Progress), and several very messy domiciles, in New York, in Greece, and in Austria. Despite infidelities on both sides, the relationship was to continue throughout their lives, though Kallman's neglect contributed substantially to the loneliness of the older poet's final years. Overindulgence in cigarettes, alcohol, and the amphetamine Benzedrine had caused his health to deteriorate, and his increasingly churlish manners had alienated his friends. He died in 1974; Kallman died a few months later.

Davenport-Hines's portrait of the poet is astute and sympathetic, and his extremely sophisticated literary interpretations are almost poetic in their own right: "Auden's shrewdest critics see such different strengths in his work: the honey of intellect and the imperatives of ethical commitment; romanticism; tense passion; and constant, implacable political concern. These readings are not antagonistic: the meaning is most where the interpretations lie thickest."

However, the book's emphasis on concepts rather than facts occasionally gives it a rather cryptic atmosphere; one senses that pictures are incomplete. Readers unfamiliar with Auden's life may find Carpenter's fact-filled biography more satisfying. Nonetheless, Davenport-Hines's work, obviously the product of passionate involvement with Auden's writing, contains illuminating analysis, and makes interesting connections between his beliefs and the writings of lesser-known twentieth-century thinkers. And he supplies enough biography to make it clear that Auden fulfilled the aspiration set out in his early poem "September 1, 1939," a poem he later repudiated for not meeting his high standards for "truth":

Our world in stupor lies; Yet, dotted everywhere, Ironic points of light Flash out wherever the Just Exchange their messages: May I, composed like them Of Eros and of dust, Beleaguered by the same Negation and despair, Show an affirming flame.

A Review of The Country Between Us by Carolyn Forche'

In the introduction to The Poet's Tongue, W.H. Auden and J. Garrett state that "Poetry is not concerned with telling people what to do, but with extending our knowledge of good and evil, perhaps making the necessity for action more urgent and its nature more clear, but only leading us to the point where it is possible for us to make a rational and moral choice." Carolyn Forche lives up to W. H. Auden's and J. Garrett's definition of the nature of poetry with the heart of a humanist and the power of her words, she gives voice to El Salvador that is waiting to be heard. Sometimes this voice is delightful and rich with charm and sometimes it wails of horriffic human torture. The Country Between Us is a collection of experiences that occurred during the late Seventies. The first poem, "San Onofre, California" ends with two haunting lines that immediately capture the sympathy of the reader: "the cries of those who vanish/ might take years to get here." It is this idea of "the cries" and "the voices" of the people of El Salvador that dominates the imagery and theme in this collection.

Forche', as the narrator, plays the role of observer, being objective when appropriate and sentimental when called for. These poems contain a great deal of honesty, perfect detail, and brutish truth while never ceasing to be beautiful. She writes: "You will fight/ and fighting, you will die. I will live/ and living cry out until my voice is gone/ to its hollow earth, where with our/ hands and by the lives we have chosen/ we will dig deep into our deaths."

In a world where death is not only expected to come unnaturally but sometimes welcomed as an end to suffering, passion for a cause can enable the loss of one life to become a sacrifice for the better of others. This may be a statement that we can call "political" from the outside but in El Salvador to die for rights is honour. "These are the flowers we bought/ this morning, the dahlias tossed/ on his grave and bells/ waiting with their tongues cut out/ for this particular silence." Silence is Forche's enemy and the enemy of the peoples this country. In the poem "Endurance," we find a person loved dearly by the narrator. Forche' described the voice of a women named Anna and with images that wouldn't seem to be associated at all with a human voice but fit perfectly to produce an audial image. " Anna. Peeling her hands/ with a paring knife, saying in your country/ you have nothing. Each word was the husk/ of a vegetable tossed to the street/ or a mountain rounded by trains/ with cargoes of sheep-dung and grief." Sometimes it is hard to see clearly what it is that Forche' sees as important. But it is not hard to realise that she finds a special richness among the Salvador people and their culture. She compares American culture with that of El Salvador: "To my country I ship poetry instead/ of bread, so I cut through nothing./ I give nothing, so you see I have/ nothing, according to myself/... I am xaloc, a wind/ from the southwest as far away/ as my country and there is nothing/ to help me in or out of it." In awe of the people and event surrounding her, detachment can be sensed in the tone of some of the poems like this one.

The second half of the book seems to change focus from the actual experienced of the narrator to the person the narrator becomes and life the narrator lives with the knowledge of true human suffering and joy. The poems turn inward from the lives and politics of El Salvador to the childhood, adolescence and adulthood of the narrator. In the poem "Departure," this progression is documented with the opening lines "We take it with us, the cry/ of a train slicing a field/ leaving a stiff suture, a distant/ tenderness as when rails slip/ behind us and our windows/ touch the field, where it seems/ the dead are awake and so reach/ for each other." Although she wrote for the spirit of the people of El Salvador, she continued to live, travel, and write with that spirit in mind.

There is amazing skill in the writings of Carolyn Force'. Her words are inspiring and engrossing. Reading The Country Between Us is like reading a novel or watching a movie that never fails to surprise you with something new each time. She can breath life into words with phrases like "the black and white collapse of hours," "behind the blind/ whit hills and a scant/ snow ticking in the stars," and "in a city of liquor bottles and light." And there is much to learn from her abrasive use of rhythm that can make you feel as if you are reading another language or a language translation. In many ways, this collection of twenty-two poems is a translation of poetry from another language. Rather, it is a translation of the language of the people of El Salvador into poetry.

Bibliography

- *Humphrey Carpenter. W. H. Auden*: a biography (1981)
- *Richard Davenport-Hines*. Auden (1995)
- *Edward Mendelson*. Early Auden (1981)
- *Edward Mendelson*. Later Auden (1999)
- *Norman Page Auden and Isherwood*: The Berlin Years (2000)
- Thekla Clark. "*Wystan and Chester: A Personal Memoir of W. H. Auden and Chester Kallman*" (1996)
- Dorothy J. Farnan. "*Auden in Love*" (1985)